Woman's Day
Crochet Showcase

Woman's Day
Crochet Showcase

Edited by Nancy Schraffenberger

Robert J. Kasbar
Book Coordinator/Production Manager

Designed by Allan Mogel Studios

Columbia
House
New York

PHOTOGRAPHY CREDITS

Carmen Schiavone	All photography except as follows:
Tito Barberis	page 72
Didier Dorot	pages 49, 78, 115, 118, 119, 120
Frederick Eberstadt	page 61
Douglas Kirkland	page 34
Mort Mace	page 144
Frances McLaughlin-Gill	pages 105, 106, 110, 122, 123, 124
Sigrid Owen	page 164
Rakan/Scribe International	pages 53, 133
Leif Schiller	page 39
Steen Svensson	pages 37, 38, 41, 46, 48, 172
Transworld Feature Syndicate	page 160
Woman's Day Studio	pages 129, 151, 153, 154, 155, 156, 162 (Jute Baskets), 163

DESIGNER CREDITS

Marianne Ake, pages 34, 37, 38, 71, 172
Irene P. Albee, page 146
Ann Anderson, page 44
Linda Osborne Blood, pages 17, 30, 100
Lorraine Bodger, page 163
Beattie Bodenstein, page 50
Casey Bradford, page 125
A. Breth, page 78
Gary Brouwer, pages 170, 171 (Tweedy slippers)
Nan Jennes Brown, page 49
Carmella Cannarozzi, page 73 (Hat)
Patti Cappalli, page 61
Sally DeGaetano, page 113
Edith d'Errecalde, page 24
Gail Diven, page 45
Dorothy Feder, page 69
Ellen Fine, page 112
Phoebe Fox, page 110
Liselotte Fruehwirth, page 162 (Mitt Potholders)
Agnes Gaynor, page 51
Sally Gronsand, page 63
Carol Hasselriis, page 67
Ruth G. Hill, page 139
Shani Jacobs, pages 68, 101, 103
Jacqueline Jewett, pages 75, 76

Veronica Kiem, page 74 (Silvery Necktie)
Minnie Kramer, pages 108, 166
Marjorie Kratz, page 157
Annette Lep, pages 18, 22, 25 105, 115, 118, 119, 120
Erika Loeb, pages 16, 19, 26, 28, 77, 105, 127, 144
Nancy Marshall, page 42
Natalie Matott, page 129
Patricia McCann, page 114
Arlene Mintzer, pages 41, 72 , 73 (Scarf and Gauntlets)
Barbara Muccio, pages 98, 121, 154, 162 (Jute Baskets)
Sharon Mullin, page 143
Nili, page 58
Susan Perricone, page 149
Jan Pileggi, pages 122,123,124
Maggie Ramsay and Sondra Miller, pages 46, 48
M. D. Rodrigue, page 99
Kathryn Roose, page 138
Alison Schiff, pages 74 (Drawstring Purse), 164
Cynthia Sinclair, page 128
Josephine Springer, pages 33, 155, 156, 171 (Bulky Scarf)
Mary Ellen Thompson, page 147
Marilyn Wein, page 97
Woman's Day Staff, pages 39, 151, 153
Sheila Zagar, page 169

Copyright © 1980 CBS Publications,
the Consumer Publishing Division of CBS Inc.
ISBN: 0-930748-14-X
Printed in the United States of America
Published by Columbia House, a Division of CBS Inc.,
1211 Avenue of the Americas, New York, New York 10036

CONTENTS

YARN INFORMATION

If you have difficulty in obtaining any of the yarns specified in these projects, write to the following addresses for information on mail-order sources:

Aunt Lydia
American Thread Co.
Hi Ridge Park
Stamford, Connecticut 06905

Bernat
Emile Bernat & Sons
Depot and Mendon Streets
Uxbridge, Massachusetts 01569

Berroco
Stanley Berroco, Inc.
140 Mendon Street
Uxbridge, Massachusetts 01569

Brunswick
Brunswick Yarns
230 Fifth Avenue
New York, New York 10001

Bucilla
Bucilla Yarns
30–20 Thomson Avenue
Long Island City, New York 11101

Coats & Clark
J. & P. Coats
Coats & Clark
75 Rockefeller Plaza
New York, New York 10019

Columbia-Minerva
Columbia-Minerva Yarns
295 Fifth Avenue
New York, New York 10016

D. M. C.
D. M. C. Corporation
107 Trumbull Street
Elizabeth, New Jersey 07206

Joseph Galler
Joseph Galler, Inc.
149 Fifth Avenue
New York, New York 10010

Kentucky
January & Wood Co.
Maysville, Kentucky 41056

Lily
Belding Lily Co.
Shelby, North Carolina 28150

Lion Brand
Lion Brand Yarn Co.
1270 Broadway
New York, New York 10001

Ludlow Macramé Welt Cord
Ludlow Textiles
Ludlow, Maine 01056

Reynolds
Reynolds Yarns
15 Oser Avenue
Hauppage, New York 11787

Spinnerin
Spinnerin Yarns
230 Fifth Avenue
New York, New York 10001

Unger
William Unger & Co.
230 Fifth Avenue
New York, New York 10001

INTRODUCTION

In the following pages, the editors of *Woman's Day* present a collection of more than 90 superb crochet designs featured in the magazine, none ever before published in book form. Women who have already mastered this simple and satisfying needlecraft will find fresh challenges and inspiration here—and those who may be waiting for the right moment to take up crochet will find our beautifully detailed "Crochet Lesson" a persuasive argument for not delaying any longer.

The selection of projects includes one-of-a-kind fashions for women, children and men, and accessories that contribute a special look to almost every area of your home. The range is vast: a magnificent filet wedding gown and a child's granny-square poncho, a rugged Aran pullover and a dainty camisole, a dramatic afghan and a whimsical sailor-suited toy duckling. Many are quick and easy items (such as jute baskets for hot casserole dishes) that you'll want to make in quantity for gifts or for money-raising events; others are heirloom designs—like the christening dress and bonnet—that are truly a labor of love.

In the famous *Woman's Day* tradition, the directions for each project are meticulously prepared and diagrams are provided, where necessary, to ensure clarity. In addition, the teaching unit is a model of precise information and instruction on crochet tools, terms and materials, beginning techniques, basic stitches and finishing procedures. It is abundantly illustrated with more than 30 diagrams showing hand positions.

Finally, the designs are marked (*) if suitable for a beginner or (**) if considerable experience is needed. Most of the projects, can be undertaken by anyone who has acquired intermediate skills.

Crochet Hooks come in many sizes, which sometimes go by number, sometimes by letter, sometimes by both. Aluminum or plastic hooks, recommended for beginners, usually come in letter sizes B (smallest) through K (largest) or number sizes 1 through 10½.

Crochet Materials depend on what you're making. Wool, metallic and synthetic yarns are usually chosen for clothes or decorating accessories such as afghans or pillows; fine cotton for lacy filet work; heavy cotton, wool and jute yarns for rugs.

Gauge means the number of stitches to an inch and the number of rows to an inch. The gauges specified in directions must be maintained to assure proper size in the finished piece.

Always check gauge before starting a project. To do this, make a 3″ practice square, using the hook, yarn and stitch specified. Measure the square with a ruler. If it's less than 3″, change to a larger size hook; more than 3″, change to a smaller size hook.

ABBREVIATIONS, TERMS AND SYMBOLS

beg	beginning
ch	chain
cl	cluster
dc	double crochet
dec	decrease
h dc	half double crochet
inc	increase
lp	loop
pc	popcorn
rnd	round
sc	single crochet
sl	slip
sl st	slip stitch
sp	space
st	stitch
sts	stitches
tog	together
tr	treble
y o	yarn over hook

* Asterisk means repeat the instructions following the asterisk as many times as specified, in addition to the first time.

Even When directions say "work even," continue without increasing or decreasing.

( ) Parentheses mean repeat the instructions in parentheses as many times as specified. For example,

"(Ch 5, sc in next sc) 5 times," means to crochet stitches specified 5 times in all.

TO BEGIN CROCHET

The following 7 diagrams with accompanying step-by-step directions show you how to make a slip knot, which anchors yarn on the hook, exact positions for holding the yarn and the hook, and how to do the chain stitch, which is a foundation for other stitches. To practice, use knitting worsted and a size G aluminum or plastic hook.

While you learn, hold your hands in the positions shown in the diagrams. As you become more proficient, you will adjust to the positions most comfortable for you.

Left-handed crochet work comes out in reverse. If you are left-handed, try to crochet with your right hand—directions are written for right-handed crocheters and you'll find it easier to follow more complex patterns and shaping later on. However, if using your right hand is impossible, hold diagrams in front of a mirror to reverse hands.

Hold the hook in your right hand as you would a pencil; bring middle finger forward to rest on hook near tip (Diagram 1).

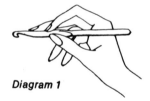

Diagram 1

Slip Knot: *A.* To make a slip knot, hold yarn end with left thumb and forefinger. Bring yarn up and around to make a ring—with yarn dropping behind ring. Put hook through ring; catch yarn and draw it through ring toward you (Diagram 2).

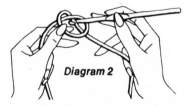

Diagram 2

B. With yarn loop on hook, pull short yarn end and long working yarn in opposite directions to tighten. You have now made the starting slip knot. Insert long working yarn between ring and little fingers of left hand. Wrap yarn around little finger toward back of hand and bring out between ring and middle fingers (Diagram 3).

Diagram 3

C. Weave yarn around middle finger toward back of hand; bring it forward between forefinger and thumb. This weaving of the working yarn enables you to control the tension as you feed the yarn onto the hook (Diagram 4).

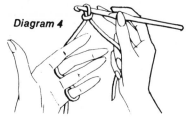

Diagram 4

D. To begin crocheting, grasp short yarn end between thumb and middle finger of left hand under knot (Diagram 5).

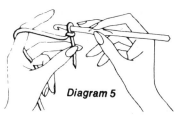

Diagram 5

Chain Stitch (CH): A. Pass hook under yarn and catch yarn with hook. This procedure is called yarn over (y o) (Diagram 6).

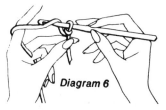

Diagram 6

B. Draw yarn through loop on hook. This makes one chain (ch) (Diagram 7).

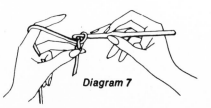

Diagram 7

Repeat steps A and B until you have as many chain stitches as you need. One loop always remains on the hook. Practice making chains until they are uniform.

THE BASIC STITCHES

Single Crochet (SC): Make a foundation chain of 10 or more stitches for practice.
A. Working from front, insert hook under 2 top threads of second chain from hook; pass the yarn over hook (Diagram 8).

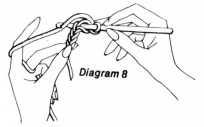

Diagram 8

B. Draw yarn through chain. There are now 2 loops on hook (Diagram 9).

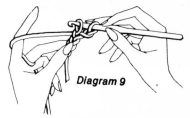

Diagram 9

C. Yarn over hook (Diagram 10).

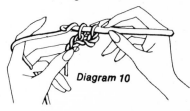

Diagram 10

D. Draw yarn through 2 loops on hook. One loop now remains on hook. One single crochet (sc) is completed (Diagram 11).

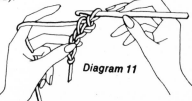

Diagram 11

E. To work next single crochet, insert hook under 2 top threads of next chain (Diagram 12).

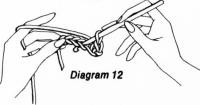

Diagram 12

9

F. Yarn over hook. Repeat steps *B* through *F* until you have made a single crochet in each chain.
G. At end of row of single crochet, chain one to turn (Diagram 13).

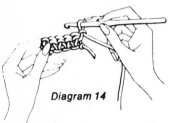

Diagram 13

H. Turn your work so the reverse side is facing you (Diagram 14).

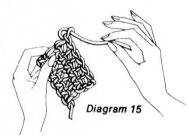

Diagram 14

I. Insert hook under 2 top threads of first single crochet. Repeat steps *B* through *F*, inserting hook into single crochet instead of chain, to complete second row of single crochet, ending with a chain one. Turn. Continue in this manner until work is uniform and the stitch is familiar.
J. On last row do not make a turning chain. Cut yarn about 3″ from work; bring cut end through remaining loop on hook. Pull tight (Diagram 15).

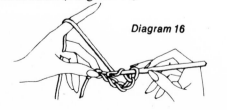

Diagram 15

Now you have completed your practice piece of single crochet.

Double Crochet (DC): Make a foundation chain of 15 stitches for practice piece.
A. Yarn over hook (Diagram 16).

Diagram 16

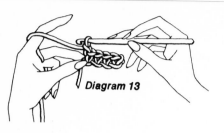

B. Insert hook under 2 top threads of fourth chain from hook. Yarn over hook (Diagram 17).

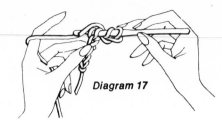

Diagram 17

C. Draw yarn through chain. There are 3 loops on hook. Yarn over hook (Diagram 18).

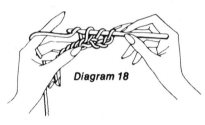

Diagram 18

D. Draw yarn through first 2 loops on hook. Two loops remain on hook. Yarn over hook (Diagram 19).

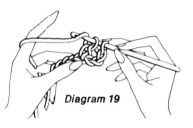

Diagram 19

E. Draw yarn through remaining 2 loops. One loop remains on hook. One double crochet (dc) is now completed (Diagram 20).

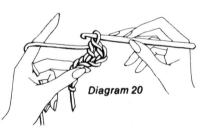

Diagram 20

F. To work next double crochet, yarn over hook, insert hook under 2 top threads of next chain. Yarn over hook and repeat steps *C* through *E*. Repeat until you have made a double crochet in each chain.

G. At end of row of double crochet, chain 3 (Diagram 21).

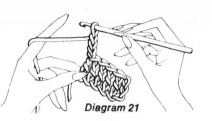
Diagram 21

H. Turn work. On next row, yarn over hook. Skip first double crochet, insert hook under 2 top threads of second double crochet (Diagram 22).

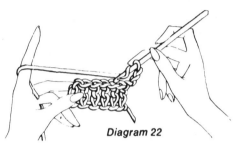
Diagram 22

I. Yarn over hook. Repeat steps *C* through *E*, inserting hook into double crochet instead of chain, to complete double crochet; work a double crochet in top of each remaining double crochet across (Diagram 23).

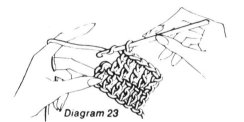
Diagram 23

J. Work a double crochet in top chain stitch of turning chain. Continue in this manner until work is uniform and you feel familiar with the stitch. On last row do not make a turning chain. Cut yarn about 3″ from work; bring cut end through remaining loop on hook. Pull tight.

Now you have completed your practice piece of double crochet.

Half Double Crochet (H DC): Make a foundation chain of 10 or more stitches for practice piece.
A. Yarn over hook; insert hook under 2 top threads of third chain from hook. Yarn over hook; draw yarn through chain. There are 3 loops on hook. Yarn over

hook; draw through all 3 loops at once. A half double crochet (h dc) is now completed (Diagram 24).

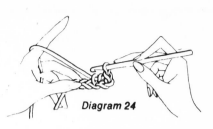
Diagram 24

B. Work a half double crochet in each remaining chain. At the end of row chain 2 to turn.
C. Skip first half double crochet; work half double crochet in each half double crochet across; half double crochet in top stitch of turning chain. Chain 2 to turn. Continue in this manner until you are familiar with the stitch. End off as before.

Now you have completed your practice piece of half double crochet.

Treble Crochet (TR): Make a foundation chain of 15 or more stitches for practice.
A. Yarn over hook twice (Diagram 25).

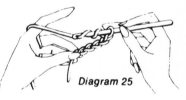
Diagram 25

B. Insert hook under 2 top threads of fifth chain from hook. Yarn over hook (Diagram 26).

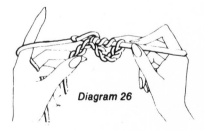
Diagram 26

C. Draw loop through chain. There are 4 loops on hook. Yarn over hook (Diagram 27).

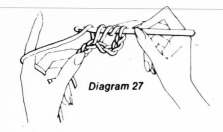

Diagram 27

D. Draw yarn through first 2 loops on hook. Three loops remain. Yarn over hook (Diagram 28).

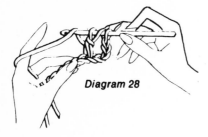

Diagram 28

E. Draw through next 2 loops on hook. Two loops remain. Yarn over hook (Diagram 29).

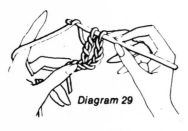

Diagram 29

F. Draw through remaining 2 loops on hook. One loop remains on hook. One treble crochet (tr) is now completed.
G. Work a treble crochet in each remaining chain. At end of row chain 4 to turn.
H. Skip first treble crochet, work treble crochet in each treble crochet across; treble crochet in top stitch of turning chain. Chain 4 to turn. Continue in this manner until you are familiar with the stitch. End off as before.

Now you have completed your practice piece of treble crochet.

BASIC TECHNIQUES

To Decrease (DEC) Single Crochet:
A. Draw up a loop in next single crochet; 2 loops on hook. Draw up loop in following single crochet. There are 3 loops on hook. Yarn over hook (Diagram 30).

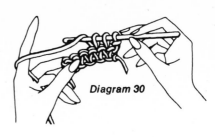

Diagram 30

B. Draw yarn through all 3 loops at once. One single crochet decrease is completed (Diagram 31).

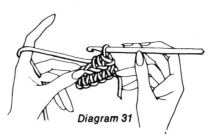

Diagram 31

To Increase (INC): Where directions indicate an increase, work 2 stitches in the same stitch. This forms one extra stitch.

Slip Stitch (SL ST): Make a foundation chain of 10 or more stitches for practice.
A. Insert hook under top thread of second chain from hook. Yarn over hook. With one motion draw yarn through both chain and loop on hook. One slip stitch (sl st) is completed.
B. Insert hook under top thread of next chain (Diagram 32).

Diagram 32

C. Yarn over. Draw through chain and loop on hook. Work a slip stitch in each remaining chain.

Slip Stitch for Joining Rings: Use when directions say join in a ring. Make a chain of 10 stitches for practice. *A.* Insert hook through 2 top threads of last chain from hook. Yarn over (Diagram 33).

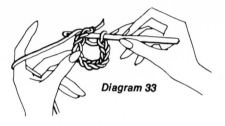

Diagram 33

B. With one motion draw yarn through chain and loop on hook (Diagram 34).

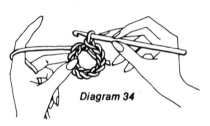

Diagram 34

Slip Stitch for Joining Rounds: Use when working around as for a hat, rather than across in rows.

Following any set of crochet directions, work to end of round; then to join, insert hook under 2 top threads of first stitch on this same round and work slip stitch. First and last stitches of round are now joined.

PATTERN STITCHES

The pattern stitches that follow are simply combinations of the basic stitches, techniques and terms you have already learned. To review the abbreviations, terms and symbols used in the directions, see page 8.

Shell Stitch: This is one of many varieties of shell stitch. Once you have learned this basic stitch, you'll find directions for others easy to follow.

Make a foundation chain of 25 stitches (or other multiple of 6 stitches plus 1) for practice piece. **1st row:** Work 2 dc in 4th ch from hook (half shell made), skip 2 ch, sc in next ch, * skip 2 ch, work 5 dc all in next ch (shell made), skip 2 ch, sc in next ch. Repeat from * across (Diagram 35). Ch 3 to turn. **2nd row:** Work 2 dc

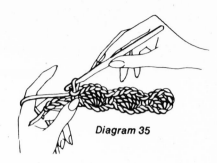

Diagram 35

in first sc (half shell), skip 2 dc of shell, sc in next dc, * skip 2 dc of same shell, work shell (5 dc) in next sc, skip 2 dc of next shell, sc in next dc. Repeat from * across, working last sc in top of turning ch. Ch 3, turn. Repeat 2nd row for pattern.

Popcorn Stitch: Make a foundation chain of 16 stitches for practice.

1st row: Sc in 2nd ch from hook and in each remaining ch across (15 sc on row). Ch 3, turn. **2nd row:** Skip first sc, work popcorn as follows: * Work 5 dc all in next sc, remove hook from loop, insert hook in top of first dc of this 5-dc group plus the dropped loop (Diagram 36). Draw dropped loop through, ch 1 to

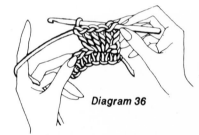

Diagram 36

fasten; popcorn made dc in each of next 3 sc. Repeat from * across to last 2 sc, work popcorn in next sc, dc in last sc. Ch 1, turn. **3rd row:** Sc in first dc, * sc in ch-1 of popcorn, sc in each of next 3 dc between popcorns. Repeat from * across to last popcorn, sc in ch-1 of popcorn, sc in top st of turning ch. Be sure to have 15 sc at end of row. Ch 3, turn. **4th row:** Skip first sc, dc in each of next 2 sc, * popcorn in next sc, dc in each of next 3 sc. Repeat from * across. Ch 1, turn. **5th row:** Sc in each dc and each popcorn across, working last sc in turning ch (15 sc). Ch 3, turn. Repeat 2nd through 5th rows for pattern.

FINISHING

Fastening Ends: After you have completed an article, thread each loose yarn end in a needle and weave about 1″ through solid part of reverse side of the crochet to fasten. Cut off remaining yarn end close to work. If yarn ends are too short for needle, use crochet hook to weave them into work.

Laundering: If your work has become soiled, wash it by hand before blocking. Wash woolens in cold-water soap or mild soap and lukewarm water. Squeeze out water but do not wring. Rinse in lukewarm water several times until all soap is removed. Roll in a towel to absorb some of the moisture.

Blocking: Since blocking is not always recommended for all yarns, especially synthetics, read the information on yarn wrapper. If blocking is suggested and an article is made up of several pieces, block each piece before sewing.

If you have laundered your work, block it while still damp. Place article wrong side up on a flat, padded surface. Gently pat into shape; pin with rustproof pins. Let dry thoroughly before unpinning.

If you have not had to launder your work, pin the dry article, wrong side up, on a padded surface. Press through a damp cloth with a hot iron; do not let weight of iron rest on article. Let work dry.

Sewing: With right sides together, pin edges to be sewn, matching any pattern in rows or stitches. Use matching yarn. Begin sewing by anchoring yarn to work with several small stitches. Sew straight edges with a whipped stitch at edge of work. Sew shaped or uneven edges with a backstitch, sewing just inside edges of work. On woolen articles, work stitches loosely enough to match elasticity of garment.

When sewing is completed, press seams lightly on the wrong side and give article a light final blocking.

HOW TO ENLARGE PATTERNS

You will need brown wrapping paper (pieced if necessary to make a sheet large enough for a pattern), a felt-tipped marker, pencil and ruler. (**Note:** If pattern you are enlarging has a grid around it, first connect lines across pattern with a colored pencil to form a grid over the picture.) Mark paper with grid as follows: First cut paper into a true square or rectangle. Then mark dots around edges, 1″ or 2″ apart (or whatever is indicated on pattern), making same number of spaces as there are squares around the edges of pattern diagram. Form a grid by joining the dots across opposite sides of paper. Check to make sure you have the same number of squares as shown in diagram. With marker, draw in each square the same pattern lines you see in corresponding squares on diagram.

If you want to avoid the trouble of drawing a grid to enlarge your pattern, you can order a package of four 22″ x 34″ sheets of 1″ graph paper for $2.00 postpaid from Sewmakers, Inc., 1619 Grand Avenue, Baldwin, New York 11510.

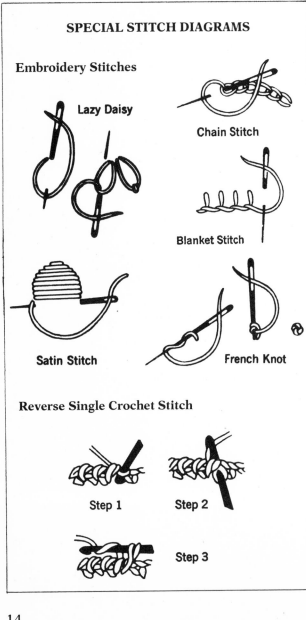

SPECIAL STITCH DIAGRAMS

Embroidery Stitches

Lazy Daisy

Chain Stitch

Blanket Stitch

Satin Stitch

French Knot

Reverse Single Crochet Stitch

Step 1

Step 2

Step 3

1

*Fashions
For Women*

TEXTURED SMOCK SWEATER

Chains and double crochets form interlocking Vs in a textured pattern with five accent colors. Two buttons close the back of the neck.

SIZES: (6–8) [(10–12)–(14–16)]. Sweater measures about 15½″ [17½″–19½″] across back at underarms; 21½″ from back of neck to lower edge.

MATERIALS: Bucilla Winsom Orlon acrylic yarn, 5 [5–6] (2-oz.) skeins larkspur No. 312 (color M), 1 skein each deep rose (dusty rose) No. 42 (color D), royal blue No. 292 (color B), Pompeii (rust) No. 339 (color R), almond (olive) No. 377 (color O), antique rose No. 43 (color P); aluminum crochet hook size H (or international size 5.00 mm) **or the size that will give you the correct gauge.**

GAUGE: 5 V-sts = 4″; 2 rows V-sts = 1″.

To dec 1 dc: (Y o hook, pull up lp in next st, y o and draw through 2 lps on hook) twice, y o and draw through all 3 lps on hook.

BODY (make 2): Starting at lower edge with M, ch 76 [82–88]. **Border: 1st row (right side):** Dc in 4th ch from hook and in each ch across (74 [80–86] dc, counting turning ch as 1 dc); ch 3, turn. **2nd row:** Dc in each dc; ch 3, turn. Repeat 2nd row twice more.

To Establish Pattern: 1st row (V-st row): *Skip 2 dc, in next dc work dc, ch 1 and dc (V-st made). Repeat from * across, ending by skipping next st, dc in last dc (24 [26–28] V-sts); ch 3, turn. **2nd and 3rd rows:** Work 1 V-st in each ch sp of V-sts on previous row, dc in last dc; ch 3, turn. **4th row:** Dc in each dc and in each ch, decreasing 3 sts evenly across (71 [77–83] dc); ch 3, turn.

Repeat last 4 rows 4 times more, then work 3 rows of 19 [21–23] V-sts. Break off M.

Stripe Band: 1st row (wrong side): With D, work dc in each dc and in each ch, decreasing 6 sts evenly across. Break off; turn. **2nd row:** With B sl st in 1st dc, ch 3; repeat from * on 1st pattern row (17 [19–21] V-sts), dc in last dc. Break off; turn. **3rd row:** With R, sl st in ch sp of 1st V-st, ch 3; work V-st in each of next 15 [17–19] V-sts, dc in ch sp of next V-st. Break off; turn. **4th row:** With B sl st in 1st dc, ch 3; work V-st in each V-st, dc in ch 3. Break off; turn. **5th row:** With O repeat 1st stripe row. Break off; turn. **6th row:** With P sl st in 1st dc, ch 3; repeat from * on 1st pattern row (13 [15–17] V-sts), dc in last dc. Break off; turn. **7th row:** With B repeat 4th stripe row. Repeat last row once more with M. Break

off. Mark center V-st on one body piece for center back.

SLEEVES: Cuff Ribbing: Ribbing is worked vertically. With M ch 11. **1st row:** Sc in 2nd ch from hook and in each ch across; ch 1, turn. **2nd row:** Working in back lps only, sc in each sc across; ch 1, turn. Repeat 2nd row 20 [20–22] times more. Break off.

Sleeve Section: 1st row (right side): With M work 29 [29–32] sc evenly spaced along one long edge of cuff ribbing; ch 3, turn. **2nd row:** Skip 1st sc, work V-st in next sc, * skip next sc, work V-st in each of next 2 sc. Repeat from * 7 [7–8] times more. Skip next sc, V-st in next sc, dc in last sc; ch 3, turn (18 [18–20] V-sts). **3rd**

and 4th rows: Work V-st in each V-st across, dc in last dc; ch 3, turn. **5th row:** Dc in each dc and in each ch across (56 [56–62] dc, counting turning ch as 1 dc); ch 3, turn. **6th row:** Work as for 1st pattern row of body to establish V-sts; ch 3, turn.

Repeat 3rd through 5th sleeve pattern rows once, then work 3 V-st rows. **Next row:** Repeat 5th sleeve pattern row, decreasing 6 dc evenly spaced across. Work 3 rows of 16 [16–18] V-sts. Break off M; turn.

Stripe Band: Continuing to work in established pattern and decreasing 3 sts on next row **only**, work in the following color sequence: 1 row each D, B, R, B, O and P.

With M work even in pattern for 4 more rows (15 [15–17] V-sts ending with 6th sleeve pattern row). Break off M; turn.

To Shape at Armholes: Next row: With M sl st in 1st V-st, ch 3; work V-st in each V-st to within last V-st, dc in last V-st. Break off; turn. Repeat last row once more (11 [11–13] V-sts). Do not break off; ch 3, turn. **Next row:** Work dc in each dc and ch, decreasing 6 sts evenly. Work 3 rows of 9 [9–11] V-sts. Break off.

Sew sleeves to body pieces, matching armhole-shaping rows. Sew side and sleeve seams.

YOKE: 1st row (right side): With M, dc in marked V-st at center back; skipping dc's at joinings of pieces, work as follows: Dc in each st to left sleeve decreasing 3 sts evenly; dc in each st across left sleeve; dc in each st across front, decreasing 9 sts evenly; dc in each st across right sleeve; dc in each remaining st across back decreasing 3 sts evenly, dc in marked st; ch 3, turn. **2nd row:** Work as for 1st pattern row of body to establish V-sts (38 [42–50] V-sts), dc in last dc; ch 3, turn. **3rd row:** Work V-st in each V-st, dc in last dc; ch 3, turn. **4th row:** Work 2 dc in each V-st, dc in last dc; ch 3, turn. **5th row:** * Dc in each of next 2 dc, dec 1 dc. Repeat from * . ast 2 dc, dc in each of last 2 dc; ch 3, turn.

Repeat 2nd row once (19 [21–25] V-sts), then repeat 3rd row O [1–2] times. Repeat 4th row once, omitting ch 3. Break off.

COLLAR: 1st row: Skip 2 dc, dc in each dc to within last 2 dc; ch 3, turn. **2nd row:** Skip 1st dc, dc in each dc across; ch 3, turn. Repeat last row once more, omitting ch 3. Break off.

Sl st along 1st collar row on wrong side to keep neckline from stretching. Sc evenly around neck edges. Sew on hooks and eyes at back neck edge if desired.

COLLARED MOHAIR PULLOVER

Worked in lacy crochet stitch, this sweater has bell sleeves, slit sides and a convertible collar.

SIZES: (8–10) [(12–14)–(16–18)]. Pullover measures 16″ [18″–20″] across back at underarms; 14½″ from underarm to lower edge.

MATERIALS: Bucilla Melody (50% mohair/50% acrylic), 10 (1-oz) balls tea rose No. 34; aluminum crochet hooks sizes H and J (or international hooks sizes 5.00 mm and 6.00 mm) **or the size that will give you the correct gauge.**

GAUGE: On size J hook: 7 pattern st = 2″.

Directions for back follow cluster-st directions below.

CLUSTER ST: 1st row: Draw up lp in 2nd ch from hook, draw up lp in 3rd ch, y o and draw through all 3 lp on hook (1st cl made); * ch 1, draw up lp in each of next 2 ch, y o and draw through all 3 lp on hook (another cl made). Repeat from * across; ch 1, turn. **2nd row:** Draw up lp in top of 1st cl, draw up lp in next ch-1 sp, y o and draw through all 3 lp on hook (cl made), ch 1; * cl over next cl and ch-1 sp, ch 1. Repeat from * across,

ending last repeat with cl worked in last cl and in turning ch; ch 1, turn. Repeat 2nd row for pattern.

BACK: Starting at lower edge with size J hook, ch 55 [63–71] to measure 16" [18"–20"]. Work even in cl st on 27 [31–35] cl for 14½". Mark each end of last row for underarm. Continue in cl st for another 4". Change to size H hook.

Yoke: Back has yoke worked in rows of sc. **Next row:** Sc in top of 1st cl, * sc in next ch-1 sp, sc in top of next cl. Repeat from * across; sc in top of turning ch (54 [62–70] sc); ch 1, turn. Work even in sc for 4" [4½"–5"]. Break off. Mark off center 22 sc for back neck.

FRONT: Work as for back until piece measures same as back to underarm markers. Mark front for underarms.

To Divide for Neck Opening: Left Side: Work in pattern across 11 [13–15] cl, ending ch 1, turn. Work even on these cl for 7" [7½"–8"], ending at arm edge. Change to size H hook.

To Shape Neck: Next row: Sc in 1st cl, * sc in next ch-1 sp, sc in next cl. Repeat from * until 15 [19–23] sc have been made; ch 1, turn. Work even in sc for 1". Break off.

Right Side: Skip center 5 sc on last full row worked, work in pattern across row (11 [13–15] cl). Complete to correspond to left side.

SLEEVES: Starting at lower edge with size J hook, ch 57 [61–65] to measure 16" [17"–18"]. Work even in cl st for 16". Break off.

FINISHING: Sew shoulder seams. Sew sleeves between markers. Sew sleeve and side seams, leaving 7" slits at sides.

NECKBAND AND COLLAR: 1st row: With right side facing you, with size H hook, sc evenly along right front neck opening, work 3 sc at upper right corner, sc evenly around neck edge, work 3 sc at upper left corner, sc evenly along left front neck opening; ch 1, turn. **2nd row:** Sc in each sc across; ch 1, turn. **3rd row:** Sc in each sc across, working 3 sc at each corner; ch 1, turn. Repeat 2nd and 3rd rows 5 times more, then repeat 2nd row once again. Break off. Lap end of right neckband over left and sew in place.

COWL-NECK PULLOVER

One of the easier patterns to do: single- and half double-crochet stitches in a pretty mix of stripes on a solid background.

SIZES: (6–8) [(10–12)–(14–16)–(18–20)]. Sweater measures 16" [18"–20"–22"] across back at underarms. Length is adjustable.

MATERIALS: Bucilla Win-Knit (Orlon acrylic knitting-worsted-weight) yarn, 4 [4–5–5] (4-oz) twin-paks almond green No. 464 (color G), 1 twin-pak each American beauty No. 427 (color A), purple No. 493 (color P) and medium turquoise No. 412 (color T); aluminum crochet hook size J (or international hook size 6.00 mm) **or the size that will give you the correct gauge.**

GAUGE: 3 sts = 1"; 3 rows = 1".

BACK: With G, starting at lower edge, ch 49

[55–61–67] to measure about 16″ [18″–20″–22″]. **1st row:** Sc in 2nd ch from hook, h dc in next ch, * sc in next ch, h dc in next ch. Repeat from * across (48 [54–60–66] sts); ch 1, turn. **2nd row:** Sc in 1st h dc, h dc in next sc, * sc in next h dc, h dc in next sc. Repeat from * across; ch 1, turn. Repeating 2nd row for pattern st, work 1 more row G, 2A, 1P, 2G, 2A, 3T, 2A, 2G, 1P and 2A, then with G, work even until piece measures 15″ from beg, or desired length to underarms. Mark beg and end of last row worked for underarms.

Yoke: Keeping in established pattern, work 2 rows A, 1P, 2G, 2A, 3T, 2A, 2G, 1P and 1A. Break off; turn.

To Shape Neck and Shoulders: 1st Shoulder: With G, work in pattern across 1st 14 [17–20–23] sts. Work 2 [2–3–3] more rows in pattern on these sts. Break off. Mark but do not work center 20 sts for back neck. **2nd Shoulder:** With G, work in pattern across remaining 14 [17–20–23] sts. Complete as for 1st shoulder.

FRONT: Work same as back.

SLEEVES: Starting at lower edge with G, ch 43 [43–47–47] to measure about 14″ [14″–16″–16″]. Work even in pattern with G until piece measures 12″ [12″–12½″–12½″]. Continuing in pattern, work 2 rows, A, 3T, 2A, 2G, 1P and 2A. Break off.

FINISHING: Sew shoulder seams. Sew sleeves to front and back between markers. Sew underarm and sleeve seams.

Turtleneck: 1st row: With G, starting at right shoulder seam and working in pattern, work 3 [3–4–4] sts along back neck edge of right shoulder, work across 20 sts on back neck, work 6 [6–8–8] sts along left neck edge, work across 20 sts on front neck, work 3 [3–4–4] sts along front neck edge of right shoulder (52 [52–56–56] sts); ch 1, turn. Work even in pattern for 7″. Break off. Sew neck seam. Fold collar down.

FUZZY-WUZZY PULLOVER/FUZZY-WUZZY CARDIGAN

MATCHING SCARF**

* **Beginner project**
** **Expert project**

General Directions

Mix single and double crochet to produce a wavy row and add double-loop stitiches and popcorns as you go along.

The pattern of these garments is made simply by working rows of dcs and scs as desired and inserting a random number of popcorns and loops. Be sure to work the pattern sample first (see below) before starting the garments.

To Change Colors: If last st is sc, work across in pattern to within last st, insert hook in last st, y o and draw up lp; * break off old color, leaving 3″ end for weaving back into work. Make lp on hook with new color and draw it through 2 remaining lps of old color. * **If last st is dc,** work across in pattern to within last st, y o, insert hook in last st, y o and draw up lp, y o and draw through 2 lps on hook; repeat from * to * above.

To Increase: Work 2 sc (or 2 dc) in same st.

To Decrease: To dec 1 sc draw up lp in each of next 2 sts, y o and draw through all 3 lps on hook. **To dec 1 dc** (y o, insert hook in next st, y o and draw up lp, y o and draw through 2 lps on hook) twice, y o and draw through all 3 lps on hook. **To dec more than 1 st at beg of row** sl st in each st to be decreased, then start pattern

with sc in next st. **To dec more than 1 st at end of row** work across row to within the number of sts to be decreased, then turn or ch 1 and turn.

To Make Popcorn: Y o, insert hook in next st, y o and draw up lp, y o and draw through 2 lps on hook; (y o, insert hook in same st, y o and draw up lp, y o and draw through 2 lps on hook) twice; y o and draw through 3 lps on hook, y o and draw through remaining 2 lps on hook. (**Note:** The next st worked will make popcorn "pop" out on right side.)

To Make Double-Loop Stitch (d lp st): Wrap yarn loosely around 1st 2 fingers of left hand twice (each wrap = 1 lp), insert hook in next st and draw a bit of both lps through st, drop lps from fingers, y o and draw through all 3 lps on hook (2 lps formed on right side).

PATTERN: Sample: Make this before starting a garment. With J hook and 1st color ch 25. **1st row (right side):** Sc in 2nd ch from hook, sc in next ch, dc in each of next 3 ch, sc in next ch, dc in each of next 2 ch, (sc in next ch, dc in next ch) 6 times; sc in each of last 4 ch, changing to 2nd color in last sc (24 sts); ch 1, turn. **2nd row (wrong side):** Sc in each of 1st 2 sts, * work d lp st in each of next 3 sts *, sc in each of next 2 sts, d lp st in each of next 2 sts, dc in each of next 2 sts, (popcorn in next st, sc in next st) 3 times. Repeat from * to * once; popcorn in next st, sc in each of last 3 sts, changing to 3rd color in last st; ch 1, turn. **3rd row:** Work 2 sc, 1 dc, sc in next (popcorn) st, * 2 dc, 1 sc *, 1 dc, 1 sc. Repeat from * to * once; 3 dc, 1 sc. Repeat from * to * twice; 2 sc, changing to 4th color in last st (24 sts); ch 1, turn. **4th row:** Work 3 sc, 3 d lp sts, 1 sc, (1 popcorn, 1 sc) 3 times; 2 d lp sts, (1 sc, 1 popcorn) 3 times; 2 d lp sts, 1 sc, changing to 5th color; ch 1, turn. **5th row:** Work 2 sc, 2 dc, 4 sc, 2 dc, 2 sc, (1 dc, 1 sc) 4 times; 2 dc, 2 sc, changing to 1st color in last st; ch 3, turn. **6th row:** Skip 1st st (the one directly under the ch 3), dc in next st, (1 popcorn, 1 sc) twice; 3 d lp sts, (1 popcorn, 1 sc) twice; 5 d lp sts, (1 popcorn, 1 sc) twice; 2 sc, changing to 2nd color; ch 1, turn. **7th row:** Work 2 sc, 2 dc, 1 sc, 2 dc, 2 sc, 2 dc, (2 sc, 1 dc) twice; 1 sc, 2 dc, 1 sc, 1 dc, dc in last (ch-3) st, changing to 3rd color; ch 1, turn. **8th row:** Work 1 sc, * 3 d lp sts, (1 sc, 1 popcorn) twice; 1 sc *. Repeat from * to * once more; 3 d lp sts, 1 sc, 1 popcorn, 2 sc, changing to 4th color; ch 1, turn. **9th row:** Work 3 sc, * 1 dc, 1 sc, 2 dc, 2 sc *. Repeat from * to * once more; (1 dc, 1 sc) 3 times, 2 dc, 1 sc. Break off. Piece should measure about 4" × 9".

Tips on Pattern: After you have made the sample, you should have a good understanding of the pattern. Further important reminders:

The stitches are worked at random. You decide how many scs, dcs, lps and popcorns you want to make and where you want to place them.

The lps and popcorns are always worked on wrong-side rows.

Only scs and dcs are worked on right-side rows.

Always change colors at end of each row and break off old color.

Always work sc or d lp st, not dc, following popcorn in order to make popcorn "pop" out.

FUZZY-WUZZY PULLOVER

In order to familiarize yourself with the pattern, read and follow **General Directions**, before starting sweater.

SIZES: (6–8) [(10–12)–(14–16)]. Sweater measures 15" [17"–19"] across back at underarms.

MATERIALS: Spinnerin 4 Ply (Orlon/acrylic knitting-worsted-weight yarn), 2 [2–3] (4-oz) skeins cranberry No. 3273 (main color), 1 skein each red No. 3253, camel No. 3206, vermilion No. 3270, watermelon No. 3263 and light rust No. 3258; aluminum crochet hook sizes H and J (or international sizes 5.00 mm and 6.00 mm) **or the sizes that will give you the correct gauges;** tapestry needle.

GAUGES: Pattern worked with J hook, 11 sts = 4"; 5 rows = 2". Sc worked with H hook, 3 sc = 1"; 4 rows = 1".

See **General Directions** to work pattern, change colors, increase and decrease.

BACK: Ribbed Band: Band is worked vertically. Starting at side seam with main color and H hook, ch 15. **1st row:** Sc in 2nd ch from hook and in each ch across (14 sc): ch 1, turn. **2nd row:** Working in back lp only of each st, sc in each sc across; ch 1, turn. Repeat 2nd row until piece measures 15" [17"–19"] when slightly stretched. Break off and set aside.

Starting at lower edge above ribbing, using J hook and any color except main color, ch 43 [47–53] loosely. Using all colors in random sequence, work pattern on 42 [46–52] sts until piece measures 14" from beg or 3" less (to allow for waistband) than desired length to underarms, ending with a right-side row. Attach new color (except main color); ch 1, turn.

To Shape Armholes: Next row (wrong side): Working in pattern, dec 3 sts at beg and end of row (36 [40–46] sts). Break off; turn.

Yoke: Work in sc and main color only. **Next row (right side):** With H hook and main color, sc in each st across; ch 1, turn. Dec 1 st at beg and end of next 1 [1–2] rows, then work even in sc on 34 [38–42] sts until armhole measures 6¾" [7¼"–7¾"] from beg.

To Shape Shoulders: Dec 5 [6–7] sts at beg of next 4 rows (14 sts remain).

FRONT: Work as for back through 1st 3 rows of yoke (34 [38–42] sc).

To Shape Neck Opening: Next row (wrong side): Sc in 1st 17 [19–21] sc; ch 1, turn. Work even for right front yoke on 17 [19–21] sc for 5″ [5½″–6″], ending with wrong-side row. Dec 4 sts at beg (neck edge) of next row. Work 1 row even. Dec 3 sts at beg of next row (10 [12–14] sc). Work even until armhole measures same as back armholes, ending at armhole edge; turn.

To Shape Shoulder: Dec 5 [6–7] sts at beg of next row. Work 1 row even. Dec remaining 5 [6–7] sts. Break off.

Work left front yoke to correspond to right yoke, reversing shaping.

SLEEVES: Ribbed Band: Work as for back ribbed band until piece measures 7½″ [9″–10½″] when slightly stretched. Break off and set aside.

Starting at cuff edge above ribbing, using J hook and any color except main color, ch 21 [25–27]. Work in pattern and random color sequence, increasing 1 st at beg and end of row every 2″ six times. Work even in pattern on 32 [36–38] sts until piece measures 15″ from beg or 3″ less (to allow for cuff) than desired length to underarm.

To Shape Cap: Keeping in pattern, dec 3 sts at beg of next 2 rows (26 [30–32] sts). Dec 1 st at beg and end of next 4 rows. Work even on 18 [22–24] sts for 0 [1–2] rows. Dec 3 sts at beg of next 4 rows. Break off.

FINISHING: Sew ribbed bands to lower edges of back, front and sleeves. Sew shoulder seams. Sew in sleeves, easing to fit. Sew side and sleeve seams.

Collar: With main color and J hook crochet ch to fit around neck edge. **1st row:** Sc in 2nd ch from hook and in each ch across; ch 1, turn. **2nd row:** Sc in each sc across; ch 1, turn. Repeat 2nd row until piece measures 5″. Break off. Sew 1st row of collar to neck edge.

Neck Trim and Ties: With main color and J hook ch 6″ for tie; sl st in front neck edge at collar seam, sc evenly around both edges of front neck opening, ch 6″ for other tie. Break off.

FUZZY-WUZZY CARDIGAN AND SCARF

In order to familiarize yourself with the pattern read and follow **General Directions** before starting cardigan and scarf.

SIZES: (6–8) [(10–12)–(14–16)–(18–20)]. Cardigan measures 16″ [18″–20″–22″] across back at underarms. Scarf measures 10″ × 84″, not including fringe.

MATERIALS: Spinnerin 4-ply (Orlon/acrylic knitting-worsted-weight yarn), 3 [4–4–4] (4-ounce) skeins camel No. 3205, 2 [2–3–3] skeins each beige No. 3211, natural No. 3206, cocoa No. 3210 and charcoal-brown heather No. 5933; aluminum crochet hook size J (or international size 6.00 mm) **or the size that will give you the correct gauge;** five 1″-diameter buttons; tapestry needle.

GAUGE: 11 sts = 4″; 5 rows = 2″.

See **General Directions** to work pattern, change colors, increase and decrease.

CARDIGAN

BACK: Starting at lower edge with charcoal, ch 45 [51–57–63]. Work even in pattern on 44 [50–56–62] sts in the following color sequence: 1 row each cocoa, camel, natural, beige and charcoal until piece measures 18″ or desired length to underarms.

To Shape Armholes: Dec 2 [3–3–4] sts at beg of next 2 rows, then dec 1 st at beg and end of following 2 [2–3–3] rows.

Keeping in color sequence, work even on 36 [40–44–48] sts until armholes measure 7″ [7½″–8″–8½″].

To Shape Shoulders: Dec 6 [7–8–9] sts at beg of next 2 rows, then dec 5 [6–7–8] sts at beg of following 2 rows (14 sts remain). Break off.

LEFT FRONT: Starting at lower edge with charcoal, ch 23 [26–29–32]. Work as for back on 22 [25–28–31] sts until piece measures 1½″ less than back to underarm.

To Shape Neck and Armhole: Dec 1 st at neck edge only on next row, then every other row 6 times more; while shaping neck, when piece measures same as back to underarm, shape armhole as follows: Dec 2 [3–3–4] sts once, then dec 1 st every row 2 [2–3–3] times. Keep arm edge even after armhole shaping is completed, but continue neck shaping until 11 [13–15–17] sts remain. Work even until armhole measures same as back armhole, ending at armhole edge.

To Shape Shoulder: Next row (right side): Dec 6 [7–8–9] sts; work in pattern across remainder of row. Work 1 row even. Dec remaining 5 [6–7–8] sts. Break off.

RIGHT FRONT: Work as for left front, reversing shaping.

SLEEVES: Starting at wrist edge above border with charcoal, ch 25 [25–29–29]. Work pattern in color sequence as for back on 24 [24–28–28] sts, increasing 1 st at beg and end of row every 3″ [2½″–2½″–2″] 5 [6–6–7] times.

Work even on 34 [36–40–42] sts until sleeve measures 17″ from beg or 1″ less (to allow for border) than desired length to underarm.

To Shape Cap: Dec 2 [3–3–4] sts at beg of next 2 rows. Dec 1 st at beg and end of every other row 4 [4–5–5] times, then every row 3 times (16 [16–18–18] sts remain). Break off.

Border: With camel work 5 rows sc across wrist edge of sleeve.

FINISHING: Sew shoulder, side and sleeve seams. Sew in sleeves.

Front Border: 1st row (right side): Starting at lower edge of right front with camel, sc evenly along right front edge, neckline and left front edge; ch 1, turn. **2nd row (wrong side):** Sc in each sc; ch 1, turn. Mark right front edge for 5 buttonholes evenly spaced. **3rd row:** Sc in each sc to 1st buttonhole marker, * ch 2, skip 2 sc, sc in each sc to next marker. Repeat from * 3 times more; ch 2, skip 2 sc, sc in each sc across neckline and left front edge; ch 1, turn. **4th row:** Sc in each sc across, working 2 sc over each ch-2 buttonhole lp; ch 1, turn.

5th row: Sc in each sc across; do not break off.

Lower Border: Work row of sc evenly spaced across lower edge of jacket.

SCARF

Starting at one end with charcoal, ch 26. Work even in pattern on 25 sts in color sequence as for back until scarf measures 84″ or desired length, ending with charcoal row. Break off.

FINISHING: With camel sc in edge of scarf at any place, * ch 1, skip about ⅜″ of scarf edge, sc in edge. Repeat from * around; sl st in 1st sc. Break off.

Fringe: Cut six 15″ strands camel for each tassel. Fold strands in half, draw folded end through any ch-1 sp at one end of scarf. Draw cut ends through lp formed by fold and tighten. Attach 12 tassels to each end of scarf.

SHORT-SLEEVED BOAT-NECK PULLOVER*

The simple, streamlined design is worked in an easy pattern of alternating single- and double-crochet stitches.

See **How to Determine Your Size** before making this sweater.

MATERIALS: Bucilla Win-Knit (Orlon acrylic knitting-worsted-weight yarn), 3 (4-oz.) twin-paks natural heather No. 474, 1 twin-pak each gold No. 442 and Pompeii (rust) No. 447; aluminum crochet hook size J (or international hook size 6.00 mm) **or the size that will give you the correct gauge.**

GAUGE: 3 sts = 1″.

BACK: Starting at lower edge (see diagram) with

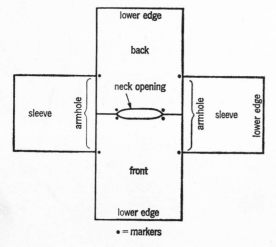

lower edge

back

neck opening

sleeve   armhole   armhole   sleeve   lower edge

front

lower edge

• = markers

heather, ch number of sts for your size (see Boat-Neck Chart). Work back and forth in rows as follows: **1st row (right side):** Work dc in 4th ch from hook and in each ch across (see chart for correct number of dc across back, counting the turning ch as 1 dc); ch 1, turn. **2nd row:** Work sc in each dc across, sc in top of turning chain; ch 3, turn. **3rd row:** Skip 1st sc (directly below the ch 3), dc in each sc across; ch 1, turn. Repeating 2nd and 3rd rows, work 2 more rows heather, 3 gold, 4 rust, then work with heather until piece measures length of back for your size (see chart), or about 3″ less than desired length to shoulders, ending with dc row. Continuing in same sc row- dc row pattern, work 3 rows gold, 4 rust and 2 heather. Break off.

FRONT: Make same as back.

SLEEVES: Starting at lower edge with heather, ch number of stitches for your size (see chart). Work back and forth in rows as for back (see chart for correct number of sts) until piece measures 7″, ending with dc row, then work 2 rows gold and 4 rows rust. Break off.

BOAT-NECK CHART

	Small (6–8)	Medium (10–12)	Large (14–16)	Extra Large (18–20)
BACK: Chain	47	53	59	65
Stitches Across Back	45	51	57	63
Length of Back	18″	18″	19″	20″
SLEEVES: Chain	44	44	47	50
Stitches Across Sleeve	42	42	45	48
Length of Armhole (front and back)	14″	14″	15″	16″

FINISHING: Mark off center 10″ along upper edge of back and front for neck opening. Sew back to front from markers to side edges (see diagram). Mark off correct length for armhole for your size along side edges of front and back (see chart). Sew upper edge of each sleeve between markers. Sew underarm and sleeve seams.

HOW TO DETERMINE YOUR SIZE

The easiest way is to take a sweater you own that you know fits well, lay it flat and measure the width across the back at the underarms. Then refer to our sizing chart to determine your size.

SIZING CHART

SIZE	Small (6–8)	Medium (10–12)	Large (14–16)	Extra Large (18–20)
Width of Garment Across Back at Underarms	15″	17″	19″	21″

DONEGAL CARDIGAN JACKET

The Irish look, accented with wooden buttons, is worked in a combination of shell and double-crochet stitches.

SIZES: (8–10) [(12–14)–(16–18)]. Jacket measures 16" [18"–20"] across back at underarms, 13½" [14"–14½"] from underarm to lower edge.

MATERIALS: Unger's Scottish Fantasy (100% Shetland wool yarn), 9 [10–11] (1.6-oz) balls beige tweed No. 100; aluminum crochet hook size E (or international hook size 3.50 mm) **or the size that will give you the correct gauge;** 5 buttons.

GAUGE: 11 dc = 2"; 5 rows dc = 2".

Note: When working in dc pattern or in shell and sc pattern, work in back lp of each st.

BACK: Starting at lower edge, ch 93 [105–117] to measure about 16" [18"–20"]. **1st row (right side):** Dc in 4th ch from hook and in each ch across (91 [103–115] dc, counting turning ch as 1 dc); ch 3, turn. **2nd row:** See note above. Skip 1st dc, dc in each dc across, dc in top of turning ch; ch 3, turn. Repeat 2nd row for dc pattern until piece measures 4½" [5"–5½"], ending with a wrong-side row. **Shell and sc pattern:** See note above. **1st row (right side):** Skip 1st 3 dc, work shell of 5 dc in next dc, skip next 2 dc, dc in next dc, * skip next 2 dc, work 5-dc shell in next dc, skip next 2 dc, dc in next dc. Repeat from * across, working last dc in top of turning ch (15 [17–19] shells); ch 3, turn. **2nd row:** Skip 1st 3 dc, * work 5-dc shell in center dc of next shell, skip 2 dc, dc in next single dc of last row. Repeat from * across, working last dc in top of turning ch; ch 3, turn. **3rd and 4th rows:** Repeat 2nd row twice, ending last row with ch 1, turn. **5th row:** Sc in each dc across; ch 1, turn. **6th through 8th row:** Sc in each sc across; ch 1, turn, ending last row with ch 3. **9th through 12th row:** Working over sc's instead of dc's, repeat 1st through 4th row of shell and sc pattern. Working in dc pattern from now on, work even on 91 [103–115] dc until piece measures 13½" [14"–14½"] from beg. Place marker at beg and end of last row for underarms. Continue to work even for another 5" [5½"–6"]; ch 3, turn.

To Shape Neck and Shoulders: 1st Side: 1st row: Skip 1st dc, dc in next 27 [33–39] sts; ch 3, turn. **2nd row:** Skip 1st dc, dc in each dc across; ch 3, turn. **3rd and 4th rows:** Repeat 2nd row, omitting ch 3 on last row; turn. **5th row:** Sl st in 1st 7 [8–10] dc, sc in next 7 [8–10] dc, dc in next 7 [9–10] dc, tr in last 7 [9–10] dc. Break off.

Skip center 35 sts on last full row for back neck. **2nd Side: 1st row:** Dc in remaining 28 [34–40] dc; ch 3, turn. **2nd row:** Skip 1st dc, dc in each dc across; ch 3, turn. **3rd and 4th rows:** Repeat 2nd row once more, ending last row ch 4, turn. **5th row:** Skip 1st dc, tr in next 6 [8–9] dc, dc in next 7 [9–10] dc, sc in next 7 [8–10] dc, sl st across remaining 7 [8–10] dc. Break off.

LEFT FRONT: Starting at lower edge, ch 45 [51–57] to measure about 8" [9"–10"]. Marking beg of 1st row for side edge, work even in dc pattern as for back on 43 [49–55] dc until piece measures 4½" [5"–5½"], ending at side edge. Repeat 1st through 12th row of shell and sc pattern of back (working on 7 [8–9] shells), then work even in dc pattern on 43 [49–55] dc until piece measures same as back to underarm marker. Mark side edge for underarm. Continuing in dc pattern from now on, work even for 5" [5½"–6"] more, ending at front edge and omitting last ch 3; turn.

To Shape Neck and Shoulder: 1st row: Sl st in 1st 13 dc, ch 3, dc in each remaining dc across (31 [37–43] dc, counting ch 3 as 1 dc); ch 3, turn. **2nd row:** Skip 1st dc, dc in each dc to last 2 dc; dec 1 dc as follows: (Y o, insert hook in next dc and pull lp through, y o and pull through 2 lps on hook) twice, y o and pull through all 3 lps on hook (1 dc dec); ch 3, turn. **3rd row:** Skip 1st dc, dec 1 dc, dc in each dc across; ch 3, turn. **4th row:** Repeat 2nd row, ending ch 4, turn. **5th row:** Skip 1st dc, tr in next 6 [8–9] dc, dc in next 7 [9–10] dc, sc in next 7 [8–10] dc, sl st in remaining 7 [8–10] dc. Break off.

RIGHT FRONT: Work as for left front, reversing shaping.

SLEEVES: Starting at top edge, ch 75 [81–87] loosely to measure about 13″ [14″–15″]. Working as for back, work even in dc pattern on 73 [79–85] sts for 4 rows.

Working in shell and sc pattern as for back, * work 3 rows (instead of 4 rows) in shell pattern on 12 [13–14] shells, work 3 rows (instead of 4 rows) in sc pattern, work 3 rows in shell pattern, then work 5 rows in dc pattern. Repeat from * twice more, ending last repeat with 3 [4–5] rows dc. Sleeve should measure 19″ [19½″–20″] from beg; adjust length of sleeve if necessary, allowing for turned-back cuff. Break off.

FINISHING: Sew shoulder seams. Sew sleeves between markers. Sew underarm and sleeve seams.

Front Bands and Collar: 1st row: With right side facing you, starting at lower right front corner, dc evenly along right front edge, neck edge and left front edge, working 3 dc at each upper front corner; ch 3, turn. **2nd row:** Work in dc pattern, increasing as necessary at upper corners so work lies flat. **3rd row:** Repeat 2nd row. Mark right front band for placement of 5 buttonholes, the 1st 2″ from lower edge, the others 2¼″ apart. **4th row:** Work as for 2nd row, working buttonhole at each marker as follows: Ch 3, skip next 3 dc, work to end. **5th row:** Work as for 2nd row, working 3 dc in each ch-3 sp and ending ch 1, turn. **6th row:** Sc in each st across; ch 1, turn. **7th row:** Repeat 6th row. Break off. Sew buttons opposite buttonholes. Turn collar down and turn up sleeves for cuffs.

TAMBOUR BOLERO JACKET

Decorative borders suggest peasant embroidery on a jacket done in easy half double crochet with almost no shaping.

SIZES: (6–8) [(10–12)–(14–16)]. Jacket measures 17″ [19″–21″] across back at underarms, 24″ [24½″–25″] from shoulder to lower edge.

MATERIALS: Bucilla Win-Knit (acrylic yarn), 3 [3–4] (4-oz) skeins natural heather No. 474 (color N), 1 skein each dusty rose No. 425 (color R), medium turquoise No. 412 (color T) and almond green No. 463 (color G); aluminum crochet hook size G (or international size 4.50 mm), **or the size that will give you the correct gauge.**

GAUGE: 3 h dc = 1″; 7 rows = 3″.

To Change Colors on Design Row: H dc in each st to within last h dc of old color, y o and draw up lp in next st, drop old color, y o with new color and draw through all 3 lps on hook. (**Note:** Leave 4″ ends when breaking off or attaching colors.) Hold color not in use along top edge of piece and work over it.

BACK: Starting at lower edge with R, ch 53 [59–65] to measure about 17″ [19″–21″].

Border Pattern: 1st row (wrong side): H dc in 3rd ch from hook and in each ch across (52 [58–64] h dc, counting turning ch 2 as 1 h dc); ch 2, turn. **2nd row:** Skip 1st h dc (directly below ch 2), h dc in next h dc, * with G (see To Change Colors, above), h dc in each of next 2 h dc, with R, h dc in each of next 2 h dc. Repeat

from * across, ending with 2 G [2 R–2 G] h dc; ch 2 R, turn. Break off G. **3rd row:** With R, h dc in each st across. Break off. Attach T; ch 2, turn.

4th row: H dc in each h dc across. Break off T. Attach R; ch 2, turn. **5th row:** H dc in each h dc across; ch 2, turn. **6th row:** Repeat 2nd row. **7th row:** Repeat 3rd row. Break off R. Attach N; ch 2, turn. Border completed. Work even in h dc with N until piece measures 11″ from beg or desired length to underarm. Mark beg and end of last row for beg of armholes.

Armholes: Continue to work even until armholes measure 5½″ [6″–6½″] from beg, ending with a right-side row. Break off N, attach R; ch 2, turn. **Next row:** H dc in each st across; ch 2, turn.

Body of jacket is made in 1 piece without shoulder seams. Continue by working over right shoulder and complete right front as follows:

RIGHT FRONT: 1st row (right side): Work as for 2nd row of Border Pattern across 16 [18–20] h dc, ending 1 G h dc in last st (17 [19–21] h dc, including ch 2). Break off G. With R, ch 2, turn. Working on right shoulder and front **only**, complete border as for back. With N, work even for 3 rows. Do not turn. Ch 10 [11–12] and mark this edge for front neckline. Turn. **Next row:** H dc in 3rd ch from hook and in each ch and h dc across (26 [29–32] h dc); ch 2, turn. Work even until front measures same as back to underarm; mark side edge for end of armhole. Continue to work even until front measures same as back to border, ending with a right-side row. Work border pattern. Break off.

Hold work so that right side is facing you. Skip 18 [20–22] sts along back neck. With R, make lp on hook, y o and work h dc in next st. Work left shoulder and front to correspond to right shoulder and front, reversing all shaping.

SLEEVES: 1st row (wrong side): Attach R to wrong side at right front armhole marker, work an even number of sts evenly spaced across armhole between markers, being careful not to draw work in.

2nd through 7th rows: Work as for border pattern, then work even with N until sleeve measures 16″ [16½″–17″] from beg or desired length, allowing 1″ extra for turned-up cuff if desired.

FINISHING: Sew side and sleeve seams.

Edging: With right side facing you, using R, work row of sc along neck, front and lower edges of garment, working 3 sc in each corner; join with sl st to 1st sc. Break off.

Neck Border: 1st row: With right side facing you, with T, work h dc in each st across neck edge. Break off. **2nd row:** With right side facing you, with R, work sc in each T st across, decreasing 1 st at each inner corner of front neck (to dec 1 st, draw up lp in each of next 2 sts, y o and draw through all 3 lps on hook). Break off.

Ties: With R, crochet 21″ chain each in T and G. Thread ends of each chain through jacket neck, following photograph for placement, and tie in bows.

REVERSIBLE WRAP JACKET AND HAT

The flip side is solid color and it's all done in double crochet; stripes are slip-stitched in at the end. Front and back are made in one piece; hat is started at crown.

SIZES: (6–8) [(10–12)–(14–16)]. Jacket measures about 16½″ [18″–20″] across back at underarms.

MATERIALS: For Jacket: Knitting worsted, 28 [32–34] ounces light oxford and Persian yarn, 35 [37–40] yards each scarlet, violet, deep rose, royal blue, magenta and teal blue; aluminum crochet hook size I (or international size 5.50 mm) **or the size that will give you the correct gauge.**

For Hat: 6 ounces knitting worsted, same color as jacket. Trim hat with leftover Persian yarn from jacket.

GAUGE: 13 dc = 4″; 3 rows = 2″.

Note: Jacket and hat are reversible, with colored stripes showing on one side only. The light oxford is used for crocheting the jacket and hat (the stitch pattern forms ridges on right side of work). The con-

trasting colors are crocheted along these ridges and show on only one side of work.

Jacket

BODY: Starting at lower edge with oxford, ch 145 [153–161] to measure about 44″ [46½″–49″]. **1st row:** Dc in 4th ch from hook and in each ch across; ch 3, turn.

2nd row: To form ridge, work as follows: Skip 1st dc, dc in **back** lp of each dc across, dc in top of ch 3 (143 [151–159] dc, counting ch 3 as 1 dc); ch 3, turn. **3rd row:** Skip 1st dc, dc in **both** lps of each dc across, dc in top of turning ch; ch 3, turn.

Repeat 2nd and 3rd rows for pattern until 6 rows are completed. **7th row (dec row):** Work in pattern until 39 [41–43] dc are completed, (y o hook, draw up a lp in next st, y o hook and draw through 2 lps on hook) twice; y o hook and draw through all lps on hook (1 dc dec), work across in pattern until 41 [43–45] dc remain, dec 1 dc, work in pattern to end of row (2 dc dec); ch 3, turn.

Work even in pattern for 3 rows more, then repeat dec row, working decreases above those made below. Repeat last 4 rows three times more (133 [141–149] dc).

Work even in pattern until 25 [25–27] rows are completed, ending with a 3rd row of pattern. Break off. Piece should measure about 17″ [17″–18½″] from beg. Put piece aside.

SLEEVES: With oxford ch 36 [37–38] for cuff. Work even in pattern as for body on 34 [35–36] dc for 6″. Inc 1 dc at beg and end of next row. Continue in pattern and repeat inc every 3″ three times more. Work even on 42 [43–44] dc until 27 rows are completed, ending with a 3rd row of pattern. Sleeve will stretch to measure 21″, including 4″ cuff to be turned back. Break off.

YOKE: Hold work with ridge side of body and sleeves facing you. Work as follows in pattern as established across last row of body and sleeves.

1st row: Make lp on hook with oxford. Dc in 1st dc of body, work in pattern across until 39 [41–43] dc are worked for front; then pick up one sleeve and work in pattern across all 42 [43–44] sleeve sts; then working on body sts, work across next 55 [59–63] sts for back. Pick up 2nd sleeve and work across all 42 [43–44] sts; then work across remaining 39 [41–43] sts of body for other front; ch 3, turn.

Place one marker at each joining between body and sleeves (4 markers in all).

2nd row: Skip 1st dc, * dc in each dc across to within 3 dc of marker, (y o, draw up lp in next dc, y o and draw through 2 lps on hook) 3 times, y o and draw through all lps on hook (this is a double dec worked across 3 sts), work another double dec across next 3 sts

following same marker. Working 1 extra double dec over center 3 sts of **back** section, repeat from * across, ending dc in each dc to end of row (18 dc dec); ch 3, turn.

3rd row: Skip 1st dc, * dc in each dc across to within 2 dc of marker, (y o, draw up lp in next dc, y o and draw through 2 lps) twice, y o and draw through all lps on hook (this is a single dec worked over 2 dc), work another single dec across next 2 sts following same marker. Repeat from * across, ending dc in each dc to end of row (8 dc dec); ch 3, turn.

Repeat 2nd and 3rd rows once more. Omitting extra dec at center back, repeat 2nd and 3rd rows 3 times more; then repeat 3rd row 2 [3–4] times more (77 [79–81] sts remain). Do not break off; ch 3, turn.

COLLAR: 1st row: Mark beg of row. Work in pattern until 22 [23–24] dc are completed; do not work remaining sts; ch 3, turn. Work even in pattern as established until 8th row is completed, ending at marked edge. Work short rows as follows: **1st row:** Work until 12 dc are completed, then h dc in each of next 4 dc, sc in each of next 4 dc; ch 1, turn. **2nd row:** Sl st in each of 1st 3 sts, sc in each of next 4 sts, h dc in each of next 4 sts, dc in each dc to end of row; ch 3, turn. **3rd row:** Dc in each of 1st 5 sts, h dc in each of next 3 sts, sc in each of next 3 sts. Break off.

Work other half of collar along neck edge of other front to correspond. To finish jacket, see Stripes and Finishing following directions for hat.

BELT: With oxford crochet a ch about 52″ [54″–56″] long. Work in pattern as for body for 2 rows, omit turning ch at end of 2nd row, turn. Sl st in each st across last row. Break off.

Hat

One size fits all.

Starting at top, with oxford ch 4. Join with sl st to form ring. **1st rnd:** Work 6 sc in ring; ch 3, turn. **2nd rnd:** Work 5 dc in 1st sc, work 6 dc in each remaining sc (36 dc). Join with sl st to top of ch 3; ch 3, turn. Always turn work at end of each round.

3rd rnd: Work in **back** lp on this rnd to form ridge. Skip 1st dc, dc in next dc, 2 dc in next dc, * dc in each of next 2 dc, 2 dc in next dc. Repeat from * around (48 dc), join as before; ch 3, turn. **4th rnd:** Work in **both** lps on this round. Skip 1st dc, dc in each of next 2 dc, 2 dc in next dc; * dc in each of next 3 dc, 2 dc in next dc. Repeat from * around (60 dc). Join; ch 3, turn. Piece should measure 6″ across.

Repeating last 2 rnds for pattern only, work even on 60 dc for 4 rnds. Continue in pattern and inc 3 dc evenly around on next 2 rnds, then continue in pattern and work even on 66 dc until 17th rnd is completed.

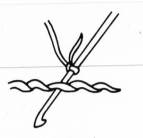

step 1

step 2

Stripe Diagram

Join and break off. Piece should measure about 10½″ from beg.

STRIPES: Stripes for Jacket Body: Use Persian yarn and work along ridges formed by pattern stitch. Hold jacket with lower edge down and start stripe pattern at lower edge.

1st Stripe: Work along 1st free ridge. With scarlet make lp on hook. Insert hook from above (see stripe diagram, step 1), y o, twist st around as in step 2 and draw lp through both lps on hook (sl st made), * ch 1, skip next st, inserting hook in same manner as before sl st in next st. Repeat from * across. Break off. **2nd Stripe:** With violet work as for 1st stripe along next free ridge. **3rd Stripe:** With deep rose work as for 1st stripe along next free ridge. Skip next ridge. **4th Stripe:** With royal blue work across next free ridge. **5th Stripe:** With magenta, work across next free ridge. **6th Stripe:** With teal blue work across next free ridge. Skip next ridge.

Continue to work stripes in color pattern as established, spacing them in same manner across body, yoke and collar.

Stripes for Sleeves: Hold jacket with yoke down and sleeve up. Starting at lower edge of yoke and working toward wrist edge of sleeve, work stripes to correspond with those on body.

Stripes for Hat: Hold hat with crown down and face edge up. Starting near center of crown, work same as for body until 6th stripe is completed.

FINISHING: Sew back seam of collar, then sew collar to neck edge. Sew sleeve seams. With main color, work 1 row of sc along front edges of jacket and edge of collar.

BLOUSON JACKET

Details include openwork sleeves, mandarin collar, drawstring waist, three pockets. Body is worked in double crochet.

SIZES: (6–8) [(10–12)–(14–16)]. Loose-fitting jacket measures 16″ [18″–20″] across back at underarms.

MATERIALS: Lion Brand Fisherman's Knit (wool knitting worsted), 4 [4–5] (4-oz.) skeins natural No. 98; aluminum crochet hook size H (or international hook size 5.00 mm) **or the size that will give you the correct gauge;** 5 buttons; 2 snaps.

GAUGE: 10 dc = 3″; 2 rows dc = 1″.

BACK: Starting at lower edge, ch 56 [62–68] to measure 16″ [18″–20″]. **1st row:** Dc in 4th ch from hook and in each ch across (54 [60–66] dc, counting turning ch 3 as 1 dc); ch 3, turn. **2nd row:** Skip 1st dc (directly below ch 3), dc in each dc across; ch 3, turn. Repeating 2nd row, work even until piece measures 18½″ [19″–19½″], omitting ch 3 on last row.

Note: There is no shaping at underarms, and shoulders are slightly dropped.

To Shape Shoulders: 1st row: Sl st across 1st 2 [3–4] sts, sc in each of next 2 sts, h dc in each of next 2 sts, dc in each st to within last 6 [7–8] sts, h dc in each of next 2 sts, sc in each of next 2 sts; turn. **2nd row:** Sl st across 1st 6 [7–8] sts, sc in each of next 2 [3–4] sts, h dc in each of next 2 sts, dc in each st to within last 10 [11–12] sts, h dc in each of next 2 sts, sc in each of next 2 [3–4] sts. Break off. Mark off center 14 [16–18] sts of last row for back of neck.

LEFT FRONT: Starting at lower edge, ch 26 [29–32] to measure 8″ [9″–10″]. **1st row:** Dc in 4th ch from hook and in each ch across (24 [27–30] dc, counting turning ch 3 as 1 dc); ch 11 for front border; turn. **2nd row:** Dc in 4th ch from hook, dc in each of next 7 ch, dc in each dc across (33 [36–39] dc); ch 3, turn. **3rd row:** Skip 1st dc, dc in each dc across; ch 3, turn. Repeating 3rd row, work even until piece measures 16½″ [17½″–18½″], ending at front edge and omitting ch 3 on last row.

To Shape Neck: 1st row: Sl st across 1st 10 [11–12] dc, ch 3 (counts as 1 dc), dc in each dc across; ch 3, turn. **2nd row:** Skip 1st dc, dc in each dc to within last 2 dc; turn. **3rd row:** Sl st across 1st 3 dc, ch 3 (counts as 1 dc), dc in each dc across. Work 2 rows even on 20 [22–24] dc, ending at shoulder edge.

To Shape Shoulder: 1st row: Sl st across 1st 2 [3–4] sts, sc in each of next 2 sts, h dc in each of next 2 sts, dc in each remaining st across; ch 3, turn. **2nd row:** Skip 1st st, dc in each st to within last 10 [11–12] sts, h dc in each of next 2 sts, sc in each of next 2 [3–4] sts. Break off.

RIGHT FRONT: Starting at lower edge, ch 26 [29–32] to measure 8″ [9″–10″]. **1st row:** Dc in 4th ch from hook and in each ch across (24 [27–30] dc, counting turning ch 3 as 1 dc). Drop lp from hook. With another ball of yarn, ch 9, sl st in top of turning ch at beg of row. Break off. Pick up dropped lp at end of row; ch 3, turn. **2nd row:** Skip 1st dc, dc in each dc across, dc in each of next 9 ch (33 [36–39] dc); ch 3, turn. Work even in dc until piece measures same as left front, ending at side edge; ch 3, turn.

To Shape Neck: 1st row: Skip 1st dc, dc in each dc to within last 9 [10–11] dc; turn. **2nd row:** Sl st across 1st 3 dc, ch 3 (counts as 1 dc), dc in each dc across; ch 3, turn. **3rd row:** Skip 1st dc, dc in each dc to within last 2 dc; ch 3, turn. Work 2 rows even on 20 [22–24] dc, ending at neck edge; ch 3, turn.

To Shape Shoulder: 1st row: Skip 1st dc, dc in

each dc to within last 6 [7–8] sts, h dc in each of next 2 sts, sc in each of next 2 sts; turn. **2nd row:** Sl st across 1st 6 [7–8] sts, sc in each of next 2 [3–4] sts, h dc in each of next 2 sts, dc in each dc across. Break off.

SLEEVES: Starting at lower edge above cuff, ch 58 [62–66] to measure 16½″ [17½″–18½″]. **1st row:** Dc in 6th ch from hook, (ch 1, skip next ch, dc in next ch) 26 [28–30] times (27 [29–31] sps); ch 4, turn. **2nd row:** Skip 1st sp, dc in next dc, * ch 1, skip next sp, dc in next dc. Repeat from * to within last sp (turning ch on last row); ch 1, skip next ch, dc in next ch; ch 4, turn. Repeat 2nd row until piece measures 13″ [13½″–13½″]. **Next row (inc row):** Dc in 1st dc, * ch 1, skip next sp, dc in next dc (1 sp inc). Repeat from * to within last sp, ch 1, skip next ch, work dc, ch 1 and dc in next ch (1 sp inc); ch 4, turn. Repeat 2nd row across 29 [31–33] sps until piece measures 16″ [16½″–16½″] or desired length to underarm without 1″ cuff. (Top of sleeve is straight to fit into dropped shoulder; there is no cap.) Break off.

Cuff: 1st row: With right side facing you, work 21 [22–23] sc as evenly spaced as possible across lower edge of sleeve; ch 1, turn. **2nd row:** Sc in each sc across; ch 1, turn. Repeat 2nd row 3 times more. Break off.

COLLAR: Starting at inner edge, ch 43 [47–51] to measure 13″ [14″–15½″]. **1st row:** Sc in 2nd ch from hook and in each ch across (42 [46–50] sc); ch 1, turn. Work 4 more rows sc. Break off.

LARGE POCKET (make 2): Starting at lower edge, ch 22 to measure 6½″. **1st row:** Dc in 6th ch from hook, (ch 1, skip next ch, dc in next ch) 8 times (9 sps); ch 4, turn. **2nd row:** Skip 1st sp, dc in next dc, (ch 1, skip next sp, dc in next dc) 7 times; ch 1, skip next ch, dc in next ch; ch 4, turn. Repeat 2nd row 4 times more, ending last row with ch 3; turn. **Flap: 1st row:** Skip 1st sp, dc in next dc (1 sp dec), ch 1, * skip next sp, dc in next dc, ch 1. Repeat from * to within last 2 sps, y o, insert in next dc and draw up lp, y o and draw through 2 lps on hook, skip next ch, y o, insert hook in next ch and draw up lp, y o and draw through 2 lps on hook, y o and draw through all 3 lps on hook (1 sp dec); ch 3, turn. **2nd row:** Skip 1st sp, dc in next dc (1 sp dec), ch 1, * skip next sp, dc in next dc, ch 1. Repeat from * to within last 3 sp, (y o, insert in next dc and draw up lp, y o and draw through 2 lps on hook) twice; y o and draw through all 3 lps on hook (1 sp dec); ch 3, turn. **3rd row:** Repeat last row. **4th row:** Dec 1 sp as at beg of last row, ch 1, dec 1 sp as at end of last row. Break off. Work 1 row sc across sides of pocket flap.

SMALL POCKET: Ch 16 to measure 5″. **1st row:** Dc in 6th ch from hook, (ch 1, skip next ch, dc in next ch) 5 times (6 sps); ch 4, turn. **2nd row:** Skip 1st sp, dc in next dc, (ch 1, skip next sp, dc in next dc) 4 times, ch 1, skip next ch, dc in next ch; ch 4, turn. Repeat 2nd row twice more, ending last row with ch 3; turn. **Flap:**

Repeat 1st and 2nd rows of large pocket flap. **3rd row:** Dec 1 sp as at end of last row. Break off. Work 1 row sc across sides of pocket flap.

FINISHING: Mark off 7″ [7½″–8″] from beg of shoulder shaping along each side edge of fronts and back for armholes. Sew shoulder seams, side seams below markers, and sleeve seams. Sew in sleeves. Turn 4 sts along each front edge to inside to form facing and sew in place. Turn up 1st row along lower edge to form casing for drawstring. Leaving 1″ free at front corner of each front edge, sew collar to neck edge. With right side facing you, work 1 row sc along right front edge, around collar and along left front edge, working 3 sc at corners.

To make drawstring, with 2 strands of yarn held together, crochet 60″ chain. Run through casing along lower edge. Sew buttons on left front. Button through sps between sts on right front. Sew snaps at upper and lower edges of fronts. Sew pockets in place.

HOODED SWEATER-COAT AND MITTENS**

A burnoose-like hood falls back into a flattering collar on a sweater with a handsome yoke pattern and rib texture. Crocheted ties keep it closed.

SIZES: Small (6-8) [medium (10–12)–large (14–16)]. Jacket measures about 16½″ [18″–20″] across back at underarms and 21″ from lower edge to underarm. Mittens fit all sizes

MATERIALS: For Jacket: Bernat Berella Husky (60% Orlon-40% Antron nylon), 10 [11–12] (118 yard-4 ounce) balls No. 6193 birch (natural mix—color NM), 5 [6–7] balls No. 8559 natural (color N), 2 balls rust (color R), 1 ball each black (color B), yellow (color Y) and green (color G). **For Mittens:** 1 ball each of Berella Husky birch and natural. **For Both:** Aluminum crochet hooks sizes K for sweater-coat and mittens and J for sweater-coat border (or international sizes 7.00 mm and 6.50 mm) **or the sizes that will give you the correct gauges.**

GAUGES: With size K hook: 5 sc = 2″; 6 rows sc = 2″. With J hook: 11 sc = 4″; 7 rows sc = 2″.

2nd row. Break off white. Do not turn, form lp on hook with yellow and work next row from wrong side of work. **6th row (wrong side):** Do not work in 1st sc, work popcorn as follows: Insert hook in next sc, y o and draw lp through, y o and draw through 1 lp on hook, (insert hook in same sc, y o and draw lp through, y o and draw lp through 1 lp on hook) 4 times, y o and draw through all 6 lps on hook (1 popcorn made); (ch 1, skip next sc, work popcorn in next sc) twice; * ch 3, skip next 3 sc, work popcorn in next sc, (ch 1, skip next sc, make popcorn in next sc) twice. Repeat from * to within last sc, ch 1, do not work in last sc (10 [11–12] 3 popcorn groups). Break off yellow, attach white; turn. **7th row (right side):** Working over yellow ch 1 of previous row, h dc in 1st skipped sc *on the row below*, * work 5 sc over next 3-popcorn group as follows: Sc in sp after next popcorn, (sc in sp before next popcorn, sc in sp after same popcorn) twice (5 sc completed); working over yellow ch 3 of previous row, h dc in each of next 3 white skipped sc *on the row below*. Repeat from * across, ending h dc in last skipped white sc *on the row below* (79 [87–95] sts); ch 1, turn. **8th row (wrong side):** Sc in each sc across. Break off white; attach green and ch 1, turn. **9th row (right side):** Sc in each sc across, increasing 1 st in last sc (80 [88–96] sc). Break off; do not turn.

Cluster Pattern: 1st row: With right side facing you, with size F hook and white, form lp on hook. * Working in back lp only of each st, draw up lp in each of next 2 sc, y o and draw through all 3 lps on hook, ch 1 (cl made). Repeat from * across, omitting ch 1 after last cl, sc in same place as last st was worked (40 [44–48] cl); ch 1, turn. (**Note:** See diagram for pattern stitch. We used 2 colors in the diagram so that the stitches show more clearly. Between each pair of cl there is a vertical bar. Always insert hook in sp before or after this bar, as specified. These vertical bars form a vertical stripe effect that will become apparent after a few inches of pattern are completed.) **2nd row:** Change to size H hook. Insert hook in sp before 1st cl and draw up lp, insert hook in sp after same cl (just before vertical bar) and draw up lp, y o and draw through all 3 lps on hook, ch 1 (1st cl made), * insert hook in sp before next cl (right after vertical bar), insert hook in sp after same cl (just before next bar), y o and draw through all 3 lps on hook, ch 1 (cl made). Repeat from * across, omitting ch 1 after last cl; sc in same place as last st was worked; ch 1, turn. Repeating 2nd row for cl pattern, work even until piece measures 12″ [12″–12½″] from beg, ending with a right- [wrong—right-] side row and omitting last ch1; turn.

To Shape Underarms: 1st row: Sl st across 1st 4 sts, work in pattern to within last 4 sts, ending with sc in same place as last st was worked (4 cl dec in row);

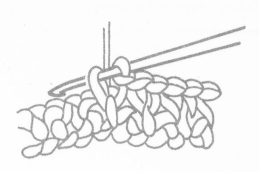

turn. Repeat last row 2 [3–4] times more (28 cl). Last row worked is a wrong-side row. Break off and set aside.

FRONT: Work as for back.

RIGHT SLEEVE: Border Pattern: Starting at lower edge with size F hook and green, ch 56 [64–64] to measure 11″ [12½″–12½″]. **1st row (right side):** Sc in 2nd ch from hook and in each ch across (55 [63–63] sc). Break off green; do not turn. With white, work next row from right side of work. **2nd row:** Sc in each sc across; ch 1, turn. **3rd through 5th row:** Repeat 2nd row 3 times. Break off white; do not turn. With yellow, work next row from wrong side of work. **6th row (wrong side):** Do not work in 1st sc, * work popcorn in next sc, (ch 1, skip next sc, work popcorn in next sc) twice; ch 3, skip next 3 sc. Repeat from * to within last sc, ch 1, do not work in last sc (7 [8–8] popcorn groups). Break off yellow, attach white; turn. **7th through 9th row:** Work as for 7th through 9th row on Back Border Pattern, inc 0 [1–1] st at end of last row (55 [64–64] sc). Break off. Do not turn.

Cluster Pattern: 1st row (right side—inc row): With right side facing you, with size F hook and white, form lp on hook. Working in back lps only, * draw up a lp in each of 1st 2 sc, y o and draw through all 3 lps on hook, ch 1 (1st cl made). * Draw up lp in each of next 2 sc, y o and draw through all 3 lps on hook, ch 1 (cl made), draw up a lp in same place as last st was worked, draw up a lp in next sc, y o and draw through all 3 lps on hook, ch 1 (cl made). Repeat from * to within last 2 sts, work cl over last 2 sts (36 [42–42] cl), sc in same place as last st was worked; ch 1, turn. Change to size H hook. Work even in Cluster Pattern for 1″, ending with a right- [wrong- —right-] side row and omitting ch 1 at end of last row.

To Shape Underarm: 1st row: Sl st across 1st 4 [6–6] sts, work in Cluster Pattern to within last 4 [6–6] sts, sc in same place as last st was worked (4 [6–6] cl dec in row); turn. **2nd row:** Sl st across 4 sts, work in Cluster Pattern to within last 4 sts (4 cl dec in row); turn. Repeat last row 0 [1–1] times (28 cl). Work even on 28 cl for 1 [1–2] rows more. Last row worked is a wrong-side row. Break off. Set piece aside.

LEFT SLEEVE: Work as for right sleeve, but do not break off after last row; ch 1, turn. Continue as follows, joining all pieces for yoke.

YOKE: With right sides of left sleeve, front, right sleeve and back facing you, with size H hook and white, work as follows: **1st row (right side):** Work 28 cl across left sleeve, 28 cl across front, 28 cl across right sleeve and 28 cl across back (112 cl); sc in same place as last st was worked; ch 1, turn. **2nd through 17th row:** Work even in Cluster Pattern. **18th row (dec row):** * Draw up lp in sp before next cl, draw up lp in sp after next cl, y o and draw through all 3 lps on hook (1 cl dec). Repeat from * across, ending with sc in same place as last st

was worked (113 sts). Break off white, attach green; ch 1, turn.

Border Pattern: 1st row (right side): Sc in each st across, decreasing 2 sts evenly spaced (111 sc). Break off green. Do not turn. **2nd row (right side):** With white, sc in back lp of each sc across; ch 1, turn. **3rd through 9th row:** Working on 111 sc, work as for Back Border Pattern (omit inc on last row and do not break off); ch 1, turn (14 popcorn groups). **10th row:** With green, sl st in each st across. Break off.

FINISHING: Sew yoke and underarm seams. Sew side and sleeve seams. Following photograph, with tapestry needle and 2 strands of green, work 3 lazy-daisy-st leaves below each popcorn flower group. (See Special Stitch Diagrams, page 14.)

SCALLOP-EDGE CAMISOLE**

The single-crochet/double-crochet pattern with post-double-crochet ridges and leaves shows off your skills.

NOTE: This camisole is recommended for experienced crocheters.

SIZES: (6–8) [(10–12)–(14–16)]. Snug-fitting camisole measures 29″ [32″–35″] around bust; 12″ [12½″–13″] from underarm to lower edge.

MATERIALS: J. & P. Coats Knit-Cro-Sheen, 7 [8–8] (175-yd) balls Spanish red No. 126; aluminum crochet hook size F (or international hook size 4.00 mm) **or the size that will give you the correct gauge.**

GAUGE: 9 sts = 2″.

Note: Use 2 strands thread held together throughout.

PATTERN STITCHES: Back Post Dc (b dc): Y o; reaching over top of piece and working on opposite side (right side) of work, insert hook from right to left around vertical post (upright part) of next dc, y o and draw yarn through, y o and complete dc in usual manner. Horizontal ridge will form across side facing you (wrong side).

Front Post Dc (f dc): Y o; insert hook from front to back and to front again around vertical post of next dc; y o and draw yarn through, y o and complete dc. Horizontal ridge will form across opposite side (wrong side) of work.

Dec 1 f dc: * Y o; insert hook from front to back and to front again around vertical post of next dc; y o and draw yarn through, y o and draw through 2 lps on hook. Repeat from * once more, y o and draw through all 3 lps on hook.

BACK: Starting at lower edge, ch 68 [72–80] to

measure about 14½″ [16″–17½″]. **1st row (right side):** Sc in 2nd ch from hook, * dc in next ch, sc in next ch. Repeat from * across (67 [71–79] sts); ch 3, turn. **2nd row:** Skip 1st sc, (sc in next dc, dc in next sc) 1 [2–1] times; b dc around next dc, * dc in next sc, (sc in next dc, dc in next sc) twice; b dc around next dc. Repeat from * to last 3 [5–3] sts, (dc in next sc, sc in next dc) 1 [2–1] times; dc in next sc; ch 1, turn. **3rd row:** Sc in 1st dc, (dc in next sc, sc in next dc) 1 [2–1] times; f dc around next dc, * sc in next dc, (dc in next sc, sc in next dc) twice; f dc around next dc. Repeat from * to last 3 [5–3] sts, (sc in next dc, dc in next sc) 1 [2–1] times; sc in next dc; ch 3, turn. Repeat 2nd and 3rd rows for background and post dc patterns until piece measures 11½″ [12″–12½″]. Break off.

FRONT: Work same as back until piece measures 9½″ [10″–10½″], ending with a 2nd pattern row.

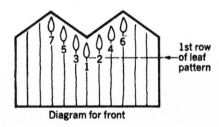

Diagram for front

First Leaf Pattern: See diagram. **1st row (right side):** Work in background pattern across 1st 32 [34–38] sts, dc in next st; to start **1st leaf,** ch 1, f dc around next dc, ch 1, dc in next st, work background pattern across next 32 [34–38] sts; ch 3, turn. (**Note:** Unless otherwise specified, if row ends with sc, ch 3 and turn; if row ends with dc, ch 1 and turn.) **2nd row:**

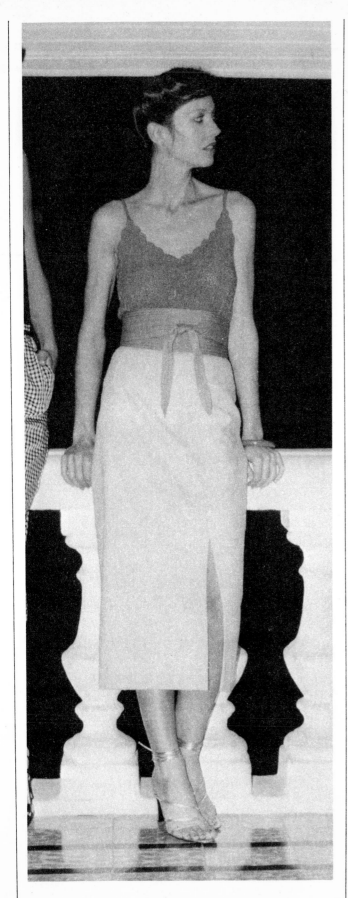

Counting turning ch 3 as 1 st, work 32 [34–38] background sts, 1 b dc, (dc in next ch 1, 1 b dc) twice; work 32 [34–38] background sts. **3rd row:** Work 32 [34–38] background sts, 2 f dc, ch 1, 1 f dc, ch 1, 2 f dc, 32 [34–38] background sts. **4th row:** Work 32 [34–38] background sts, 2 b dc, dc in next ch, 1 b dc, dc in next ch, 2 b dc, 32 [34–38] background sts.

5th row: Work 26 [28–32] background sts, 1 dc; to start leaf **No. 2,** ch 1, 1 f dc, ch 1, 2 dc, 1 sc, 1 dc; dec 1 f dc over next 2 sts as follows: (Y o, insert hook around post of next dc, y o and draw yarn through, y o and draw through 2 lps on hook) twice, y o and draw through all 3 lps on hook (1 f dc dec); work 3 f dc, dec 1 f dc, work 1 dc, 1 sc, 2 dc; to start **leaf No. 3,** ch 1, 1 f dc, ch 1, 1 dc, 26 [28–32] background sts. **6th row:** Work 26 [28–32] background sts. * (1 b dc, dc in next ch) twice; 1 b dc. * 1 sc, 1 dc, 1 sc, 5 b dc, 1 sc, 1 dc, 1 sc. Repeat from * to * once; work 26 [28–32] background sts. **7th row:** Work 26 [28–32] background sts, * 2 f dc, ch 1, 1 f dc, ch 1, 2 f dc; * 1 dc, 1 sc, 1 dc, dec 1 f dc, work 1 f dc, dec 1 f dc, work 1 dc, 1 sc, 1 dc. Repeat from * to * once; work 26 [28–32] background sts. **8th row:** Work 26 [28–32] background sts, * 2 b dc, dc in next ch, 1 b dc, dc in next ch, 2 b dc; * (1 sc, 1 dc) twice; 1 b dc, (center leaf completed—mark this last st); (1 dc, 1 sc) twice. Repeat from * to * once; work 26 [28–32] background sts; ch 1, turn.

Left Side: Shape neck and armhole edges at same time as follows: **9th row:** Sl st across 1st 5 [7–11] sts, ch 1, work 15 background sts, 1 dc; to start **leaf No. 4,** ch 1, 1 f dc, ch 1, 2 dc, 1 sc, 1 dc, dec 1 f dc, work 3 f dc, dec 1 f dc, (work 1 dc, 1 sc) twice; ch 1, turn. **10th row:** Skip 1st st, work 1 sc, 1 dc, 1 sc, 5 b dc, 1 sc, 1 dc, 1 sc, 1 b dc, (dc in next ch, 1 b dc) twice; work 14 background sts; ch 1, turn. **11th row:** Skip 1st st, work 13 background sts, 2 f dc, ch 1, 1 f dc, ch 1, 2 f dc, 1 dc, 1 sc, 1 dc, dec 1 f dc, work 1 f dc, dec 1 f dc, work 1 dc; ch 1, turn. **12th row:** Skip 1st st, work 1 dc, 1 b dc, (1 dc, 1 sc) twice; 2 b dc, dc in next ch, 1 b dc, 1 dc, 2 b dc, 12 background sts; ch 1, turn. **13th row:** Skip 1st dc, work 5 background sts, 1 dc; to start **leaf No. 6,** ch 1, 1 f dc, ch 1, 2 dc, 1 sc, 1 dc, dec 1 f dc, work 3 f dc, dec 1 f dc, (work 1 dc, 1 sc) twice; ch 1, turn. **14th row:** Skip first st, work 1 sc, 1 dc, 1 sc, 5 b dc, 1 sc, 1 dc, 1 sc, 1 b dc, (dc in next ch, 1 b dc) twice; work 4 background sts; ch 1, turn. **15th row:** Skip 1st st, work 3 background sts, 2 f dc, ch 1, 1 f dc, ch 1, 2 f dc, 1 dc, 1 sc, 1 dc, dec 1 f dc, work 1 f dc, dec 1 f dc, work 1 dc; ch 1, turn. **16th row:** Skip 1st st, work 1 dc, 1 b dc, (1 dc, 1 sc) twice; 2 b dc, dc in next ch, 1 b dc, dc in next ch, 2 b dc; 2 background sts; ch 1, turn. **17th row:** Skip 1st st, work 1 dc, dec 1 f dc, work 3 f dc, dec 1 f dc, (work 1 dc, 1 sc) twice; ch 1, turn. **18th row:** Skip 1st st, work 1 sc, 1 dc, 1 sc, 5 b dc, 1 sc; ch 1, turn. **19th row:** Skip 1st st, dec 1 f dc, work 1 f dc, dec 1 f dc, work 1 dc; ch 1, turn.

20th row: Skip 1st st, work 1 dc, 1 b dc, 1 dc. Do not break off.

For strap, crochet long enough ch to fit over shoulder and diagonally across back. **1st row:** Sc in 2nd ch from hook and in each ch across; sl st in next st on 20th row; turn. **2nd row:** Sl st in each st across. Break off.

Right Side: Starting at marked center st on 8th row, work as follows: **9th row:** Sl st in marked st, ch 1, (work 1 sc, 1 dc) twice; dec 1 f dc, work 3 f dc, dec 1 f dc, work 1 dc, 1 sc, 2 dc; to start **leaf No. 5,** ch 1, 1 f dc, ch 1, 1 dc, work 15 background sts (do not work remaining sts); ch 1, turn. **10th row:** Skip 1st st, work 14 background sts, (1 b dc, dc in next ch) twice; 1 b dc, 1 sc, 1 dc, 1 sc, 5 b dc, 1 sc, 1 dc, 1 sc; ch 1, turn. **11th row:** Skip 1st st, work 1 sc, 1 dc, dec 1 f dc, work 1 f dc, dec 1 f dc, work 1 dc, 1 sc, 1 dc, 2 f dc, ch 1, 1 f dc, ch 1, 2 f dc, work 13 background sts; ch 1, turn. **12th row:** Skip 1st st, work 12 background sts, 2 b dc, dc in next ch, 1 b dc, dc in next ch, 2 b dc, (1 sc, 1 dc) twice; 1 b dc, 1 dc; ch 1, turn. **13th row:** Skip 1st st, sl st in next st, (work 1 sc, 1 dc) twice; dec 1 f dc, work 3 f dc, dec 1 f dc, work 1 dc, 1 sc, 2 dc; to start **leaf No. 7,** ch 1, 1 f dc, ch 1, 1 dc, work 5 background sts; ch 1, turn. **14th row:** Skip 1st st, work 4 background sts, (1 b dc, dc in next ch) twice; 1 b dc, 1 sc, 1 dc, 1 sc, 5 b dc, 1 sc, 1 dc, 1 sc; ch 1, turn. **15th row:** Skip 1st st, sl st in next st, work 1 dc, dec 1 f dc, work 1 f dc, dec 1 f dc, work 1 dc, 1 sc, 1 dc, 2 f dc, ch 1, 1 f dc, ch 1, 2 f dc, work 3 background sts; ch 1, turn. **16th row:** Skip 1st st, work 1 dc, 1 sc, 2 b dc, dc in next ch, 1 b dc, dc in next ch, 2 b dc, (1 sc, 1 dc) twice; 1 b dc, 1 dc; ch 1, turn. **17th row:** Skip 1st st, sl st in next st, (1 sc, 1 dc) twice; dec 1 f dc, work 3 f dc, dec 1 f dc, work 1 dc; ch 1, turn. **18th row:** Skip 1st st, work 5 b dc, 1 sc, 1 dc, 1 sc, ch 1, turn. **19th row:** Skip 1st st, sl st in next st, work 1 dc, dec 1 f dc, work 1 f dc, dec 1 f dc; ch 1, turn. **20th row:** Dc in 1st st, work 1 b dc, 1 dc. Make strap as for left side.

FINISHING: Sew side seams.

Upper Edging: With wrong side facing you, sc at top of right underarm seam, * skip 2 sts, work 5 dc in next st (shell made), skip 2 sts, sc in next st. Repeat from * across back. Continuing in this manner, skip about ½" between sc's and shells along front edge, working shell in front of each strap and sc at center front; join. Break off.

Cross straps in back and sew in place.

TANK-TYPE CAMISOLE**

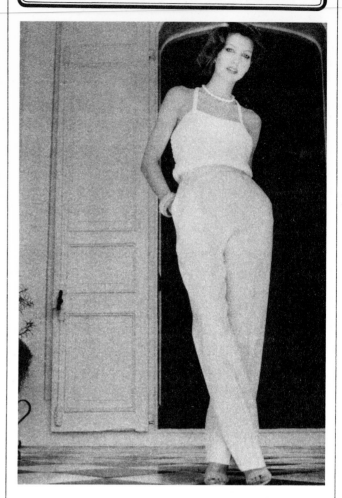

A challenging bit of workmanship: the subtly textured surface is composed of crossed-post-double-crochet stitches.

NOTE: This camisole is recommended for experienced crocheters.

SIZES: (6–8) [(10–12)–(14–16)]. Snug-fitting camisole measures 28" [31"–34"] around bust, 12" [12½"–13"] from underarm to lower edge.

MATERIALS: Joseph Galler's RBC Parisian Cotton (100% cotton knit and crochet thread), 10 [11–12] (1-oz—about 120-yd) balls blanc (white) No. 8009; aluminum crochet hook size F (or international hook size 4.00 mm) **or the size that will give you the correct gauge.**

GAUGE: 8 st = 1"; 4 rows = 1".

PATTERN STITCH: Post DC: This st is worked from right side of work. Y o, insert hook from front (right side), to back and to front again around vertical post (upright part) of next dc, y o and draw thread through, y o and complete dc in usual manner. Horizontal ridge will form across wrong side of piece.

BACK: Starting at lower edge, ch 110 [122–134] to measure about 14″ [15½″–17″]. **1st row (wrong side):** Dc in 4th ch from hook and in each ch across (110 [122–134] dc, counting turning ch as 1 dc); ch 1, turn. **2nd row (right side):** Work post dc around each of 1st 4 dc, * skip next 3 dc, post dc around each of next 3 dc; following Diagram 1, work post dc around 1st skipped

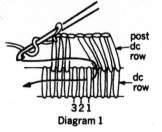

Diagram 1

dc, bringing hook down to right and under the st in direction of arrow; work post dc around 2nd skipped dc and then around 3rd skipped dc. This group of 3 post dc should cross over 3 post dc made previously (see Diagram 2). Repeat from * to last 4 dc, work post dc

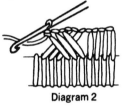

Diagram 2

around each of last 4 dc. (You will have a row of post dc groups—3 sts crossed over 3 sts in each group—and 4 single post dc at beg and end of row.) Ch 3, turn. **3rd row:** Straighten top of last row as much as possible. Skip 1st dc (directly below ch 3), dc in each st across (110 [122–134] dc); ch 1, turn. **4th row:** Work post dc around 1st dc, * skip next 3 dc, post dc around each of next 3 dc, post dc around 1st, 2nd, then 3rd skipped dc. Repeat from * to last dc, post dc around last dc. You will have a row of crossed groups and a single post dc at beg and end of row. Ch 3, turn. **5th row:** Repeat 3rd row.

Repeat 2nd through 5th row until piece measures 11½″ [12″–12½″], ending with a right-side row. **Next row:** Sc across, dec evenly to 80 [88–96] sc; ch 1, turn. **Following row:** Sc in each st across; ch 1, turn. Repeat last row twice more. **Last row:** Sl st in each st across. Break off.

FRONT: Work same as back.

FINISHING: Sew side seams.

Straps (make 2): Crochet an 18″ chain. **1st row:** Sc in 2nd ch from hook and in each ch across; ch 1, turn. **2nd row:** Sc in each sc across; ch 1, turn. Repeat 2nd row twice more. Sl st in each sc across. Break off. Sew straps in place, crossing in back.

SHELL-PATTERN CAMISOLE

Satin ribbon is beaded through a romantic design that's mostly double crochet in an open shell pattern.

SIZES: (6–8) [(10–12)—(14–16)]. Garment measures 14½″ [16¼″–18″] across bust from underarm to underarm for snug fit, 13″ [14¼″–14¼″] from underarm to lower edge including armhole border.

MATERIALS: DMC Brilliant crochet cotton (knit and crochet yarn), 4 [4–5] (218-yd) balls light pink No. 8777; steel crochet hook No. 0 **or the size that will give you the correct gauge;** 1½ yds ¼″-wide blue satin ribbon.

GAUGE: In shell pattern: 5 shells = 4½″; 4 rnds = 1¼″. **In sc pattern:** 7 sc = 1″; 8 rnds = 1 ″.

BODY: Body is worked in rounds, starting at lower edge; there are no side seams. Ch 204 [228–252] to measure 29″ [32½″–36″]. Being careful not to twist chain, join with sl st in 1st ch st to form ring.

1st rnd: Ch 1, sc in same ch st as sl st, sc in each ch st around; join with sl st in 1st ch st. **2nd rnd:** Ch 1, sc

in 1st sc, * ch 2, skip 2 sc, sc in next sc. Repeat from * around, ending ch 2, skip last 2 sc, sl st in 1st sc (68 [76–84] ch lps). **3rd rnd (1st shell rnd):** Sl st in 1st ch-2 sp, ch 3, in same ch-2 sp work dc, ch 2 and 2 dc for 1st shell, * ch 2, skip next sc, skip next ch-2 and next sc, in next ch-2 sp work a shell of 2 dc, ch 2 and 2 dc. Repeat from * around, ending ch 2, skip last ch 2; join with sl st in top of 1st ch 3 (34 [38–42] shells).

4th rnd: Sl st in next dc, sl st in ch-2 sp of 1st shell, ch 3, in same sp work dc, ch 2 and 2 dc for 1st shell, * ch 2, work shell of 2 dc, ch 2 and 2 dc in ch-2 sp of next shell. Repeat from * around, ending ch 2; join with sl st to top of ch 3. **5th rnd:** Repeat 4th rnd. **6th rnd:** Sl st in next dc, sl st in ch-2 sp of 1st shell, ch 3, work dc, ch 2 and 2 dc in same sp for 1st shell, * ch 2, insert hook in sp below ch-2 lps 2 rnds below and sc tightly (working over both ch-2 lps of last 2 rnds), ch 2, shell in next shell. Repeat from * around, ending ch 2, sc over next 2 ch-2 lps, ch 2; join with sl st to top of ch 3. **7th rnd:** Sl st in next dc, sl st in sp of 1st shell, ch 3, complete 1st shell, * ch 2, shell in ch-2 sp of next shell. Repeat from * around, ending ch 2; join as before.

Repeat 4th through 7th rnd for pattern until piece measures about 12½″ [13¾″–13¾″], ending with a 6th rnd of pattern. **Next rnd:** Repeat 7th rnd, but ch 1 (instead of ch 2) in center of each shell (34 [38–42] shells). Break off.

To Divide Work: Skip next 2 [3–3] shells for half of 1st armhole, sc in sp of next shell, (ch 1, shell of 2 dc, ch 1 and 2 dc in next shell) 11 [12–13] times (mark 1st shell); ch 1, sc in next shell (back section completed). Break off, then skip next 4 [5–6] shells for 2nd armhole, sc in sp of next shell, (ch 1, shell of 2 dc, ch 1 and 2 dc in next shell) 11 [12–13] times (mark 1st shell); ch 1, sc in next shell (front section completed), leaving last 2 [2–3] shells free to complete 1st armhole. Break off.

YOKE: 1st rnd: Make lp on hook and, starting at shoulder edge, ch 40 [40–41], then sc in sp on marked shell on back, * sc in each of next 2 dc on same shell, (sc in sp before next shell, sc in each of next 2 dc on next shell, sc in sp on same shell, sc in each of next 2 dc of same shell) 9 [10–11] times; sc in sp before next shell and in each of next 2 dc on shell, sc in sp on same shell *, then ch 79 [80–81]; skip armhole shells, sc in sp on marked shell on front, then repeat from * to * once, ch 39 [40–40]; join with sl st to 1st ch st of 1st long ch made.

2nd rnd: Ch 1, sc in same ch st as sl st, sc in each ch st and in each sc of last rnd (280 [294–308] sc); join with sl st in 1st ch st. **3rd rnd (dec rnd):** Ch 1, sc in same ch st as sl st, sc in each of next 17[18–19] sc, draw up lp in each of next 2 sc, y o and draw through all 3 lps on hook (1 sc dec); * sc in each of next 18 [19–20] sc, dec 1 sc. Repeat from * around; join (14 sc dec).

4th rnd: Sc in each sc around. **5th and 6th rnds (dec rnds):** Work in sc and, spacing decs evenly apart, dec 14 sc, being sure that the decs do not fall directly over those below.

7th through 9th rnd: Repeat 4th, 5th and 6th rnds (210 [224–238] sc at end of 9th rnd).

10th rnd (beading rnd): Ch 3, dc in each sc around; join with sl st in top of ch 3.

Continue working in sc rnds for 3 [4–5] rnds more and, at same time, dec 10 [11–12] sc evenly spaced on each rnd. **Last rnd (picot rnd):** Sc in 1st sc, * ch 3, sc in 1st ch st to make picot; skip 1 sc, sc in next sc. Repeat from * around; join and break off.

FINISHING: Underarm Border: Work same border across free space left at each underarm between front and back yoke. Work all rows from right side of work, breaking off at end of 1st and 2nd rows and starting next row at beg of previous row, as follows: Work 2 rows sc, decreasing 4 sc on 2nd row, then repeat picot rnd around entire armhole; join and break off.

Starting at center front of beading rnd, weave ribbon (over 1 dc and under 2 dc's) around neckline. Tie ends in bow.

COUNTRY VEST

The richly textured pattern is mostly single and double crochet. The buttons are crocheted balls.

SIZES: (6–8) [(10–12)–(14–16)]. Vest measures about 16″ [18″–20″] across back at underarms.

MATERIALS: Bucilla Win-Knit (Orlon acrylic knitting-worsted-weight yarn), 2 (4-oz) skeins natural heather No. 474 (color N), 2 [2–3] skeins each parchment No. 453 (color P) and beige No. 455 (color B); aluminum crochet hooks size J for vest and size F for buttons (or international sizes 6.00 mm and 4.00 mm) **or the sizes that will give you the correct gauges.**

GAUGE: Pattern St: With size J hook: 3 sts = 1″. **Border St:** 5 sc = 2″.

Note: Work with yarn double throughout.

BACK: Starting at lower edge with color N and size J hook, ch 49 [57–61] sts to measure about 16″ [18″–20″]. Work in pattern as follows: **1st row (right side):** Sc in 2nd ch from hook and in each ch across (48 [56–60] sts); ch 1, turn. **2nd row:** Sc in each st across (48 [56–60] sc); ch 3, turn. **3rd row (right side):** Skip 1st st directly below ch 3, dc in next st, * skip next 3 sts, h dc in next st: with thumb hold h dc down toward you and, working behind this st, work 1 dc in each of 3 skipped sts, starting with 1st skipped st (h dc crosses over 3 dc). Repeat from * across to within last 2 sts, dc in each of last 2 sts; ch 3, turn. **4th row (wrong side):** Skip 1st st, dc in next st, * skip next 3 sts, h dc in next st; holding h dc away from you, work 1 dc in each of 3 skipped sts (h dc crosses over 3 dc on right side of work). Repeat from * across to within last 2 sts, dc in each of last 2 dc (**Note:** Ch 3 always counts as dc); ch 1, turn.

5th row: Repeat 2nd row. **6th row:** Repeat 4th row. **7th row:** Repeat 2nd row. **8th row:** Repeat 4th row, but end ch 3 instead of ch 1, turn. **9th row:** Repeat 3rd row, but end ch 1, turn. **10th row:** Repeat 2nd row. **11th row:** Repeat 3rd row, but end ch 1, turn. **12th, 13th and 14th rows:** Repeat 2nd, 3rd and 4th rows. Piece should measure about 8″ from beg. At end of last row do not ch. Break off; turn.

Work next 8 rows with color P as follows: **15th row (right side):** With P, make lp on hook, draw up lp in 1st st, y o and draw through 2 lps on hook (1st sc made), sc in each st across (48 [56–60] sc); ch 3, turn. Repeat 6th through 12th rows of pattern once, omitting ch at end of last row. Break off; turn.

Work next 7 rows with color B as follows: With B, make lp on hook, y o hook and draw up lp in 1st st, (y o and draw through 2 lps) twice (1st dc made), dc in next st; repeat from * on 3rd row of pattern to end of row. Repeat 4th through 9th rows once, omitting ch at end of last row. Break off; turn. Piece should measure 16″ from beg.

To Shape Armholes: Continue with color B to end of back as follows: Skip 1st 5 [8–8] sts, sc in each st across to within last 5 [8–8] sts; ch 3, turn. Work even in pattern as established on 38 [40–44] sts until armholes measure 5″ [6″–7″] from beg; turn.

To Shape Neck and Shoulders: Work across 1st 11 [12–14] sts only for 1″. Break off. Skip next 16 sts for back of neck, work across remaining 11 [12–14] sts for 1″. Break off.

RIGHT FRONT: Starting at lower edge with N, ch 21 [25–29] to measure about 7″ [8″–9″]. Working in pattern as for back on 20 [24–28] sts, work 14 rows with N, 8 rows with P and 7 rows with B, ending at side edge. Piece should measure same length as back to armhole. Break off; turn.

To Shape Armhole: Continue with color B to end of front as follows: Starting at side edge, skip 1st 5 [8–8] sts, sc in each st to end of row. Work even in pattern as established on 15 [16–20] sts until armhole measures 5" [6"–7"] from beg, ending at front edge. Break off; turn.

To Shape Neck and Shoulder: Skip 1st 4 [4–6] sts, work to end of row. Work even on 11 [12–14] sts for 1". Break off.

LEFT FRONT: Work same as for right front until end of 7th row of color-B stripe, ending at front edge. Piece should measure same length as back to armhole. Do not break off; ch 1, turn.

To Shape Armhole: Continue with B as follows: Starting at front edge, sc in each st across to within last 5 [8–8] sts; ch 3, turn. Work even in pattern on 15 [16–20] sts until armhole measures 5" [6"–7"] from beg, ending at armhole edge.

To Shape Neck and Shoulder: Work across 1st 11 [12–14] sts only for 1". Break off.

FINISHING: Sew side and shoulder seams. Work with yarn double for all finishing, except buttons.

Right Front Border: 1st row (right side): Starting at lower edge of right front and using color P and size J hook, work 52 [54–56] sc evenly spaced along front edge to beg of neck shaping; ch 1, turn. Work even in sc for 2" [2"–1½"]. Do not ch 1 at end of last row. Break off.

Left Front Border: Starting at neck edge, repeat same 2" [2"–1½"] border along front edge. Break off.

Vest Edging: With right side facing you, using color P and size J hook, work as follows around entire vest: Start at corner st of border on neck edge of right front; sc evenly along neck edge (easing to fit if necessary), work 3 sc in next corner, sc in each sc along front edge of left border, work corner, sc evenly spaced along lower edge, work corner; then working along front edge of right border, sc in each sc to within 36 sc of neck edge.

Continue as follows for button loops: * Ch 5, skip next sc, sc in each of next 4 sc. Repeat from * 6 times more; work 2 sc in last sc; join with sl st to 1st sc. Break off.

Armhole Borders: With right side of work facing you and starting at underarm seam, using color P, sc evenly around one armhole. Continue to sc in each sc around for 1". At end of last rnd, join with sl st to next sc. Break off. Repeat around other armhole.

Buttons (make 7): Use size F hook. With 1 strand of P, ch 2. **1st rnd:** Work 6 sc in 2nd ch from hook. **2nd rnd:** (Work 2 sc in next sc, sc in next sc) 3 times (9 sc). **3rd rnd:** Sc in each sc around. Stuff firmly with yarn. **4th rnd:** * Sc in next sc, skip next sc. Repeat from * around; sl st in last sc. Add more stuffing if necessary. Break off, leaving 12" end. Using end, sew opening closed. Sew buttons in place.

EVERGREEN VEST

A festive pattern of trees is worked in single crochet around a vest done in double crochet.

SIZES: (6–8) [(10–12)–(14–16)]. Vest measures 15" [17"–19"] across back at underarms.

MATERIALS: Bucilla Winsom (Orlon acrylic yarn), 3 [3–4] (2-oz.) skeins white No. 330 (color W), 2 skeins green No. 297 (color G) and 1 skein red No. 309 (color R); aluminum crochet hook size G (or international size 4.50 mm) **or the size that will give you the correct gauge.**

GAUGE: 4 sts = 1"; 2 rows dc = 1".

Note: Make bobbins for trunks, trees and background areas when working Tree Band. Do not carry colors across rows. **To change color within row,** work as follows: Sc to within last st of old color, y o, insert hook in next st, pull up lp, y o with new color, draw through both lps on hook.

BACK: Ribbing (worked vertically): With G, ch 13 to measure about 3″. **1st row:** Sc in 2nd ch from hook and in each ch across (12 sc); ch 1, turn. **2nd row:** Working in back lp only of each st, sc in each sc; ch 1, turn. Repeat 2nd row for 15″ [17″–19″]. Break off.

Starting at lower edge above ribbing with G, ch 60 [68–76] to measure 15″ [17″–19″]. **1st row (wrong side):** Sc in 2nd ch from hook and in each ch across (59 [67–75] sc). Break off, turn. **2nd row:** With R, sc in each sc; ch 1, turn. **3rd row:** Sc in 1st sc and each remaining sc. Break off, turn. **4th row (right side):** With W, sl st in 1st sc, ch 3, dc in each remaining sc (59 [67–75] dc, counting ch 3 as 1 dc); ch 3, turn. **5th row:** Skip 1st dc, dc in each remaining dc; ch 3, turn. Repeat last row until piece measures 7½″ from beg, ending with a wrong-side row. Break off, turn.

Tree Band: Next row (right side): With R, sc m each dc; ch 1, turn. **Following row:** Sc in each sc. Break off, turn. Continuing in sc, work the 10 rows of chart. **Next row:** With R, sc in each sc; ch 1, turn. **Following row:** Sc in each sc. Break off, turn.

To Shape Armholes: Next row (right side): Skip 6 [7–8] sc; with W, sl st in next sc and ch 3, dc in each remaining sc to within last 6 [7–8] sts; ch 3, turn. Work even in dc on 47 [53–59] dc until armholes measure 7″ [7½″–8″], ending with a wrong [right–wrong] side row. Turn.

To Shape Shoulders: Sl st across 5 [6–7] sts, sc in each of next 5 [6–7] sts, h dc in each of next 27 [29–31] sts, sc in each of next 5 [6–7] sts, sl st across 5 [6–7] sts. Break off.

FRONT: Work same as for back to underarm, marking center st on last row of Tree Band.

Upper Left Front: Next row (right side): Skip 5 [6–7] sts; with W, sl st in next st, ch 3, dc in next st and in each st to within 1 st of marked sc (23 [26–29] dc); ch 3, turn. **Following row:** Skip 1st 2 dc, dc in each remaining dc (1 dc dec at beg of row); ch 3 turn. **Next row:** Skip 1st dc, dc in each dc to within last 2 dc; (y o, insert hook in next st and pull up lp, y o and draw through 2 lps on hook) twice, y o and draw through all 3 lps on hook (1 dc dec at end of row); ch 3, turn.

Repeat last 2 rows until 15 [17–19] sts remain. Work even in dc until armhole measures same as back, ending with a wrong [right–wrong] side row; ch 0 [2–0], turn.

To Shape Shoulder: For sizes (6–8) and [14–16] only, sl st across 5 [7] sts, sc in each of next 5 [7] sts, h dc in each of remaining 5 sts. Break off. **For size (10–12) only,** skip 1st st, h dc in each of next 4 sts, sc in each of next 6 sts, sl st across remaining 6 sts. Break off.

Upper Right Front: Next row (right side): Skip marked st and next st on last row of Tree Band; with W, sl st in next st, ch 3, dc in each of next 23 [26–29] sts; ch 3, turn. Work to correspond to upper left front, reversing all shaping.

FINISHING: Sew ribbing pieces to front and back. Sew shoulder and side seams.

Neck Trim: 1st rnd (right side): Starting at right shoulder seam, sc evenly around neck edge, working as follows at lower point of V: Draw up lp in last dc, draw up lp in 1st sc, y o and draw through all 3 lps on hook (joined sc made), sc in marked st, work joined sc in next 2 sts; join to 1st sc; do not turn. **2nd rnd:** Sc in each sc, working joined sc by pulling up lp in each of 3 sts at lower point; join and break off. **3rd rnd:** With G, sc in each sc, working joined sc at lower point; join; break off.

Armhole Trim: Work as for neck trim, working joined sc's at lower corners.

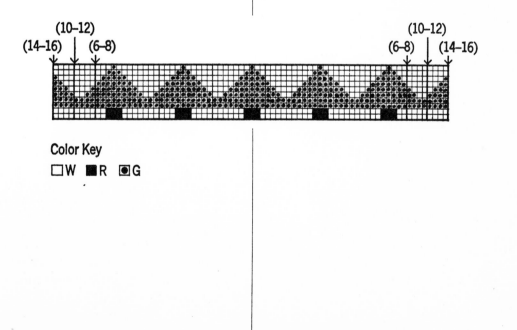

Color Key
□ W ■ R ◉ G

CAP-SLEEVED VEST*

The easy design is mostly done in half double-crochet stitch using a textured ombré yarn.

SIZES: (8–10) [(12–14)]. Snug-fitting vest measures 13½″ [15½″] across back at underarms; 11″ [11½″] from underarm to lower edge.

MATERIALS: Stanley Berroco Que Linda, 5 (2-oz.) skeins white/gold/melon No. 3012; aluminum crochet hook size F (or international hook size 4.00 mm) **or the size that will give you the correct gauge;** 7 buttons about ⅝″ diameter.

GAUGE: 7 h dc = 2″; 5 rows h dc = 2″.

BACK: (Note: As for any fabric vest, back is narrower than front.) Starting at lower edge, ch 42 [48] to measure 11½″ [13½″]. **1st row:** H dc in 3rd ch from hook and in each ch across (41 [47] h dc, counting turning ch 2 as 1 h dc); ch 2, turn. **2nd row:** Skip 1st h dc (directly below ch 2), h dc in each h dc across; ch 2, turn. Repeat 2nd row until piece measures 11″ [11½″] from beg, omitting ch 2 on last row.

To Shape Armholes: 1st row: Sl st across 1st 4 sts, ch 2 (counts as 1st h dc), h dc in each h dc to within last 3 h dc (35 [41] h dc); ch 2, turn. **2nd row:** Skip 1st h dc; (y o and draw up lp in next st) twice, y o and draw through all 5 lps on hook (1 h dc dec); h dc in each h dc to within last 2 h dc, dec 1 h dc over last 2 h dc; ch 2, turn. Repeat 2nd row twice more, then work even on 29 [35] h dc until armholes measure 5″ [5½″].

To Shape Neck: 1st side: Work across 1st 9 [11] sts. Working across these sts only and continuing in h dc, dec 1 st at neck edge every row 2 [3] times, then work even on 7 [8] h dc until armhole measures 7½″ [8″]. Break off. Skip center 11 [13] h dc. Sl st in next h dc, ch 2, h dc in each h dc across (9 [11] sts). Complete as for 1st side, reversing shaping.

Side Panels: With right side facing you, work 38 [40] h dc, as evenly spaced as possible, along left side edge of back. Work even in h dc for 3 rows more. Break off. Repeat along right edge of back.

LEFT FRONT: Starting at lower edge, ch 23 [27] to measure 6¼″ [7¼″]. **1st row:** H dc in 3rd ch from hook and in each ch across. Mark beg of row for side edge. Work even in h dc on 22 [26] sts as for back until piece measures same as back to underarm, ending at side edge. Omit last ch 2.

To Shape Armhole and Neck: 1st row: Sl st across 1st 4 sts, ch 2, h dc in each h dc to within last 3 [4] h dc; ch 2, turn. Dec 1 st at arm edge every row 3 [4] times and, **at same time,** dec 1 st at neck edge every row 6 times. Work even on 7 [9] h dc until armhole measures same as back to shoulder. Break off.

RIGHT FRONT: Work as left front, reversing shaping. (Mark end of 1st row for side edge.)

FINISHING: Sew shoulder and side seams.

Cap Sleeves (make 2): Mark off 10″ along each armhole (5″ on each side of shoulder seam). **1st row:** Work 1 sc, 28 dc and 1 sc evenly spaced between markers; turn. **2nd row:** Sl st in 1st st, sc in next st, dc in each st to within last 2 sts, sc in next st, skip last st; turn. **3rd row:** Sl st in 1st st, sc in next st, dc in each st to within last 3 sts, sc in next st, skip last 2 sts; ch 1, turn. **4th row:** Sc in 1st st, (dc in next st, 3 tr in next st, dc in next st, sc in next st) 5 times. Break off.

Left Front Band: 1st row: With right side facing you, work 38[40] sc evenly spaced along left front edge. Work even in sc for 3 rows more. Break off. Mark band for placement of 7 buttons.

Right Front Band: Work as for left front band until 2 rows have been completed. **Next row (buttonhole row):** * Sc in each sc to marker, ch 1, skip next sc. Repeat from * across, sc to end of row. On the following row, sc in each sc and in each ch-1 sp across. Break off. With right side facing you, work 1 row sc along neck and front bands and around each armhole and cap sleeve. Sew on buttons.

FUZZY VEST

Embroidery floss is used for the medallions and ties; the vest is worked vertically in single crochet and gently shaped.

SIZES: (6–8) [(10–12)–(14–16)–(18–20)]. Vest measures 14″ [16″–18″–20″] across back at underarms, 10″ [10½″–10½″–11″] from underarms to lower edge.

MATERIALS: Stanley Berroco Mirabella (wool and nylon yarn), 4 [4–4–5] (2-oz.) skeins beige No. 1506; for medallions, Bucilla Glossilla (rayon 4-strand embroidery floss) 4 (10-yd) skeins toast No. 5; aluminum crochet hook size K (or international hook size 7.00 mm) **or the size that will give you the correct gauge;** steel crochet hook size 0; cardboard.

GAUGE: 2 sts = 1″; 2 rows = 1″ with Mirabella on size K hook.

Note: Vest is worked in vertical rows.

BACK: Starting at left side edge with Mirabella and size K hook, ch 33 [35–35–37] to measure 16″ [17″–17″–18″]. **1st row (right side):** Sc in 2nd ch from hook and in each ch across; ch 1, turn. **2nd row:** Sc in each sc across; ch 1, turn. Repeat 2nd row 4 [5–6–7] times more, ending at lower edge. **1st short row:** Sc in each of 1st 8 sc, turn. **2nd short row:** Sc in each sc across (8 sc); ch 1, turn. Repeat 2nd row 16 [18–20–22] times, ending at lower edge. Repeat 1st and 2nd short rows. Repeat 2nd row 6 [7–8–9] times more. Break off. Mark off 6 rows at center of upper edge for back of neck with 2 pin markers.

LEFT FRONT: Starting at side edge with size K hook, ch 33 [35–35–37] to measure 16″ [17″–17″–18″]. Work as for back until 2nd short row has been completed. **3rd short row:** Sc in each of 1st 14 sc; turn. **4th short row:** Sc in each sc across (14 sc); ch 1, turn. **5th short row:** Sc in each of 1st 20 sc; turn. **6th short row:** Sc in each sc across (20 sc); ch 1, turn. **7th short row:** Sc in each of 1st 26 sc; turn. **8th short row:** Sc in each sc across (26 sc); ch 1, turn. Repeat 2nd row 4 [5–6–7] times more. Break off.

RIGHT FRONT: Work as for left front (pattern st is reversible).

FINISHING: Sew shoulder seams between markers and side edges. Sew side seams, leaving 7″ [7½″–7½″–8″] open below each shoulder seam for armhole. With right side facing you with size K hook, work 1 row sc around lower, front and neck edges, working 3 sc at each corner. Join; break off. With size K hook, work 1 row sc around each armhole edge. Join; break off.

Medallions (make 2): With double strand of floss and size 0 hook, crochet chain the length of 2 skeins of floss, leaving about 18″ end for sewing. Measure off 18″ of chain for tie. Beginning at this point, with wrong side of chain facing upward and working against a piece of cardboard, wind chain in a coil to form oval, sewing adjacent edges of chain together as you go. Oval should measure about 2¾″ × 3″. Turn right side up and press; sew to one front as pictured. Knot end of tie. Repeat for other side.

CRISSCROSS VEST

Mohair yarn is used to work the body in one piece in half double-crochet stitch; shoulders are softly gathered.

SIZES: (8–10) [(12–14)–(16–18)]. Vest measures 17″ [19″–21″] across back at underarms, 17¾″ [18¼″–18¾″] from shoulder to lower edge.

MATERIALS: Bucilla Melody (50% mohair/50% acrylic), 6 [6–7] (1-oz) balls tea rose No. 34; aluminum crochet hook size I (or international hook size 5.50 mm) **or the size that will give you the correct gauge;** 1 large button; 2 pieces of self-fastening tape such as Velcro.

GAUGE: 3 sts = 1″.

Note: Vest is worked in one piece in vertical rows (see layout diagram).

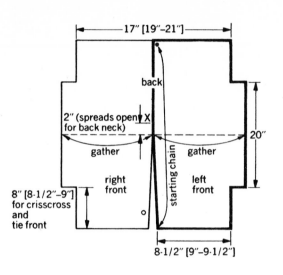

LEFT FRONT AND LEFT HALF OF BACK: You will be working the left front and left half of the back first (area outlined in heavy line on layout diagram). Note starting chain down center of vest. Starting at lower edge of center back (dot on diagram), ch 107 [110–113] to measure about 35½″ [36½″–37½″] (distance from ½″ above back waist, over shoulder and down front to ½″ above front waist). **1st row:** H dc in 3rd ch from hook and in each ch across (105 [108–111] h dc); ch 2, turn. **2nd row:** Working in back lp only of each st, h dc in each h dc across; ch 2, turn. Repeat 2nd row until piece measures 8½″ [9½″–10½″]. Break off; turn. Mark off center 61 [62–63] sts on last row for sleeve.

Sleeve: 1st row: Working in back lps only, h dc across these 61 [62–63] sts; ch 2, turn. Repeat 2nd row until sleeve measures 3½″. Break off.

RIGHT FRONT AND RIGHT HALF OF BACK: Turn work so that opposite side of starting chain is facing upward. **1st row:** Starting at lower edge of center back and working in opposite side of starting chain, h dc in each of 1st 46 [47–48] ch (to X on

diagram); ch 61 [63–65] for right front edge; turn. **2nd row:** H dc in 3rd ch from hook and in each remaining ch; working in back lps only, h dc in each h dc across (105 [108–111] h dc); ch 2, turn. Starting with 2nd row, complete as for left side. Break off.

RIGHT FRONT EXTENSION: 1st row: Working along opposite side of starting ch, h dc in 15th st from lower edge of right front (circle on diagram) and in each of next 14 sts to lower edge; ch 2, turn. **2nd row:** Working in back lps only, h dc to within last 2 sts of last row, dec 1 h dc as follows: (Y o, insert hook in next st, y o and draw lp through) twice, y o and draw through all 5 lps on hook (1 h dc dec); ch 2, turn. **3rd row:** Working in back lps only, dec 1 h dc over 1st 2 sts, h dc in each st across; ch 2, turn. Repeat 2nd and 3rd rows once more. Break off.

FINISHING: Sew underarm and sleeve seams. **Edging: 1st row:** With right side facing you, work 1 row sc evenly spaced along lower, front and neck edges, easing along lower edge to fit waist when overlapped; join. Do not turn. **2nd row:** Working from left to right, work reverse sc (see stitch diagram, page 14) in each sc around as follows: Work 1 sc in an sc, * insert hook under edge to *right* of st (Step 1), draw yarn through (Step 2), y o and draw through both lps on hook (Step 3). Repeat from * around (ropelike edging is formed); join. Break off.

To Gather Shoulders: Run double strand of yarn through upper edge of each shoulder and sleeve (broken line on diagram). Pull up and adjust gathers to fit. Secure ends.

Sew button at tip of right front extension. Overlap right front and sew pieces of self-fastening tape at each lower front corner.

TIE-FRONT CHENILLE VEST

The chenille look in a design with four ties at the front. The one-piece body is worked in easy single-crochet stitch.

SIZES: (8–10) [(12–14)–(16–18)]. Vest measures 17″ [19″–21″] across back at underarms, 17¾″ [18¼″–18¾″] from shoulder to lower edge.

MATERIALS: Unger's Chenille de Luxe (100% acrylic), 5 [5–6] (1-7/10 oz) balls russet No. 212; aluminum crochet hook size I (or international hook size 5.50 mm) **or the size that will give you the correct gauge.**

GAUGE: 3 sts = 1″.

Note: Vest is worked in one piece in vertical rows.

LEFT FRONT AND LEFT HALF OF BACK: You will be working the left front and left half of the back first (area outlined in heavy line of layout diagram). Note starting chain down center of vest. Starting at lower edge of center back (dot on diagram), ch 106 [109–112] to measure about 35½″ [36½″–37½″] (distance from ½″ above back waist, over shoulder and down front to ½″ above front waist). **1st row:** Sc in 2nd ch from hook and in each ch across (105 [108–111] sc), ch 1, turn. **2nd row:** Working in back lp only of each st, sc in each sc across; ch 1, turn. Repeat 2nd row until piece measures 8½″ [9½″–10½″]. Break off; turn. Mark off center 61 [62–63] sts on last row for sleeves.

Sleeve: 1st row: Working in back lps only, sc in each sc across sleeve sts; ch 1, turn. Repeat 2nd row until sleeve measures 1¼″. Break off.

RIGHT FRONT AND RIGHT HALF OF BACK: Turn work so that opposite side of starting chain is facing upward. **1st row:** Starting at lower edge of center back and working in opposite side of starting chain, sc in each of 1st 46 [47–48] ch (to X on diagram); ch 60 [62–64] for right front edge; turn. **2nd row:** Sc in 2nd ch from hook and in each remaining ch; working in back lps only, sc in each sc across (105 [108–111] sc); ch 1, turn. Starting with 2nd row, complete as for left side. Break off.

FINISHING: Sew underarm and sleeve seams.

Edging: 1st row: With right side facing you, work 1 row sc evenly spaced along lower, front and neck edges, easing along lower edge to fit waist; join. Do not turn. **2nd row:** Working from left to right, work reverse sc (see stitch diagram, page 14) in each sc around as follows: Work 1 sc in an sc, * insert hook under edge to *right* of st (Step 1), draw yarn through (Step 2), y o and draw through both lps on hook (Step 3). Repeat from * around (ropelike edging is formed); join. Break off.

To Gather Shoulders: Run double strand of yarn through upper edge of each shoulder and sleeve (broken line on diagram). Pull up and adjust gathers to fit. Secure ends.

Ties: Make 4 ties on each center front edge as follows, placing the 1st tie at lower corner and the others about 3″ apart. To make 1 tie, crochet a 7″ chain, sl st in edge of work. Break off.

TRIANGULAR FRINGED SHAWL

The combination of cluster stitches and single crochet resembles weaving; it's finished with loop fringe.

SIZE: About 66″ × 43″ × 43″.

MATERIALS: Reynolds Kali Mousse (light-weight, nubby wool yarn), 7 (about 1½-oz) balls lavender No. 37; aluminum crochet hook size I (or international size 5.50 mm) **or the size that will give you the correct gauge.**

GAUGE: 5 cl = 3″; 2 rows = 1″.

Starting at top edge, crochet a 66″ ch loosely, with an uneven number of sts. **1st row:** Sc in 3rd ch from hook and in each ch across; ch 2, turn. **2nd row:** Draw up lp in each of 1st 2 sc, (y o and draw through 2 lps on hook) twice (cl made); * ch 1, cl in next 2 sc. Repeat from * across, working last cl in last sc and in turning ch; ch 2, turn. (**Note:** Spread a section of work flat and notice that between each pair of cl there is a vertical thread. From now on you will be working in each sp between vertical thread and cl, as specified.) **3rd row:** Draw up lp in sp after 1st vertical thread and just before 2nd cl, skip cl, draw up lp in sp before next thread, complete cl as before (cl made directly over cl on previous row); * ch 1, skip thread, draw up lp in next sp, skip cl, draw up lp in next sp, complete cl. Repeat from * to within last thread and last cl (there should be 2 less cl than on previous row), skip thread and cl, dc in turning ch; ch 2, turn. Repeat last row until 1 cl remains. Break off.

Border: 1st row: Work sc in a top corner of shawl and, working along shaped edge, * ch 4, skip about ½″ of edge, sc in edge. Repeat from * along edge to lower point, around point and along other shaped edge to corner; turn. **2nd row:** Sl st to center of 1st lp, * ch 4, sc in next lp. Repeat from * across, working extra lps at lower point, if necessary, to keep piece flat; turn.

Fringe: Sl to center of 1st lp, * crochet 10″ ch, sc in same lp, ch 1, sc in next lp. Repeat from * across, make 10″ ch, sc in same lp. Break off.

RUFFLED SHAWL

Lover's knots make a lavish double ruffle on a semi-circle of double crochet that ripples from shoulder to elbow.

SIZE: Shawl measures 46″ across top edge and 20″ from top to center back point, including border.

MATERIALS: Bucilla Perlette (Orlon acrylic yarn), 3 (1¾-oz) balls peacock No. 18 and 1 ball sand No. 7; aluminum crochet hook size G (or international size 4.50 mm) **or the size that will give you the correct gauge.**

GAUGE: 7 dc = 2″; 7 pattern rows in dc = 3″.

Starting at center of top edge with peacock, ch 10. **1st row:** Dc in 4th ch from hook and in each ch across (8 dc, counting turning ch as 1 dc); ch 3, turn. (**Note:** From now on work each dc into sp between 2 dc.) **2nd row:** Dc in sp between 1st 2 dc, (work 2 dc in next sp—inc st made) 6 times (14 dc); ch 3, turn. **3rd row:** Dc in sp between 1st 2 dc, (dc in next sp, inc st in next sp) 6 times (20 dc); ch 3, turn. **4th row:** Dc in sp between 1st

2 dc, * dc in each of next 2 sp, inc st in next sp. Repeat from * across, marking sp in each inc st (26 dc and 6 markers); ch 3, turn. **5th row:** Dc in 1st sp (1st marked sp), * dc in each sp to next marked sp, inc st in marked sp, move marker up to sp in inc st just made. Repeat from * 4 times more; dc in each sp to last sp, inc st in last sp (32 dc); ch 3, turn.

Repeat 5th row for pattern 31 times more (218 dc on last row). Break off. Turn.

Border: Border is made in 2 sections, one overlapping the other.

1st section: With sand work lover's-knot stitch (see stitch diagram) along lower curved edge of shawl as follows: **1st row:** Working in last row of shawl, sc between 1st 2 dc, * pull up lp on hook to ¾″, y o and draw through this long lp on hook (Step 1); insert hook between long lp and single strand (Step 2), y o hook and draw lp through, y o and draw through both lps on hook (Step 3), pull up lp on hook to ¾″, y o and draw through (Step 4), work Steps 2 and 3 (double knot st made); skip next sp on shawl, sc in next sp (1 knot lp

Step 1 Step 2

Step 3 Step 4

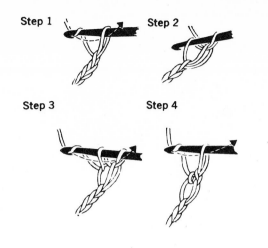

made). Repeat from * across. Break off; turn. **2nd row:** Attach sand to st at center of 1st double knot lp, * work double knot st, sc in st at center of next double knot lp. Repeat from * across. Break off; turn. Repeat 2nd row 3 times more.

    2nd Section: Work 1 row above last row of shawl as follows: Repeat 1st row of border once, then repeat 2nd row twice.

TASSELED PONCHO

A striking design combines squares and triangles in afghan stitch and easy popcorns with mesh-loop joining.

    SIZE: Poncho measures about 30″ from back of neck to point at lower edge, omitting fringe.

    MATERIALS: Bucilla Wonder-Knit (knitting-worsted-weight yarn), 7 (4-oz) balls winter white No. 3; aluminum afghan hook size H and aluminum crochet hook size G (or international afghan hook size 5.00 mm and crochet hook size 4.50 mm) **or the sizes that will give you the correct gauges.**

    GAUGES: In afghan stitch, 4 sts = 1″; 11 rows = 3″. Using G hook, each ch-4 mesh lp = 1″; 2 rows of mesh lps = 1″

    AFGHAN STITCH SQUARE (make 10): Starting at one edge of square with afghan hook, ch 33. **1st row**

(right side): Keeping all lps on hook, draw up lp in 2nd ch from hook and in each ch across (33 lps on hook); for 2nd half of row work off lps as follows: Y o and draw through 1 lp on hook, * y o and draw through 2 lps on hook. Repeat from * across (1 lp remains on hook for 1st st on next row).

2nd row: Insert hook under vertical "bar" of 2nd st on row below, y o and draw up lp; keeping all lps on hook, draw up loop in each bar across; for 2nd half of row work as follows: y o and draw through 1 lp on hook, (y o and draw through 2 lps on hook) twice; * ch 3, y o and draw through 2 lps on hook (ch lp made), y o and draw through 2 lps on hook *. Repeat from * to * 6 times more; y o and draw through 2 lps on hook. Repeat from * to * 7 times; y o and draw through last 2 lps on hook (14 ch lps made; 33 sts in all).

3rd row: Draw up lp in 2nd vertical bar and each remaining vertical bar across, pushing ch-3 lps to right side of work to form "popcorns" (33 lps on hook); work off lps as for 1st row.

4th row: Draw up lps as before; y o and draw through 1 lp, (y o and draw through 2 lps) twice. Repeat from * to * on 2nd row 6 times; (y o and draw through 2 lps) 5 times; repeat from * to * on 2nd row 6 times, y o and draw through last 2 lps.

5th row: Repeat 3rd row.

Starting with 6th row and following Chart 1 for placement of popcorns (each vertical line on grid equals 1 vertical bar, each dot equals 1 popcorn), work until 29 rows are completed. Sl st in each st of last row. Break off. Block pieces to measure 8″ square.

Mesh Loop Trim: 1st rnd (right side): Make lp on crochet hook and sc in any corner of square; (ch 4, skip about ¾″ on side of square, work sc) 10 times across 1 side, ending with sc in next corner (10 lps made). In same manner work 10 more lps on remaining 3 sides, ending with sl st in 1st sc. 2nd rnd: Sl st to center of 1st lp, sc in lp, * ch 4, sc in center of next lp. Repeat from * around, working ch 6 at each corner and ending with sl st in 1st sc (40 lps). Break off.

AFGHAN STITCH TRIANGLE (make 4): 1st row: Work as for 1st row of square until 3 lps remain on hook at end of row; y o and draw through all 3 lps on hook (1 st dec). 2nd row: Skip 1st 2 vertical bars (they look like inverted V), pick up lp in next vertical bar; work as for 2nd row of square, decreasing 1 st at end of row as before.

Follow Chart 2 for placement of popcorns, working 1 dec at end of every row until 29 rows are completed. Sl st across last row. Break off. Block to measure 8″ × 8″ × 9½″.

Mesh Loop Trim: 1st rnd: Work as for square, making 12 lps on diagonal side (32 lps in all). 2nd rnd: Work as for 2nd mesh loop rnd of square.

TO ASSEMBLE: Following Assembly Diagram lay out squares and triangles so that all vertical bars

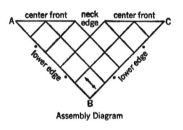

Assembly Diagram

run in same direction (see arrow).

To Join Pieces: Hold 2 squares tog with right sides facing. Using crochet hook and working through both lp trims tog, sl st through center of 2 matching corner lps, * ch 3, sl st through center of next 2 matching lps. Repeat from * across 1 side of pieces, ending with sl st in corner lps. Join all pieces in this manner, following Assembly Diagram. Then bring center front edges tog and, leaving corner lps free at A and C, join pieces along center front.

LOWER BORDER: 1st row (right side): Starting at A on diagram (center front), sc in center of free corner mesh lp, * ch 4, sc in next lp *. Repeat from * to * to lp before center lp at back point B; ch 4, sc in center lp, ch 4, sc in same lp. Repeat from * to * to last lp at C

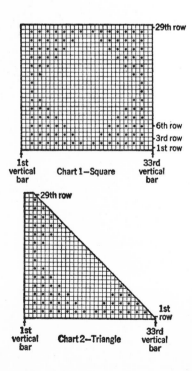

Chart 1—Square

Chart 2—Triangle

on diagram; turn. **2nd row:** Sl st to center of 1st lp, sc in lp. Repeat from * to * on 1st row across entire lower edge of poncho, working 2 ch-5 lps at lower back point. Break off; turn.

There are short rows of mesh loops along lower side edges of poncho (between dots on Assembly Diagram). Work them as follows: **1st short row (right side):** Sc in center mesh lp on square at 1st dot on 1 side of poncho, * ch 5, sc in next lp. Repeat from * to next dot (center lp on square); turn. **2nd short row:** Sl st to center of 1st lp, sc in same lp, * ch 5, sc in next lp. Repeat from * to last lp of short row; turn. Repeat 2nd short row 4 times more. Break off. Work between dots on other side of poncho in same manner.

Next row (right side): Starting at A, sc in 1st lp, * ch 5, sc in next lp *. Repeat from * to * across entire lower edge of poncho, working lps along edges of short rows and working 1 ch-6 lp at lower back point; turn. **Following row:** Sl st to center of 1st lp, sc in same lp, repeat from * to * on last row across lower edge, working 2 ch-6 lps at lower back point. Break off.

NECK BORDER: Starting at center front, work 1 row of ch-4 lps along neck edge. Break off.

FINISHING: Neck Tie: Crochet 30" chain. Break off. Run it through 2 lps at center front neck and tie in bow.

Tassels: To make tassel, cut six 12" strands of yarn. Hold strands tog and fold in half. Insert fold through a mesh lp at front seam, draw loose ends through fold and pull. Make 7 tassels along center front seam. Using 9 strands yarn for each tassel, attach 62 tassels along lower edge of poncho.

WEDING GOWN**

This challenging project requires experience and patience, but the dress can be used for formal evening wear afterward. The magnificent filet background is accented with tiny popcorns.

SIZE: Work to desired measure.

MATERIALS: No. 8 Pearl Cotton, about 100 (⅓–ounce—53–yard) balls for size 10–12; steel crochet hook No. 8, 9, or 10, depending on desired gauge; neck opening type zipper, 22" long; about ½ yd nylon organdy for facings (the larger the piece, the fewer seams will be necessary in making bias strips); graph paper for planning motifs; muslin (optional).

GAUGE: Work at about 6½ sps (dc, ch 1) per inch. Although almost any other gauge can be used, this gives a finer crochet.

NOTE: Specific instructions are given only for the stitch constructions. For planning and working the various sections of the dress, and for finishing, the instructions are general.

STITCH CONSTRUCTIONS

BASIC FILET: Over a foundation chain, **Row 1:** Dc in 6th ch from hook, * ch 1, skip 1 ch of foundation ch, dc in next ch; repeat from * across turn. **Row 2:** Ch 4 (counts as dc, ch 1, or first sp), * dc in next dc, ch 1; repeat from * ending dc in 4th ch of foundation ch, turn. **Row 3:** Ch 4, * dc in next dc, ch 1; repeat from * ending dc in 3rd ch of turning ch, turn. Repeat Row 3 for basic filet.

To Dec One SP at Each End of Row: At beg of row, ch 3, dc in next dc, ch 1, then continue across as for Row 3; at end of row, work to within last 2 dc, work the first half of a dc in next-to-last dc, the first half of a dc in the last dc, y o and draw through 3 lps on hook, turn.

To Inc One SP at Each End of Row: At beg of row, ch 4, dc in last dc of previous row, ch 1, dc in next dc, and continue as for Row 3; at end of row, complete as before, then work (ch 1, dc) again in last dc of previous row, turn.

To Dec More Than One SP at Each End: At beg of row sl st across to and in desired dc, ch 4 (counts as first sp) and continue as for Row 3; at end of row, simply work over to and in desired dc, turn.

To Inc More Than One SP at Beg and End of Row: The most simple of the many ways requires a little planning. Two rows before inc sps are needed, end off thread at end of row, turn. Ch 2 for each desired sp to be increased, then dc in last dc of previous row, ch 1, and continue as for Row 3; at the end of row after dc in turning ch, ch 2 for each desired additional sp, plus 3 ch, turn; dc in 6th ch from hook, ch 1, continue across foundation as for Row 1, then ch 1, dc in last dc of previous row, and continue as for Row 3; at the end of the row in the same manner, work desired number of sps across new ch.

POPCORNS (PC) are used in this pattern to fill in sps as blocks on charts. Mark right side (face) of work.

To Work PC on Right Side: Work as for Row 3 to desired sp for blocks, ending dc in dc of row below, work 4 dc in next ch-1 sp, drop lp from hook, insert hook from front to back under the top lps of first of 4 dc, and draw dropped lp through, ch 1 tightly, dc in next dc.

To Work PC on Wrong Side of Work: Work as above, except insert hook from back to front under the lps of first dc to draw dropped lp through. When a stitch or another pc is to be worked directly over a pc, work it in closing st of previous pc.

Note: In working the pc-dot pattern and alternate pc's and sps, keep the sps at each edge unfilled for easier seaming when the gown is finished.

Read charts from right to left for odd-numbered rows, and from left to right for even-numbered row.

To Avoid Counting a Large Number of Ch Sts: Work with 2 balls of thread as follows: With the first, crochet a ch which would seem to be long enough for piece, but do not cut off thread. Drop loop from hook (a bobby pin is good to keep the lp from raveling). With the second ball of thread, place a starting lp on hook, then beg in the first ch st made with dc, * ch 1, skip next ch, dc in next ch; repeat from * until either the desired number of sps have been worked or end of the ch is reached. If chain was not long enough, drop lp of last dc from hook; with the first ball continue the foundation ch for necessary length, drop lp, then continue to work the filet with the second ball. When desired number of sps have been worked, end off the first ball, and continue the work with the second. The last dc on the next row will be worked in the starting dc of the first row.

DRESS PATTERN

Compare your (or the bride's) measurements with those on our sample pattern. Seam allowance is not needed. (If the finished dress is slightly large, it can be taken in at the seams.) On wrapping or tissue paper, draw an actual-size pattern similar in shape to ours, to the exact measurements to be worked. The empire waistline is curved to fit under the bust at front and is straight at back. The bodice darts under the bust are sewn in; therefore, the bodice is crocheted to the bust measurement at the underarm. In drawing the skirt pattern, allow about ½" for an edging at the hemline—no turned up hem is needed. Draw sleeve pattern about 2½" shorter than desired length; the bottom of the sleeve should be only about ¾" to 1" narrower than at its fullest width, so that it can be gathered and puff a little over the cuff, which is worked separately. Pin the pattern parts together and fit to the bride. Make necessary corrections. A better fit might be had by cutting a muslin pattern from the paper, or you might buy a sewing pattern of a similar empire gown and work from that.

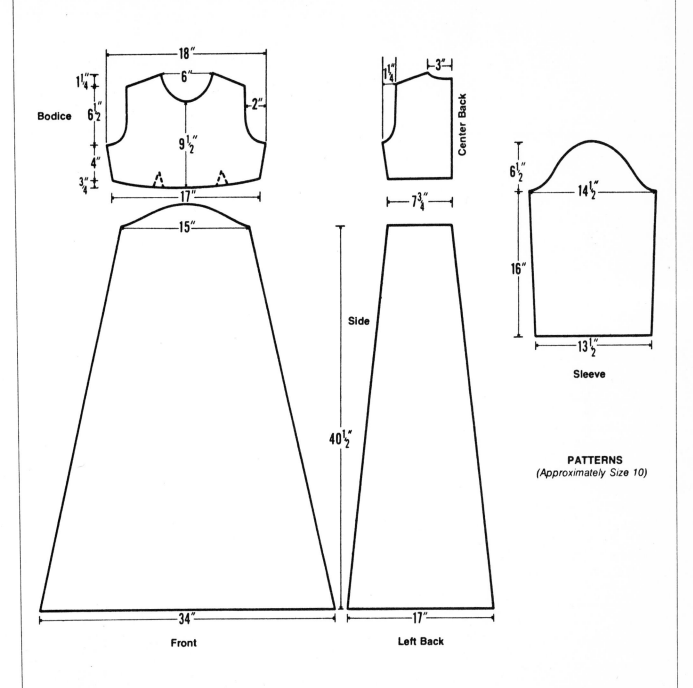

Bodice

18"

1¼"

6½"

6"

2"

9½"

4"

¾"

17"

Center Back

1¼"

3"

7¾"

15"

Side

40½"

34"

Front

17"

Left Back

6½"

14½"

16"

13½"

Sleeve

PATTERNS
(Approximately Size 10)

STITCH KEY

☐ = 1 sp

☒ = pc blocks

CHART FOR WEDDING GOWN

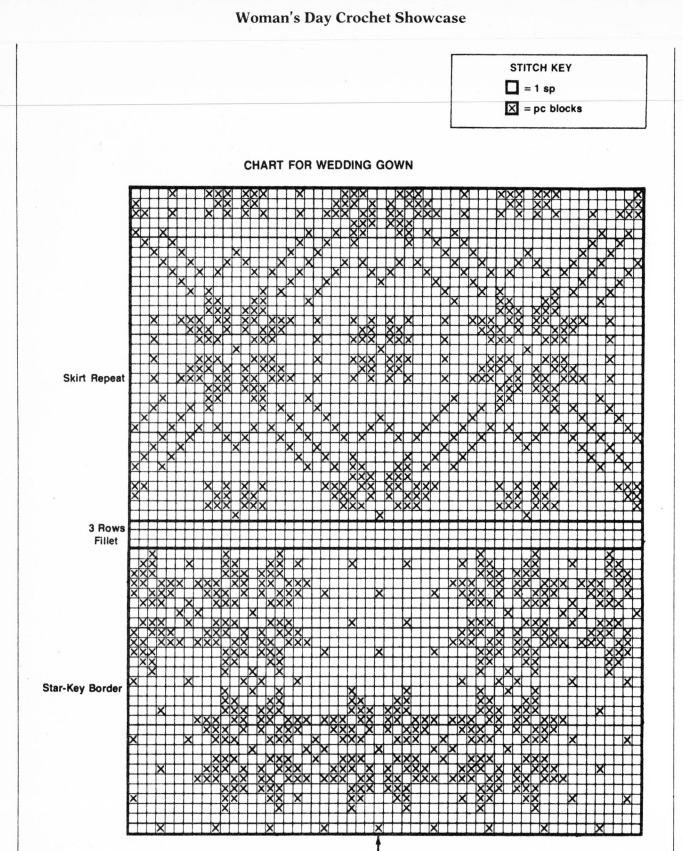

Skirt Repeat

3 Rows
Fillet

Star-Key Border

Center Front

The dress is crocheted in accordance with the pattern, increasing and decreasing so that the two coincide in size and shape. Check the crochet frequently against pattern.

PLANNING AND WORKING STEPS

Before you begin, crochet a swatch of basic filet at least 4″ square for exact gauge in planning the placement of the design motifs. On graph paper count out the number of sps which will be needed for ½ of the bottom of the skirt front. Starting at the center, plot the pc-dot pattern starting on the 3rd row of filet. Start the star-key border about 5″ to 6″ from the bottom. Work entire height of pattern. Work 3 rows of basic filet; then chart a few vertical repeats of the diamond-star motif. Plan back of skirt so that the border of each of its 2 pieces will match at the front in depth. Each of these motifs should be centered both front and back. For the bodice front and back, chart a star yoke: at least 5 stars across below the neckline at front; at least one star more over each end star on the shoulder; and 2½ stars

across each shoulder at the back. The sleeves need not be charted since they are worked all in pc-dot pattern. Crochet each piece from bottom to top, checking crochet against pattern.

FINISHING: Use back stitch for all seaming and topstitching, being sure to keep the same tension as the crochet. Seam the back of the skirt at the center allowing for a zipper opening at the top. Seam the skirt back to the front.

Hem Edge: Work as follows: Starting at the center back seam, with wrong side of work facing, * sc in next dc, sc in next ch-1 sp, sc in next dc, ch 5, skip next (ch-1, dc, ch-1, dc, ch-1); repeat from * around, turn. **Next row:** Ch 1, then in each group of 3 sc work sc in first, ch 3, skip next sc, sc in 3rd sc; in each of the ch-5 lps work (sc, h dc, 3 dc, tr, 3 dc, h dc, sc); sl st to first sc, end off.

Sew shoulder and side seams of bodice.

Collar: Crochet a neck band about 1¾″ wide and about ½″ less than the entire neckline edge. Work an odd number of alternate pcs and sps, and end on a right side row, turn. Starting on the wrong side, crochet an edging as for the hem around 3 sides of the collar, leaving one long edge (neckline) free; finish the long

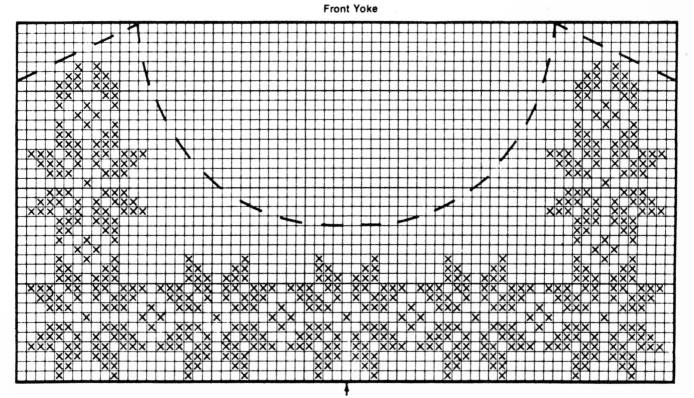

Popcorn-Dot Pattern

Row 1

Front Yoke

Center Front

free edge with 2 sc in each sp. Starting at the center back neck edge, topstitch the neck band over the neckline along the sc'd edge.

Sleeves: In the same way, work sleeve bands about 2¾" wide and long enough not only to fit above the wrist, but to get the hand through when seamed. Work the scalloped edge over the wrist side of the cuff only and sc across the long edge which will be sewed to the sleeve. Seam the short ends together. Seam each sleeve. Gather in the bottom edge of the sleeve to fit the cuff; topstitch the cuff over the gathered edge of the sleeve.

Bodice: Sew darts in the bodice to fit the waistline of the skirt. Starting at the center back, with right side of bodice facing, work a row of alternate pcs and sps across the waistline edge, turn. Now crochet a scalloped edge as for the hem. Set sleeves into armholes, adjusting extra fullness in the cap around the top of armholes, topstitch bodice over the waistline of the skirt matching side seams and center back edges.

Cut the nylon organdy into bias strips about 3" wide for the hem edge and the neck band, about 4½" wide for each of the cuffs, about 1" wide to face each side of the zipper opening, and reinforce the waistline; turn under the edges and hem to the parts to be faced. It may be necessary to hold in the shoulder seams too; do this with a narrow bias strip in the same way. Set the zipper into the back opening and topstitch in place.

TWEED COSTUME

Worked double, the hat and smartly detailed jacket are done in double-crochet stitch—the jacket has single-crochet trim and an elasticized waist. Skirt is half double crochet.

SIZES: (8–10) [(12–14)–(16–18)]. Jacket measures 17" [19"–21"] across back at underarms, 16" [16½"–17¼"] from underarm to lower edge. Skirt has adjustable waistband; finished length from waistband to lower edge is 25" and can be shortened or lengthened as you work. Skirt measures 72" [75"–78"] around lower edge. One size hat fits all.

MATERIALS: Columbia-Minerva Nantuk 4-Ply (Orlon acrylic knitting-worsted-weight) yarn.

For Jacket Only: 4 [5–5] (4-ounce) skeins black No. 5912 (color B) and 4 [5–5] skeins beige (natural) No.

5918 (color N); thin, round, black cord elastic; 4 buttons 1 ⅜" in diameter.

For Skirt Only: 3 [4–4] (4-ounce) skeins black; thin, round, black cord elastic; **7" black** skirt zipper.

For Hat Only: 1 (4-ounce) skein each black (B) and natural (N); thin, round, black cord elastic.

For all items: Aluminum crochet hook size J (or international size 6.00 mm) **or the size that will give you the correct gauge.**

GAUGE: For Jacket: 5 dc = 2"; 5 dc rows or rnds = 4½"

For Hat: 5 dc = 2"; 1 dc rnd = 1".

For Skirt: With 1 strand of yarn, 3 h dc = 1"; 4 h dc rnds = 3".

Note: For jacket and hat use yarn doubled throughout. Use either 1 strand of each color or 2 strands of same color where specified. For skirt use only 1 strand of yarn.

Jacket

Jacket is worked without side seams and starts at waistline. Top section is worked first; peplum is added later after top section is completed.

Note: To get gauge for jacket, always draw up ¾" lp for each dc throughout.

BODY: Top Section: Starting at waistline with 1 strand each of B and N, ch 90 [98–110] to measure about 36" [39"–43"]. Cut a piece of elastic 12" longer than length of starting ch.

1st row: Leaving 6" end of elastic at beg and end of this row, work over elastic as follows: Sc in 2nd ch from hook and in each remaining ch (89 [97–109] sc); ch 3, turn. When jacket is completed, elastic will be drawn up tightly to fit waistline.

2nd row: See note above for length of dc lp. Skip 1st sc, dc in each sc across; ch 3, turn. **3rd row:** Skip 1st dc, dc in each dc across, dc in top of turning ch (89 [97–109] dc, counting ch 3 as 1 dc); ch 3, turn.

Repeat 3rd row until piece measures 8" [8"–8¾"] from 1st row (sc row); ch 3, turn. Peplum will be added later.

To Divide Work: Right Front: 1st row: Skip 1st dc, dc in each dc until 19 [21–23] sts have been worked. Mark last dc worked. Do not work across remaining sts; ch 3, turn.

2nd row: Dec 1 dc at beg and end of row as follows: Skip 1st st, (y o hook, draw up long lp in next st, y o hook and draw through 2 lps) twice, y o hook and draw through all 3 lps on hook (1 dc dec at armhole edge); dc in each dc across to within last 2 sts, dec 1 dc; ch 3, turn.

Repeat last row 3 [3–4] times more, then dec 1 dc at front edge only 3 [3–4] times more. Work even, if necessary on 8 [9–10] dc until armhole measures 7"

[7¾"–7¾"] from beg. Break off.

BACK: With 1 strand each of B and N, make lp on hook. Starting at marker, skip next 8 [8–10] dc, dc in next dc and in each dc across until 35 [39–43] dc have been worked. Place 2nd marker on last dc worked. Do not work remaining sts; ch 3, turn.

Dec 1 dc at beg and end of next 4 [5–5] rows. Work even on 27 [29–33] dc until armholes measure 7" [7¾"–7¾"] from beg; ch 1, turn.

Shoulder Shaping: Sl st across 1st 9 [10–11] sts, ch 3, dc in each dc across to within last 8 [9–10] sts, ch 3, sl st in each st to end of row. Break off.

LEFT FRONT: Make lp on hook with 1 strand each of B and N. Starting at 2nd marker, skip next 8 [8–10] dc, dc in next dc and in each dc across; ch 3, turn. Finish to correspond to right front, reversing all shaping.

PEPLUM: Turn work so that foundation ch is at top of work. Work along opposite side of foundation ch for 1st row.

1st row: With 1 strand each of B and N, make lp on hook and work 1 dc in each st across (89 [97–109] dc); ch 3, turn.

Work even in dc until peplum measures 8" [8½"–8½"] in all. Break off.

SLEEVES: Starting at lower edge above cuff, with 1 strand each of B and N, ch 32 [34–36] loosely to measure 13" [13½"–14"]; join with sl st in 1st ch st.

1st rnd: Ch 1, sc in same st as sl st, sc in each remaining ch (32 [34–36] sc). Join with sl st in 1st sc. **2nd rnd:** See note for length of dc lp. Ch 3, dc in each dc around; join with sl st in top of ch 3. **3rd rnd:** Ch 3, dc in each dc around; join as for last rnd (32 [34–36] dc), counting ch 3 as 1 dc.

Repeat last rnd until sleeve measures 5" from beg. **Next row (inc row):** Work in dc as before, but work 2 dc in last dc. Repeat inc rnd every 3" twice more. Work even on 35 [37–39] dc until sleeve measures 15½" from beg or ½" less than desired length from underarm to wrist.

To Shape Cap: Work in rows from now on. **1st row:** Sl st in each of next 3 sts, sc in each of next 2 sts, dc in next 25 [27–29] sts, sc in each of next 2 sts, sl st in each of last 3 sts. Break off.

2nd row: Make lp on hook. Skip 1st 5 sts of last row. Starting with 1st dc of last row dec 1 dc dec; dc in each dc across to within last 2 dc, dec 1 dc (leaving last 5 sts of last row unworked); ch 3, turn.

3rd row: Dec 1 dc at beg and end of row; ch 3, turn. **4th row:** (Y o hook, draw up lp in next dc, y o hook and draw through 2 lps on hook) 3 times, y o hook and draw through all 4 lps on hook (2 dc dec), dc in each dc across to within last 3 dc, dec 2 dc. Break off.

COLLAR: With 2 strands of B, ch 66 [67–68] to

measure about 26″ [26¼″–26½″]. **1st row:** Sc in 2nd ch from hook and in each remaining ch (65 [66–67] sc); ch 1, turn. **2nd row:** Sc in each sc across, drop B; attach 2 strands of N, ch 1, turn.

Work even in sc, working 2 rows N, 2 rows B alternately until 11th row is completed. Break off. With 2 strands N, sc evenly across 1 short edge, across last row of collar and across other short edge, working 3 sc at each corner. Break off.

POCKET (make 2): Using 2 strands B or N, work in stripe pattern of 1 row B, 1 row N. All rows are right-side rows. Break off at end of each row and start each row at beg of last row.

With B, ch 13. **1st row:** Sc in 2nd ch from hook and in each ch across (12 sc). Break off B. **2nd row:** Make lp on hook with N; starting at beg of last row, sc in each sc across (12 sc). Break off N.

Continue in stripe pattern as established until 13th row is completed. Break off. **Border:** With right side facing you, with N, work 1 rnd sc across all sides, working 3 sc at each corner; join and break off. With B, work 1 rnd and break off.

CUFF: Work around lower edge of sleeve, starting at underarm (beg of rnds), with right side of work facing you. Use 2 strands yarn. Make lp on hook with B.

1st rnd: Sc in each st of foundation ch, drop B. Make lp with N and draw through B lp on hook. **2nd rnd:** With N, sc in each sc around, changing to B at end of rnd.

Continue to work 1 rnd B, 1 rnd N until 10th rnd is completed. Join with sl st; break off. Turn cuff to right side of sleeve. Wrong side of work is right side of cuff.

FINISHING: Trim: With 2 strands N, work 2 rnds sc evenly around each armhole and sleeve cap. To join sleeves to body, hold sleeve and body with wrong sides tog and pin sleeve cap in armhole. Working on right side of work with 2 strands B, sl st both pieces tog.

Border: Using 1 strand each B and N, with right side of body facing you, work 1 rnd sc evenly around all edges, working 3 sc at corners; join.

Mark left front edge for placement of 4 buttons, the 1st at waistline (sc row), the 4th ½″ below start of neck shaping, and the others evenly spaced between.

2nd rnd (buttonholes): Sc in each sc around, working 3 sc in each corner and working buttonholes on right front edge opposite markers as follows: * Sc in each sc to within ½″ of marker, ch 3, skip 3 sc, sc in next sc. Repeat from * 3 times more, complete rnd; join.

3rd rnd: Sc in each sc around and in each st of ch at each buttonhole, working 3 sc at corners as before. Join and break off.

Sew pockets in place, following photograph. Sew on buttons. Center and pin collar, placing each end at beg of neck shaping on each front. Sew collar in place.

Draw up elastic to fit waistline and sew ends securely.

Skirt

Note: To get gauge, for each h dc throughout skirt, draw up lp ¾″ long.

Use 1 strand black throughout.

Starting at top edge, below waistband, ch 75 [87–99] loosely to measure about 25″ [28″–32″]. **1st row:** Y o hook, insert hook in 4th ch from hook and draw up lp ¾″ long, y o and draw through all lps on hook (h dc made), h dc in each remaining ch across (73 [85–97] h dc, counting ch 3 as 1 h dc); ch 3, turn.

2nd row (inc row): Skip 1st h dc, * h dc in each of next 11 [13–15] h dc, work 2 h dc in next h dc (inc made). Repeat from * across, working last inc in top of turning ch (6 inc made); ch 3, turn.

3rd row (inc row): Skip 1st h dc, h dc in each of next 5 [7–9] h dc, inc in next h dc, * h dc in each of next 12 [14–16] h dc, inc in next h dc. Repeat from * across, ending with h dc in each of last 7 sts (6 h dc inc); ch 3, turn.

4th row: Work even in h dc; ch 3, turn.

5th row (inc row): Skip 1st h dc, * h dc in each of next 13 [15–17] h dc, inc in next h dc. Repeat from * across, working last inc in top of turning ch (6 h dc inc); ch 3, turn.

6th row (inc row): Skip 1st h dc, h dc in each of next 7 [9–11] h dc, inc in next h dc. * h dc in each of next 14 [16–18] h dc inc in next h dc. Repeat from * across, ending with h dc in each of last 7 sts (6 h dc inc); ch 3, turn.

7th row: Work even in h dc; ch 3, turn.

8th row (inc row): Skip 1st h dc, * h dc in each of next 15 [17–19] h dc, inc in next h dc. Repeat from * across, working last inc in top of turning ch; join with sl st to top of 1st st at beg of this row. Work in rounds from now on.

1st rnd (inc rnd): Ch 3, h dc in each of next 9 [11–13] h dc, inc in next h dc * h dc in each of next 16 [18–20] h dc, inc in next h dc. Repeat from * around, h dc in each remaining h dc, join with sl st to top of ch 3.

2nd rnd (inc rnd): Ch 3, * h dc in each of next 17 [19–21] h dc, inc in next h dc. Repeat from * around, ending with inc in last st (6 h dc inc); join.

Being careful to alternate increases in same manner as before, * work even for 1 rnd, then inc 6 sts on each rnd for 3 rnds. Repeat from * until skirt measures 25″ from beg or 1½″ less than desired finished length. Work even for 1 rnd more. Break off.

Waistband: Cut lengths of elastic about 4″ longer than waistline measurements. Work each row of waistband over elastic.

Working across opposite edge of foundation ch, sc in each st across; ch 1, turn. Continue to work in rows of sc until waistband is 1″. Break off.

Draw up elastic to fit snugly and sew ends securely. Work 1 row sc across back opening, then pin and sew zipper in place.

Hat

Note: For hat only, to get gauge always draw up lp 1″ for each dc throughout.

Starting at top, with 1 strand each of B and N, ch 4. Join with sl to form ring.

1st rnd: Work 10 sc in ring; sl st in 1st sc.

2nd rnd: Ch 3, work dc in same place as sl st, work 2 dc in each sc around (20 dc, counting ch 3 as 1 dc); join with sl st to top of ch 3. Always count ch 3 at beg of rnds as 1 dc.

3rd rnd: Ch 3, work dc in same place as sl st, work 2 dc in each dc around (40 dc) join.

4th rnd: Ch 3, dc in next dc, * work 2 dc in next dc, dc in next dc. Repeat from * around (59 dc); join. Piece should measure 7″ in diameter.

5th rnd: Ch 3, dc in each dc around; join. Repeat 5th rnd twice more.

8th rnd: (If desired, cut a piece of elastic larger than head size and work over elastic as follows): Ch 1, sc in same place as sl st, sc in each dc around. Join with sl st in 1st sc. Mark this sc rnd.

For brim, work as follows: Turn work. Reversing direction of work and working as for 5th rnd, work even on 59 dc until brim measures 5″ from marked sc rnd. Join and break off.

Fold brim in half to right side of hat, then fold brim up again. If elastic was used, draw up to fit head size and fasten ends securely.

EMBROIDERED SUIT

Single crochet and chain-one is the stitch pattern used for both jacket and flared skirt, which is worked in four panels. The embroidered motifs are simple star stitch.

SIZES: (6–8) [(10–12)—(14–16)—(18–20)]. Jacket measures about 16″ [18″–20″–22″] across back at underarms, 23″ [23¾″–24½″–25¼″] from shoulder to lower edge. Skirt measures 17″ [18″–20″–22″] across hips, measured 7″ below waist, and 31″ [32″–34″–36″] across hem. Skirt length is 27″ and is adjustable.

MATERIALS: Unger Nanette (100% acrylic), 20 [21–22–23] (about 1¾-oz) balls raspberry No. 42; small amounts of gold and rust for embroidery; aluminum crochet hook size H (or international size 5.00 mm) **or the size that will give you the correct gauge;** 4 buttons ¾″ in diameter; 1 yard ½″-wide elastic for skirt; tapestry needle.

GAUGE: 4 sts (sc, ch 1, sc and ch 1) = 1"; 7 rows = 2".

SKIRT

Note: Skirt is composed of 4 gores which are sewn together. Pattern is reversible.

FIRST SECTION: Starting at lower edge, ch 66 [68–72–76] to measure about 16½" [17"–18"–19"]. **1st row:** Sc in 2nd ch from hook, * ch 1, skip next ch, sc in next ch. Repeat from * across (65 [67–71–75] sts); ch 1, turn. **2nd row:** Sc in first sc, * ch 1, skip next ch-1, sc in next sc. Repeat from * across; ch 1, turn.

Repeating 2nd row for pattern, work even on 65 [67–71–75] sts until piece measures 4". To lengthen or shorten, work more or fewer rows before first dec row.

Next row (dec row): Sl st across first 2 sts, ch 1, work in pattern across row to within last 2 sts (2 sts dec at beg and end of row—59 [63–67–71] sts); ch 1, turn.

Continuing in pattern, dec 2 sts at beg and end of row every 3" 6 times more, then every 2" twice more. Work even on 29 [31–35–39] sts until piece measures 27". Break off. Work 3 more sections in same manner.

FINISHING: Treating crochet as fabric, machine stitch or hand sew side and center seams, allowing ½" for seams.

Edging: With right side of work facing you, attach yarn to lower edge at center back; spacing sc's evenly apart, work a row of ch-1 and sc around lower edge; join. Break off. Work edging in same manner around waist edge.

Casing: Thread a tapestry needle with yarn. Work ¾"-wide herringbone stitch (see diagram) around wrong side of waist edge. Cut elastic to waist measurement and insert it under herringbone stitches. Sew ends together.

Embroidery: Vertical Seam: Using yarn and tapestry needle, work chain st (see Special Stitch Diagrams, page 14) vertically over each of the 4 seams.

JACKET

BACK: Starting at lower edge, ch 72 [80–88–96] to measure about 18" [20"–22"–24"]. Work even in pattern as for skirt on 71 [79–87–95] sts until piece measures 4". Dec 2 sts at beg and end of next row. Work even on 67 [75–83–91] sts until piece measures 6", ending last row with ch 4, turn.

Next row (beading row): Skip first sc and ch-1, dc in next sc, * ch 1, skip next ch-1, dc in next sc. Repeat from * across; ch 1, turn.

Following row: Sc in first dc, * ch 1, skip next ch-1, sc in next dc. Repeat from * across, ending ch 1, sc in 3rd ch of ch-4; ch 1, turn.

Continue to work even in pattern on 67 [75–83–91] sts until piece measures 16" [16½"–17"–17½"] or desired length to underarm.

To Shape Armholes: 1st row: Sl st across first 2 [4–4–4] sts; ch 1, work in pattern across row to within last 2 [4–4–4] sts (63 [67–75–83] sts); ch 1, turn. Dec 2 sts at beg and end of next 3 [3–4–5] rows. Work even in pattern on 51 [55–59–63] sts until armholes measure 7" [7¼"–7½"–7¾"] from beg; ch 1, turn.

To Shape Shoulders: 1st row: Sl st across first 8 [8–8–10] sts, ch 1, sc in next sc, work across in pattern to within last 8 [8–8–10] sts, ending with sc; turn. **2nd row:** Sl st across first 6 [8–8–8] sts, ch 1, sc in next sc, work across to within last 6 [8-8-8] sts, ending with sc. Break off (23 [23–27–27] sts remain for back of neck).

LEFT FRONT: Starting at lower edge, ch 38 [42–46–50] to measure about 9½" [10½"–11½"–12½"]. Work even in pattern as for back on 37 [41–45–49] sts until piece measures 4". Dec 2 sts at beg of next row (mark this edge for side edge), work across.

Work even on 35 [39–43–47] sts until piece measures 6", ending last row with ch 4, turn. Working as for back, repeat beading row and following row. Work even in pattern on 35 [39–43–47] sts until piece measures 8", then dec 2 sts at side edge. Work even in pattern on 33 [37–41–45] sts until piece measures 1" less than back to armholes, ending at front edge.

To Shape V-Neck and Armholes: Next row (dec row): Continuing in pattern, dec 2 sts at neck edge, work across; ch 1, turn at neck edge every 6th row 2 [2–3–3] times, then every 4th row twice more and, **at same time,** when piece measures same as back to armhole, sl st across first 2 [4–4–4] sts at armhole edge once, then dec 2 sts at armhole edge every row 3 [3–4–5] times.

When neck decreases are completed, work even in pattern on 15 [17–17–19] sts until armhole measures same as back to shoulder, ending at arm edge.

To Shape Shoulder: Next row: Sl st across first 8 [8–8–10] sts, ch 1, sc in next sc, work across in pattern; ch 1, turn. **Following row:** Work across remaining 7 [9–9–9] sts. Break off.

RIGHT FRONT: Work as for left front, reversing shaping.

SLEEVES: Starting at lower edge, ch 34 [36–38–40] to measure about 8½" [9"–9½"–10"]. Work even in pattern on 33 [35–37–39] sts until piece measures 3".

Next row (inc row): Work sc, ch 1 and sc in first sc, work in pattern across row to within last sc, work sc, ch 1 and sc in last sc (2 sts inc at beg and end of row—37 [39–41–43] sts); ch 1, turn.

Continuing in pattern, inc 2 sts at beg and end of row every 3" 4 times more (53 [55–57–59] sts). Work even until piece measures 17½" or desired length to underarm.

To Shape Cap: Dec 2 sts at beg and end of next 2 rows. Work even for 0 [1–1–2] rows. Dec 2 sts at beg and end of every other row 7 times, then dec 2 sts at beg and end of next 3 rows (5 [7–9–11] sts). Break off.

FINISHING: Sew shoulder, side and sleeve seams. Sew in sleeves.

Front and Neck Band: 1st row: With right side of work facing you, attach yarn to lower right front corner. Work in sc and ch-1 pattern evenly along right front, back neck and left front edge; ch 1, turn. Mark right front edge for 4 buttonholes about 3″ apart with first buttonhole 3½″ from lower edge, 4th at beg of neck shaping, and the others evenly spaced between. **2nd row (buttonhole row):** Work in pattern to first marker (ending with sc), * ch 3, skip next 3 sts, sc in next sc, work in pattern up to next marker. Repeat from * 2 times more, ch 3, skip next 3 sts, sc in next st, work to end; ch 1, turn. Work 2 more rows even in pattern, omitting last ch-1. Break off.

BELT: Crochet a chain 65″ long. **1st row:** Sc in 2nd ch from hook and in each ch across; ch 1, turn. **2nd row:** Sc in each sc across. Break off. Thread belt through beading row.

EMBROIDERY: Following photograph for placement, work flower motifs in straight stitches, alternating 8 gold and rust stitches for each flower.

BIKINI IN A BAG

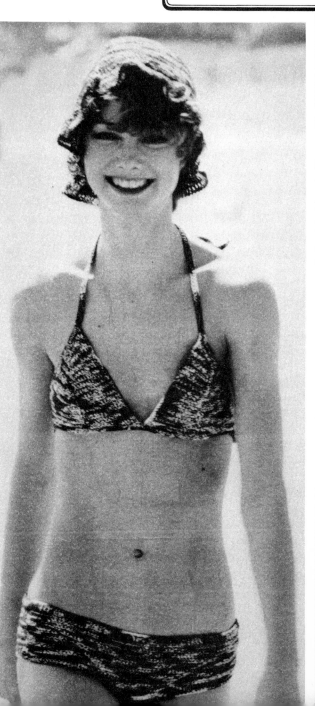

The tote bag carries the suit and can be turned into a scallop-edged hat; the outfit is all easy single-crochet stitch.

SIZES: 6 [8–10–12–14]. Bikini top ties in back; size is adjustable at bust. Pants measure 32″ [33″–34″–35″–36″] at hipline. Bag-hat is one size.

63

MATERIALS: J. & P. Coats "Knit-Cro-Sheen," 9 [9–10–10–10] (175-yard) balls Old Glory Ombré No. 176; steel crochet hook size 0 **or the size that will give you the correct gauge;** 2½ yards ⅛" flat elastic.

GAUGE: For Bikini: 11 sc = 2"; 13 rows = 2". **For Bag or Hat:** 11 average sts = 2"; 4 average rnds = 1".

Note: Use 2 strands of thread held together throughout except when noted on some of the finishing.

PANTS

FRONT: Starting at crotch, ch 11. **1st row:** Sc in 2nd ch from hook and in each ch across (10 sc); ch 1, turn. **2nd row:** Sc in each sc across; ch 1, turn. Work even in sc for 4 [4–5–5–6] rows more. **Next row (inc row):** Work 2 sc in first sc, sc in each sc across to within last sc, 2 sc in last sc; ch 1, turn. Repeat inc row every other row 4 times more, then repeat inc row every row 5 times. **Next row:** Work even on 30 sc. Piece should measure about 3¼" [3¼"–3½"–3½"–3½"] from beg. Ch 26 [27–28–29–31] for leg; turn. **Next row:** Sc in 2nd ch from hook and mark this sc, sc in each ch across, sc in each sc of last row; ch 26 [27–28–29–31] for other leg; turn. **Following row:** Sc in 2nd ch from hook and in each ch across, sc in each sc of last row; ch 1, turn.

Work even on 80 [82–84–86–90] sc until piece is 2" from marker.

Side Shaping: Next row (dec row): Draw up lp in each of first 2 sc, y o hook and draw through all 3 lps on hook (1 sc dec), sc in each sc across to within last 2 sc, dec 1 sc over last 2 sc; ch 1, turn. Work even in sc for 4 rows more, then repeat dec row once more. Work even on 76 [78–80–82–86] sc for 2 rows. Break off. Piece should measure about 6¼" [6¼"–6½"–6½"–6½"] from beg of crotch.

BACK: Back is wider than front. Work same as for front until there are 30 sc, then for each leg ch 31 [32–33–34–36] and, marking first sc on first leg, work even on 90 [92–94–96–100] sc until piece is 1" from marker. Do not ch 1 at end of last row. Break off, turn.

Shaped Section: 1st short row: Skip first 25 [26–27–28–30] sc, make lp on hook and sc in each of next 40 sc; do not work across remaining sts; ch 1, turn. Work on these center sts only for this section.

Next row (inc row): Work 2 sc in first sc, sc across to within last sc, work 2 sc in last sc; ch 1, turn. Repeat inc row 8 times more. Work even on 58 sc for 1 row. Mark with pins beg and end of last row worked, then work even in sc for 1 row more. Dec 1 sc at beg and end of next 9 rows. Work even on 40 sc for 1 row. Break off.

Make lp on hook and, starting at beg of last long sc row, sc in each of the first 13 [14–15–16–18] sc (do not work across remaining sc), then, starting at pin, work

as follows across shaped section: Work 12 sc between pin and last row, sc in each of 40 sc of last row, then work 12 sc between last row and next pin, then, leaving first 12 sc of last long sc row free, sc in each remaining 13 [14–15–16–18] sc; ch 1, turn.

Work even on 90 [92–94–96–100] sc until piece is 2" from marker. Repeat side shaping of front, then work even on 86 [88–90–92–96] sc for 2 rows. Break off. Piece should measure about 9" [9"–9¼"–9¼"–9¼"] from beg of crotch. Back is deeper than front.

FINISHING: Sew or crochet together opening on each side of shaped section to back, having seam on wrong side of work. Sew side and crotch seams.

For Leg Border: With right side of work facing you, work 2 rnds of sc around entire leg opening. **3rd rnd (beading rnd):** Ch 4, skip 2 sc, dc in next sc, * ch 1, skip next sc, dc in next sc. Repeat from * around; join with sl st in 3rd ch of ch 4. Break off. Cut a piece of elastic to fit leg opening. Place elastic on wrong side of work, then fold beading rnd over elastic and sew border in place. Adjust elastic to fit and sew ends securely. Using only 1 strand and working into scs of 2nd rnd, work 1 rnd of sc on top of folded edge. Break off. Work same border around other leg opening.

For Top Border: With right side of work facing you, work 1 rnd dc around top edge, then repeat beading rnd of leg border. Cut elastic to fit and finish as for leg border; working with 1 strand of thread, work sc in top edge of dc (instead of sc).

TOP

LEFT CUP: Each cup is worked in 2 sections.

Front Section: Starting at lower edge, ch 16 [16–17–17–17]. **1st row (right side):** Sc in 2nd ch from hook and mark beg of row for side edge, sc in each remaining ch across (15 [15–16–16–16] sc); ch 1, turn.

Working in sc, dec 1 sc at end of 7th row, dec 1 sc at beg and end of 13th row, dec 1 sc at end of 19th row, dec 1 sc at beg and end of 25th row, dec 1 sc at end of 31st row, dec 1 sc at beg and end of 37th row. Work even on 6 [6–7–7–7] sc for 2 [2–4–4–4] rows more. Break off. Do not remove marker on 1st row of work. Piece should measure about 6¼" [6¼"–6½"–6½"–6½"] from beg.

Side Section: Starting at lower edge, ch 25 [25–26–26–26]. **1st row (right side):** Sc in 2nd ch from hook and in each ch across (24 [24–25–25–25] sc). Mark end of row for front edge. Ch 1, turn. Work even in sc for 5 rows more. **7th row:** Dec 1 sc at beg of row (side edge dec), sc in each sc across to within last 2 sc, dec 1 sc (front edge dec); ch 1, turn.

Working in sc, dec 1 sc at side edge every 4th row and dec 1 sc at front edge every other row until end of 15th row. Continuing in sc, dec at side edge every other row and at front edge every row for 6 rows (7 [7–8–8–8] sts left at end of 21st row).

22nd row: Starting at front edge, draw up lp in each of next 3 sc, y o hook and draw through all lps on hook (2 sc dec), sc in each remaining sc; ch 1, turn. **23rd and 24th rows:** Sc in each sc across to within last 3 sc, dec 2 sc as before over next 3 sc; ch 1, turn.

Work even on 1 [1–2–2–2] sc for 1 [1–3–3–3] rows. Break off 1 strand only; with 1 strand ch 1, turn. Piece should measure about 4″ [4″–4¼″–4¼″–4¼″] from beg.

Joining of Sections: Easing edges to fit, pin front edge of side section to front section with both markers together at lower edge and wrong side of both sections together. Working through both thicknesses, with 1 strand sc pieces together. Break off. This seam is on right side of cup. Left cup is completed.

RIGHT CUP: Make front and side sections same as for left cup, but 1st row of work will be used as a wrong-side row instead of a right-side row and markers will be at other edge of work. When joining sections, be careful to have joining seam on right side of work.

FINISHING: Ties and Lower Border: With 2 strands crochet a chain about 20″ [20″–21″–21″–22″]. Working along lower edge of right cup, sc along opposite edge of foundation ch, then sc along lower edge of left cup; crochet a chain about 20″ [20″–21″–21″–22″]; ch 1, turn. **2nd row:** Sc in 2nd ch from hook and in each ch across one tie, sc in each sc below both cups, sc in each ch of other tie; ch 1, turn. Work even in sc for 1 row. Break off. **Top Border:** Use 1 strand. Sc evenly along top edges of both cups. Break off.

Neck Ties (make 2): With 2 strands crochet a chain about 19″ long and work even in sc for 2 rows. Break off. Sew one end of each tie to corner at top of each cup.

BAG OR HAT

Starting at center, ch 3. Join with sl st to form ring. **1st rnd:** Ch 1, work 6 sc in ring, join with sl st in ch 1. **2nd rnd:** Ch 1, work 2 sc in each sc around; join as before (12 sc). **3rd rnd:** Ch 3, dc in first sc, work 2 dc in each sc around (24 dc, counting ch 3 as 1 dc); join with sl st to top of ch 3. **4th rnd:** Ch 1, * sc in next dc, 2 sc in next dc. Repeat from * around, work 2 sc in last dc; join with sl st in 1st sc (36 sc). **5th rnd:** Ch 3, dc in each sc around (36 dc); join as for 3rd rnd. **6th rnd:** Repeat 4th rnd (54 sc). **7th rnd:** Repeat 5th rnd (54 dc).

8th rnd: Ch 1, * sc in each of next 2 dc, 2 sc in next dc. Repeat from * around to within last 2 dc, sc in next dc, 2 sc in last dc; join with sl st in 1st sc. **9th rnd:** Ch 3, work even in dc (72 dc). **10th rnd:** Ch 1, sc around and inc in every 4th dc. **11th rnd:** Ch 3, work even in dc (90 dc). **12th rnd:** Ch 1, sc around and inc in every 5th dc. **13th rnd:** Ch 3, work even in dc (108 dc). **14th rnd:** Ch 1, sc around, inc 5 sc as evenly spaced as possible. **15th rnd:** Ch 3, work even in dc on 113 dc.

Working even on 113 sts, continue to work 1 sc rnd and 1 dc rnd alternately until piece is 6¼″ from center, ending with a dc rnd. **Next rnd:** Sc around and dec evenly to 110 sc.

Beading rnd: Ch 4, skip 1 st, dc in next st (first sp made), * ch 1, skip 1 st, dc in next st (sp made). Repeat from * around, ending ch 1, skip last st, sl st in 3rd ch of ch 4 (55 spaces). Do not break off.

First Scallop: 1st row: Ch 1, sc in same st as sl st, (sc in next sp, sc in next dc) 11 times. Mark last sc worked with pin. Do not work remaining sts; ch 3, turn.

Work in rows from now on. **2nd row:** Dc in 1st sc, work 2 dc in each sc across; ch 1, turn. **3rd row:** Sc in each st across; ch 3, turn. **4th row:** Dc in each st across; ch 1, turn. Repeat 3rd and 4th rows once more.

7th row: Dec 1 sc at beg of row, sc in each sc across to last 2 sc, dec 1 sc; ch 1, turn. **8th row:** Sc in each of first 2 sc, h dc in each of next 2 sc, dc in each sc across to within last 4 sc, h dc in each of next 2 sc, sc in each of last 2 sc. Break off.

Next Scallop: 1st row: Turn, make lp on hook and work 1 sc (at pin) in same dc as last sc of last scallop, (sc in next sp, sc in next dc) 11 times. Mark last sc; ch 3, turn. Starting with 2nd row, complete as for first scallop.

Work 3 more scallops in same manner.

FINISHING: Work 1 row of sc around free edges of all 5 scallops. Break off.

Ties (make 2): Crochet a chain about 30″ long. Break off. Starting each tie at opposite edges, weave in and out of spaces on beading rnd. Tie ends in bow.

SKATING OUTFIT

A ruffle-trimmed skirt, vest with shiny brass buttons and cap are worked in a combination of single- and double-crochet stitches.

SIZES: (8–10) [(12–14)]. Vest measures 16″ [18″] across back at underarms, 10″ [10½″] from underarm to lower edge. Skirt measures 18″ [19½″] across hips, measured 7″ below waist, and 19″ [20″] from waist to lower edge. Cap fits 22″ head.

MATERIALS: Knitting-worsted-weight yarn, 12 [14] oz scarlet (color S) and 24 [26] oz French blue (color B); aluminum crochet hooks sizes J and K (or international sizes 6.00 mm and 7.00 mm) **or the sizes that will give you the correct gauges;** five ¾″-diameter buttons.

Note: Use color yarn specified doubled throughout.

GAUGE: With size J hook: 5 sc = 2″; with size K hook: 7 sc = 3″.

SKIRT

Starting at waist with size J [K] hook and color B, ch 90 to measure 36″ [39″]. Join with sl st to form circle, being careful not to twist sts. Mark for side seam. **1st row (right side):** Ch 1, sc in each ch around, join with sl st in ch 1; ch 1, turn. **2nd row:** Sc in each sc around, join; ch 3, turn. **3rd row:** Skip 1st sc (directly below ch 3), dc in each sc around, join; ch 1, turn. **4th row:** Sc in each st around, join; ch 1, turn. * Repeat 4th row 8 times more. **Next row:** Sc in each sc around, increasing 6 sc evenly spaced, join; ch 1, turn. Repeat from * twice more, ending last row ch 3, turn.

Ruffle: 1st row: Skip 1st st, dc in each st around, join; ch 3, turn. **2nd row:** Skip 1st dc, dc in each dc around, increasing 10 dc as evenly spaced as possible, join; ch 3, turn. **3rd row:** Repeat 1st row. Inc 14 dc on next row, then repeat 1st row once more. **6th row:** Skip 1st dc, 2 dc in next dc, * dc in next dc, 2 dc in next dc. Repeat from * around, join; ch 3, turn. (Repeat 1st row, repeat 6th row) twice. Break off.

Drawstring: With 3 strands B held tog, crochet 48″ chain. Weave through 3rd row. Knot ends. Tie in bow.

CAP

Starting at center with size K hook and S, ch 3. Join with sl st to form ring. **1st rnd:** Work 6 sc in ring. Mark beg of rnds, but do not join rnds. **2nd rnd:** 2 sc in each sc around (12 sc). **3rd rnd:** (Sc in next sc, 2 sc in next sc) 6 times (18 sc). Continuing in this manner, inc 6 sc on each rnd, being careful not to work inc over inc on previous rnd, until 9 rnds have been completed (54 sc). Work even in sc for 10 rnds or until hat is 7″. Break off S; attach B. Work even in sc for 2 rnds; turn.

Brim: 1st row: Work 1 row sc in back lp only of each st (forms turning ridge); join in 1st sc; ch 1, turn. **2nd row:** Sc in each sc around, join; ch 1, turn. Repeat 2nd row twice more. Break off.

VEST

BACK: Starting at lower edge with size J [K] hook and S, ch 33 to measure 13½″ [14½″]. **1st row:** Sc in 2nd ch from hook and in each ch across (32 sc); ch 1, turn. **2nd row:** Sc in each sc across; ch 1, turn. Repeating 2nd row, work 2 rows even. (Increasing 1 st at each end of next row, work 3 rows even) 4 times. Work even on 40 sts until piece measures 8½″ [9″]. Break off; turn.

To Shape Armhole and Neck: Sc to last 3 sc; to last 4 sc (32 sc); ch 1, turn. Dec 1 sc at each end of next row, then repeat this dec every other row once more. Work even on 28 sc until armholes measure 6″ [6½″].

To Shape Neck and Shoulders: Right Shoulder: Next row: Sc in 1st 5 sc; ch 1, turn. Work even on 5 sc for 4 rows. Break off. Skip center 18 st on back. **Left shoulder:** Sc in remaining 5 sc and complete same as for right shoulder.

FRONTS (make 2): Starting at lower edge with size J [K] hook and S, ch 4. **1st row:** 2 sc in 2nd ch from hook, 2 sc in last ch (4 sc); ch 1, turn. **2nd row:** 2 sc in 1st sc, sc across to last sc, 2 sc in last sc; ch 1, turn. Repeat 2nd row 5 times more (16 sc). Mark beg of last row for side edge. (Sc 3 rows even, inc 1 st at side edge on next row) 5 times. Sc even on 21 sc until piece measures 8½″ [9″] from marker, ending at front edge.

To Shape Armhole and Neck: Sc to last 3 sc; ch 1, turn. Dec 1 sc at arm edge on next row, then repeat this dec every other row twice more (15 sc). Keeping armhole edge even, dec 1 st at neck edge on next row and repeat this dec every row 9 times (5 sc). Work even until armhole measures 8″ [8½″]. Break off.

FINISHING: Sew shoulder and side seams. Mark right front edge for 5 buttonholes.

Edging: 1st rnd: With right side facing you, with size J hook and S, sc evenly around lower, front and neck edges, working 3 sc at point on each front; join. Break off. **2nd rnd:** With B, sc in each sc around, working 3 sc at each point; join. **3rd rnd:** Repeat 2nd rnd, working buttonhole at each marker as follows: Work to marker, ch 1, skip next sc, work to next marker. Join. Break off.

Armbands: With right side facing you, with size J hook, work 1 rnd S, 2 rnds B. Break off.

Pocket Flap: Starting at lower edge with size J [K] hook and S, ch 6. **1st row:** Sc in 2nd ch from hook and in each ch across (5 sc); ch 1, turn. Inc 1 sc at each end of next row, then work 5 rows even. Break off.

Edging: With size J hook and B, sc 2 rows along side and lower edges. Sew top edge to right front. Sew on buttons.

OMBRÉ BERET*

A good project for novices done in single-crochet stitch with a fluffy pompon on top.

SIZE: Fits 22″ head.

MATERIALS: Knitting-worsted-weight yarn, 1 (3½-oz) skein ombre; aluminum crochet hook size G (or international hook size 4.50 mm) **or the size that will give you the correct gauge.**

GAUGE: 3 st = 1″; 7 rnds = 2″.

Starting at center, ch 4. Join with sl st to form ring. **1st rnd:** Work 6 sc in ring. Mark beg of rnds but do not join rnds. **2nd rnd:** 2 sc in each sc around (12 sc). **3rd rnd:** (Sc in next sc, 2 sc in next sc) 6 times (18 sc). **4th rnd:** (Sc in each of next 2 sc, 2 sc in next sc) 6 times (24 sc). Continue in this manner, increasing 6 sc on each rnd until 18 rnds have been completed (108 sc). Work 5 rnds even. **24th rnd:** * Sc in each of next 16 sc; draw up lp in each of next 2 sc, y o and draw through all 3 lp on hook (1 sc dec). Repeat from * 5 times more (102 sc). **25th rnd:** (Sc in each of next 15 sc, dec 1 sc) 6 times (96 sc). Continue in this manner, decreasing 6 sc on each rnd for 6 rnds more (60 sc). **Last rnd:** Sc in each sc around; sl st in next sc. Break off. Attach 2½″-diameter pompon to center.

CARTWHEEL SCARF AND HAT

The unusual pattern is created with single crochet and long single crochet. Scarf connects two granny squares with a strip of back-and-forth crochet.

SIZES: Scarf measures 6½″ × 68″. Hat will fit about 22″ head.

MATERIALS: For hat and scarf: Bucilla Winsom, 2 (2-ounce) skeins each winter white No. 330 and Pompeii (rust) No. 339, 3 skeins Lapis Blue No. 310, aluminum crochet hooks sizes F and H (or international sizes 4.00 mm and 5.00 mm) **or the sizes that will give you the correct gauge.**

GAUGE: With size H hook: 4 sc = 1″; 1 stripe = 1″. With size F hook: 9 sc 1″; 1 stripe = 1¾″.

SCARF

Module at End of Scarf: Note: Piece may tend to cup as you work, but it can be blocked flat.

Starting at center with blue and size F hook, ch 4. Join with sl st to form ring. **1st rnd:** Ch 1, work 12 sc in ring; join with sl st to 1st sc. **2nd rnd:** Ch 1, sc in same sc as sl st, 2 sc in next sc, (sc in next sc, 2 sc in next sc) 5 times (18 sc); join. Break off. Always work with same side (right side) facing you.

3rd rnd (1st long sc rnd): Make lp on hook with rust and work sc in any sc on last rnd, sc in next sc, * make long sc as follows: Insert hook from front to back into center hole and draw lp through hole so that it lies flat against circle, y o and draw through both lps on hook to complete long sc; skip the sc on 2nd rnd behind the long sc. (**Note:** Never work into the sc that lies directly **behind** the top of a long sc. The long sc replaces this skipped st.) Sc in each of next 2 sc. Repeat from * 4 times more, make 1 more long sc (6 long sc in all); join.

4th rnd: Ch 1, sc in same place as sl st and in each st around, increasing 6 sc evenly spaced (to work inc, make 2 sc in 1 sc), (24 sc); join. From now on, when working increases on a rnd, do not work them directly over those on previous inc rnd. Repeat last rnd twice more (36 sc on last rnd). Break off. Circle should measure 2½″ in diameter.

7th rnd (2nd long sc rnd): Make lp on hook with white, work long sc in 3rd rnd as follows: Insert hook from front to back into top of any long sc on 3rd rnd, draw lp through st so that it lies flat against circle, y o and draw through both lps on hook to complete long sc; * sc in each of next 2 sc, work long sc in next sc in 5th rnd, sc in each of next 2 sc, long sc in next sc on 3rd rnd. Repeat from * around, ending in pattern; join.

8th, 9th and 10th rnds: Repeat 4th rnd, increasing 4 sc (48 sc on last rnd). Break off.

11th rnd (3rd long sc rnd): Make lp on hook with blue, work long sc in top of 1st long sc made on 7th rnd, * sc in next sc, long sc in next sc on 9th rnd, sc in next sc, long sc in next long sc on 7th rnd. Repeat from * around, ending in pattern; join.

12th, 13th and 14th rnds: Repeat 4th rnd, increasing 8 sc as evenly spaced as possible (72 sc on last rnd). Break off.

15th rnd (4th long sc rnd): Make lp on hook with rust, work long sc in any long sc on previous long sc rnd, * sc in each of next 2 sc, long sc in next long sc. Repeat from * around, ending in pattern (24 long sc); join.

16th, 17th and 18th rnds: Ch1, sc in same place as sl st and in each st around; join. Break off.

19th rnd (5th long sc rnd): Make lp on hook with blue. Repeat 15th rnd (24 long sc). Piece should measure 6¾" in diameter and will lie flat when blocked. Now shape circle into square as follows:

20th rnd: Ch 3, dc in same place as sl st, work 2 dc in next st (1st corner made), * h dc in each of next 3 sts, sc in next 10 sts, h dc in each of next 3 sts, 2 dc in each of next 2 sts (another corner made). Repeat from * twice more; complete last side in pattern (80 sts); join with sl st to 3rd ch of ch-3.

21st rnd: Sl st in 1st dc, ch 3, dc in same place as sl st, work 2 dc in next dc, * dc in next dc, h dc in each of next 3 h dc, sc in next 10 sc, h dc in each of next 3 h dc, dc in next dc, 2 dc in each of next 2 dc. Repeat from * twice more; complete last side in pattern, ending with dc in joining on ch 3; join with sl st in 1st dc.

22nd rnd: Sl st in next dc, ch 3, dc in same place as sl st, work 2 dc in next dc, * dc in each of next 2 dc, h dc in each of next 3 h dc, sc in next 10 sc, h dc in each of next 3 h dc, dc in each of next 2 dc, 2 dc in each of next 2 dc. Repeat from * twice more; complete last side in pattern, ending with last dc in sl st; join to 3rd ch of ch 3. Break off. Block piece to measure about 8" square.

Make another module in same manner.

Scarf Strip: Strip is made in 2 pieces and seamed. Starting at center back, ch 27 with size H hook and blue.

1st row: Sc in 2nd ch from hook and in each ch across (26 sc); ch 1, turn. **2nd row:** Sc in each sc across; ch 1, turn. Repeat last row twice more. Break off. Turn.

5th row (1st long sc row): Make lp on hook with white, sc in each of 1st 2 sc, * work long sc in next sc on 1st row, sc in each of next 2 sc. Repeat from * across; ch 1, turn.

6th row: Sc in each sc and long sc across; ch 1, turn. Repeat 2nd row twice. Break off.

9th row (2nd long sc row): Make lp on hook with rust, work long sc in 1st sc on 6th row, * sc in each of next 2 sc, long sc in next sc on 6th row. Repeat from * across, working sc in last sc; ch 1, turn.

Repeat 6th row once. Repeat 2nd row twice. Break off. Turn.

Continuing in stripe pattern of blue, rust, white, blue, rust, blue, white and rust, alternate 1st and 2nd long sc rows on 1st row of each stripe throughout (i.e., work next stripe repeating 1st long sc row, work following stripe repeating 2nd long sc row, and so on). Work until strip measures about 26", ending with a white stripe.

Make another strip in same manner. Sew ends tog; then sew a module to each end of scarf.

HAT

Work as for scarf module through 11th rnd.

12th, 13th and 14th rnds: Repeat 4th rnd of scarf, increasing 7 sc (69 sc on last rnd). Break off.

15th rnd (4th long sc rnd): Repeat 15th rnd of scarf (23 long sc).

16th, 17th and 18th rnds: Sc in each st around; join. Break off.

Repeat 15th through 18th rnds 5 times more, working stripe colors as follows: Blue, white, rust, blue and rust. Repeat 15th rnd again with white.

40th, 41st and 42nd rnds: Repeat 4th rnd of scarf, increasing 7 sc each on 40th and 41st rnds and 9 sts on 42nd rnd (92 sc). Break off.

43rd rnd (11th long sc rnd): Make lp on hook with blue, work long sc in any long sc on previous long sc rnd, * sc in next sc, long sc in next sc on 40th rnd, sc in next sc, long sc in next long sc. Repeat from * around, ending in pattern; join.

44th rnd: Sc in each st around, increasing 3 sc (95 sc); join. **45th rnd:** Sc in each sc around; join. Repeat last 2 rnds 3 times more (104 sc at end of last rnd). Break off.

FLUFFY SCARF AND HAT

This duo is worked in a cluster-stitch pattern and set off with bands of loopy stripes.

SIZE: Hat fits 22" head. Scarf is 8" × 72".

MATERIALS: Lion Brand Fisherman's Knit wool knitting-worsted-weight yarn: **For hat,** 1 (4-ounce) skein natural No. 98 (color W); **for scarf,** 3 skeins natural No. 98 (color W). Lion Brand Allegro acrylic/mohair yarn: **For hat,** 2 (1-ounce) skeins beige-and-white No. 55 (color M); **for scarf,** 2 skeins beige-and-white No. 55 (color M). Aluminum crochet hooks sizes F and I (or international sizes 4.00 mm and 5.50 mm) **or the sizes that will give you the correct gauge.**

GAUGE: With size I hook, 2 clusters = 1"; 2 rows of clusters = 1".

To Make Lp St: Wrap yarn around first 2 fingers of left hand to form 1"-long lp, insert hook in next st and catch a bit of both strands of lp on hook, pull hook back through work, drop lp from fingers, y o and pull through all 3 lps on hook (lps appear on opposite side of work).

HAT

Starting at center of crown with I hook and W, ch 5; sl st in 5th ch from hook to form ring. **1st rnd (right side):** Work 20 sc in ring. Do not join rnds but mark beg of each rnd. **2nd rnd (cl rnd):** Draw up lp in each of next 4 sc, y o and draw through all 5 lps on hook, ch 1 (1st cl made), * draw up lp in ch-1 sp (center of last cl made), draw up lp in same st as last lp on previous cl, draw up lp in each of next 2 sc, y o and draw through all 5 lps on hook, ch 1 (another cl made). Repeat from * 7 times more (9 cl). **3rd rnd:** Work 4 sc in center (ch-1 sp) of each cl (36 sc).

4th rnd: Repeat 2nd rnd (17 cl). **5th rnd:** Work 4 sc in 1st cl, work 3 sc in each remaining cl (52 sc). **6th rnd:** Repeat 2nd rnd (25 cl). **7th rnd:** Work 2 sc in 1st cl, work 3 sc in each remaining cl (74 sc). **8th rnd:** Repeat 2nd rnd (36 cl). **9th rnd:** Work 4 sc in 1st cl, 2 sc in each remaining cl (74 sc). Repeat last 2 rnds 8 times more. Sl st in next st. Break off.

Looped Cuff: 1st rnd: With size F hook and M work lp st in each sc around. **2nd through 7th rnds:** Working with 1 strand each M and W, work lp st in each lp st; sl st to join. Break off. Turn cuff back.

SCARF

Scarf is made in 2 pieces and sewn together at

center. Always work lp-st rows with wrong side facing you and cl rows with right side facing you.

Starting at 1 end with F hook and 1 strand each W and M held together, ch 35. **1st row (wrong side):** Work lp st in 2nd ch from hook and in each ch across (34 lp sts). Break off. Do not turn. **2nd through 7th rows (wrong side):** Starting with 1st lp st worked on last row, work lp st in each lp st; break off at end of each row through 6th row. At end of 7th row break off M only. Change to size I hook and with W ch 1; turn.

8th row (right side—cl row): Draw up lp in each of first 4 sts, y o and draw through all 5 lps on hook, ch 1 (1st cl made), * draw up lp in ch-1 sp (center of last cl made), draw up lp in same st as last lp on previous cl, draw up lp in each of next 2 sts, y o and draw through all 5 lps on hook, ch 1 (another cl made). Repeat from * 14 times more (16 cl); ch 1, turn. **9th row (wrong side):** Work 2 sc in center of each cl; ch 1, turn.

Repeat last 2 rows 3 times more. Do not turn at end of last row. Change to size F hook and attach 1 strand M.

Next row (wrong side): With 1 strand each M and W work lp st in each sc (34 lp sts). Break off. Do not turn. Repeat 2nd row 4 times. Break off M. With I hook and W ch 1; turn.

Repeat 8th and 9th rows 5 times. Turn. With F hook and 1 strand each M and W work 3 lp-st rows. Break off M. With I hook and W ch 1; turn. Repeat 8th and 9th rows 36 times. Break off. Piece measures 36" long.

Make another piece in same manner. Sew last rows together.

HOUNDSTOOTH SCARF AND HAT

The worked-in pattern has a distinctly sporting look; it's mostly single crochet stitch.

SIZE: Hat, size 22". Scarf, 6" × 44".
MATERIALS: For hat: Bucilla Deluxe Knitting Worsted (100% wool), 1 (4-oz) ball turquoise No. 310 (color A); Bucilla Persian Needlepoint and Crewel Wool, 2 (40-yard) skeins each light turquoise No. 63 (color B) and burgundy No. 145 (color C), 1 skein medium turquoise No. 64 (color D) and dark turquoise No. 65 (color E); **for scarf:** Bucilla Deluxe Knitting Worsted, 1 (4-oz) ball turquoise No. 310 (color A); Bucilla Persian Needlepoint and Crewel Wool, 3 skeins burgundy No. 145 (color C), 2 skeins dark turquoise (color E), 1 skein each light turquoise No. 63 (color B) and medium turquoise No. 64 (color D); aluminum crochet hook size F (or international size 4.00 mm) **or the size that will give you the correct gauge.**
GAUGE: 9 sc = 2".

HAT

Starting at top of crown with A, ch 4. Join with sl st to form ring. **1st rnd:** Work 6 sc in ring. Mark beg of rnds but do not join rnds. **2nd rnd:** Work 2 sc in each sc around (12 sc). **3rd rnd:** (Sc in next sc, 2 sc in next sc) 6 times (18 sc). **4th rnd:** (Sc in each of next 2 sc, 2 sc in next sc) 6 times (24 sc). **5th rnd:** Sc in each sc around, increasing 6 sc as evenly spaced as possible (30 sc). **6th through 16th rnd:** Repeat 6th rnd 11 times (96 sc). Break off A, attach D. **17th and 18th rnds:** Sc in each sc around. Piece should measure 3¾" from center.
COLOR PATTERN: To Change Colors: When working last sc of a color, draw up lp in next sc, drop old color and draw lp of new color through both lps on hook. Carry color not in use loosely across top of work and work over it. Attach C and work even in sc as follows: **1st rnd:** (Work 2 D, 2 C) 24 times. **2nd rnd:** Repeat 1st rnd. **3rd and 4th rnds:** With C, sc in each sc around. **5th rnd:** (Work 2 B, 2 C) 24 times. **6th rnd:** Repeat 5th rnd. Break off C. Work 2 rnds B, 2 E, 2 C. Piece should measure about 6" from beg. Work B,

work 8 rnds sc, increasing 3 sc on each rnd (120 sts). Working even in sc, work 2 rnds C and 4 E. **Last rnd:** With B, from left to right, work reverse sc (see Special Stitch Diagrams, page 14) in each sc around; join. Break off.

SCARF

Working lengthwise with A, ch 201 to measure 45". **1st row:** Sc in 2nd ch from hook and in each ch across; ch 1, turn. **2nd row:** Sc in each sc across; ch 1, turn. Attach C. Work even in sc from now on as follows:
COLOR PATTERN: 3rd row: (Work 2 A, 2 C) 50 times. **4th row:** Repeat 3rd row. Work 2 rows C. **7th and 8th rows:** Repeat 3rd and 4th rows. Work 2 rows A, 1 C, 1 B, 4 E, 2 B, 2 C, 2 D and 2 A.
FINISHING: Edging: 1st rnd: With A, sc around outer edge of scarf, working 3 sc at each corner; join. **2nd rnd:** From left to right, work reverse sc (see diagram) in each sc around to form ropelike edging; join. Break off.

POPCORN-TRIMMED GAUNTLETS, MATCHING SCARF AND HAT

Predominately single crochet, with popcorns on the gauntlets and a popcorn-like texture for the scarf.

SIZE: Woman's medium.

MATERIALS: For gauntlets and scarf: Bucilla Win-Knit (acrylic knitting-worsted-weight yarn), 2 (4-ounce) twin paks dark red No. 436 (color A), 1 pak each medium turquoise No. 412 (color B), red No. 434 (color C) and gold No. 442 (color D); aluminum crochet hook size G (or international hook size 4.50 mm) **or the size that will give you the correct gauge. For hat:** Bucilla Multicraft (bulky acrylic yarn), 2 (2-ounce) skeins chianti (dark red) No. 44; aluminum crochet hook size J (or international hook size 6.00 mm) **or the size that will give you the correct gauge.**

GAUGES: With Win-Knit on size G hook: 4 sc = 1″. With Multicraft on size J hook: 3 sc = 1″.

GAUNTLETS

LEFT GAUNTLET: Finger Section: Starting at tip with size G hook and color A, ch 3. Join with sl st to form ring. **1st rnd:** Work 6 sc in ring. Mark beg of rnds but do not join rnds; sl st in next sc (always end last rnd of a color in this manner). Break off. With D, make lp on hook; then work 2 rnds sc each D, C, B and D. Finish finger section with 14 rnds A (30 sc).

Thumb: Starting at tip with size G hook and A, ch 3. Join with sl st to form ring. **1st rnd:** Work 6 sc in ring. **2nd rnd:** Work 2 sc in each sc around (12 sc). Work even on 12 sc for 7 rnds, or desired length of thumb.

To Join Thumb to Finger Section: Put finger section on your left hand. Mark 1 st on last rnd for placement of thumb. Remove from hand. With right sides facing, hold edge of last rnd of each section together. Working through both thicknesses, using A, sl st in marked st and in next thumb st. **1st rnd:** Working around finger section only, sc in each of next 29 sc; continuing around thumb section, sc in each of next 11 sc (40 sc). Break off.

Upper Hand, Wrist and Arm Section: 1st row: Starting at center of palm section, with right side facing you, using A, sc in each sc around, decreasing 1 sc each side of thumb (to dec 1 sc, draw up lp in each of next 2 sc, y o and draw through all 3 lps on hook); ch 1, turn. **2nd row:** Sc in each of 1st 2 sc, * tr in next sc, sc in next sc. Repeat from * across (each tr should pop forward to

resemble a small popcorn); ch 1, turn. **3rd row (dec row):** Sc in each st across, decreasing 1 st each side of thumb. **4th row:** Sc in 1st sc, * tr in next sc, sc in next sc. Repeat from * to last sc, sc in last sc; ch 1, turn. **5th row:** Repeat 3rd row. Repeat 2nd and 3rd rows once more (32 sc). **8th row:** Repeat 4th row. **9th row:** Sc in each st across; ch 1, turn. **10th row:** Repeat 2nd row. **11th row:** Repeat 9th row. Repeat 8th through 11th rows 3 times more, working 2 rows D, 2 B, 2 C, 2 D, 2 A. With A, repeat 8th and 9th rows once more. **Last row:** Working from left to right, work reverse sc (see Special Stitch Diagrams, page 14) in each sc across. Break off, leaving 12″ end. Thread end in tapestry needle and sew seam.

RIGHT GAUNTLET: Work to correspond to left gauntlet, reversing placement of thumb.

SCARF

Starting at long edge with size G hook and color A, ch 171. **1st row:** Sc in 2nd ch from hook and in each ch across (170 sc). **2nd row:** Sc in each of 1st 2 sc, * tr in next sc, sc in next sc. Repeat from * across. **3rd row:** Sc in each st across; ch 1, turn. **4th row:** Sc in 1st sc, * tr in next sc, sc in next sc. Repeat from * across; ch 1, turn. **5th row:** Repeat 3rd row. Repeat 2nd through 5th rows 3 times more, working 2 rows D, 2 B, 2 C, 2 D, 2 A. With A, repeat 4th and 5th rows, then 2nd and 3rd rows.

Edging: With A, work 1 row sc around outer edges, working 3 sc at each corner. Break off.

HAT

Crown: Starting at center with size J hook and color E, ch 2. **1st rnd:** Work 8 sc in 2nd ch from hook. Mark beg of rnds but do not join rnds. **2nd rnd:** Work 2 sc in each sc around (16 sc). **3rd rnd:** Sc in each sc around, increasing 4 sc as evenly spaced as possible (20 sc). **4th rnd:** Sc in each sc around, increasing 8 sc (28 sc). Repeat 4th rnd 3 times more (52 sc). Work even on 52 sc until hat measures 7¼" from beg; sl st in next st, turn.

Brim: 1st rnd: Sc in each st around, increasing 18 sc as evenly spaced as possible (70 sc). **2nd rnd:** Sc in each sc around. **3rd rnd:** Sc in each sc around, increasing 6 sc (76 sc). Work 4 rnds even in sc; sl st in each sc around. Break off. Turn brim up to form cuff.

SILVERY NECKTIE, DRAWSTRING PURSE*

The tie is single and double crochet; the purse in matching silvery yarn with bright banding is all single crochet.

SIZE: 1½" × 54".
MATERIALS: Columbia-Minerva Camelot (75% metallic/25% rayon fingering-weight metallic yarn), 2 (1-ounce) balls silver No. 226; steel crochet hook No. 1 **or the size that will give you the correct gauge.**
GAUGE: 11 sts = 1½".

Starting at 1 end, ch 13. **1st row:** Dc in 4th ch from hook and in each ch across (11 dc, counting turning ch as 1 dc); ch 1, turn. **2nd row:** Sc in each dc across, sc in top of turning ch; ch 1, turn. **3rd row:** Sc in each sc; ch 1, turn. **4th row:** Sc in each sc; turn. **5th row:** Sl st in 1st sc, ch 3, dc in each sc across (11 sts); ch 1, turn.

Repeat 2nd through 5th rows for pattern until tie measures 54". Break off.

SIZE: 6" deep, without tassel.
MATERIALS: Bucilla Spotlight (83% polyester/17% nylon yarn), 1 (0.7-ounce, 130-yd) ball silver; Bucilla Glossilla (4-strand rayon embroidery thread), 4 (10-yard) skeins pink, 2 skeins blue; steel crochet hook No. 1 **or the size that will give you the correct gauge.**
GAUGE: 13 sc = 2"; 17 rnds = 2".

Starting at center of bottom with silver, ch 2. **1st rnd:** Work 5 sc in 2nd ch from hook. **2nd rnd:** 2 sc in each sc around. Mark beg of each rnd, but do not join rnds unless specified. **3rd rnd:** (2 sc in next sc, sc in next sc) 5 times (15 sc). **4th rnd:** (Sc in next 2 sc, 2 sc in next sc) 5 times (20 sc). Work 6 rnds more, increasing 5 sc evenly spaced on each rnd and being careful not to work increases directly over those on previous rnd (50 sc on last rnd). **11th rnd:** Sc in each sc around.

With pink, work even for 8 rnds; with silver, work 2 rnds; with blue, work 8 rnds; with silver, work 2 rnds; with pink, work 8 rnds; with silver, work 8 rnds, marking 3rd rnd for drawstring. **Next rnd:** * Ch 2, skip 2 sc, sc in next sc. Repeat from * around, ending ch 2, skip last 2 sc, join with sl st in 1st st of ch 2. **Following rnd:** Work 2 sc in each ch-2 sp and 1 sc in each sc around; join. Break off.

Drawstring: With silver, crochet 88" chain. Knot ends tog. Weave doubled drawstring through sts on marked rnd.

Tassel: Cut twenty 5" strands of silver. Tie tog in center, fold strands in half and tie again ½" below 1st tie. Sew to bottom of purse.

LOCKETS AND LIPSTICK HOLDERS

The lockets have openings on top into which you can tuck a coin or two; the lipstick holders may also be used to carry a tiny perfume bottle. They're mostly single and double crochet on crocheted chains.

SIZE: See gauge below.
MATERIALS: Bucilla Glossilla (100% rayon 4-strand embroidery thread), 2 (10-yard) skeins for each necklace (we used orange No. 24 and gold No. 17); steel crochet hook No. 1 **or the size that will give you the correct gauge.**
GAUGE: Locket measures 1½" in diameter.
LOCKET: Starting at center, ch 5. Join with sl st to form ring. **1st rnd:** Ch 1, work 9 sc in ring; sl st in ch 1. **2nd rnd:** Ch 4, skip next sc, sc in next sc, (ch 3, skip next sc, sc in next sc) 3 times; ch 3, skip last sc, sc in 1st ch of ch 4 (5 ch sp). **3rd rnd:** Sl st in 1st ch-3 sp, ch 3, work 5 dc in same sp, ch 1, (work 6 dc in next ch-3 sp, ch 1) 4 times; sl st in top of ch 3. **4th rnd:** Ch 1, sc in each dc and ch-1 sp around; sl st in 1st ch 1. Break off. Make another piece in same manner.
FINISHING: With wrong sides of locket pieces facing and working through both thicknesses, sl st in back lps only of corresponding sts around outer edges, leaving 1" opening; crochet chain 22"-long; sl st in 1st sl st. Break off.

SIZE: Holder is ¾" in diameter × 2".
MATERIALS: Bucilla Glossilla (100% rayon 4-strand embroidery thread), 2 (10-yard) skeins for each holder (we used royal blue No. 13 and olive green No. 20); steel crochet hook No. 1 **or the size that will give you the correct gauge.**
GAUGE: 7 sts = 1".

Starting at bottom, ch 5. Join with sl st to form ring. **1st rnd:** Ch 1, work 6 sc in ring; join with sl st in ch 1. **2nd rnd:** Ch 1, work sc in same place as sl st, (2 sc in next sc) 6 times; join. **3rd rnd:** Ch 1, sc in each sc around (13 sc); join. **4th rnd:** Ch 2, h dc in same place as sl st (1st cl made); ch 1, skip next sc, * y o, insert hook in next sc and draw lp through, y o, insert hook in same sc and draw lp through, y o and pull through all 5 lps on hook (another cl made); ch 1, skip next sc. Repeat from * around; sl st in top of ch 2 (7 cl). **5th rnd:** Ch 1, (sc in next ch-1 sp, sc in top of next cl) 6 times; sc in next ch-1 (13 sc); join. Repeat 4th and 5th rnds 4 times more. Crochet chain 22" long or desired length; sl st in opposite side of last rnd at top of holder. Break off.

FLOWERET CHOKERS

A bouquet of four single- and double-crochet posies, each on its own crocheted chain.

SIZE: Floweret measures 1½″ in diameter.

MATERIALS: Bucilla Glossilla (100% rayon 4-strand embroidery thread), 2 (10-yd) skeins for each choker (we used magenta No. 30, teal blue No. 27, purple No. 7 and candy pink No. 28); steel crochet hook No. 1 **or the size that will give you the correct gauge.**

GAUGE: 7 sts = 1″.

Starting at center of floweret, ch 5. Join with sl st to form ring. **1st rnd:** Ch 1, work 9 sc in ring; join with sl st in ch 1. **2nd rnd:** Ch 4, skip next sc, sc in next sc, (ch 3, skip next sc, sc in next sc) 3 times; ch 3, skip last sc, sl st in 1st ch of ch 4 (5 ch sp). **3rd rnd:** Ch 1, in each ch sp work petal of sc, dc, 5 tr, dc and sc; join (5 petals). **4th rnd:** Ch 1, * sc in each of next 3 sts, 2 dc in each of next 3 sts; sc in each of next 3 sts. Repeat from * 4 times more; join. Break off.

To Form Ties: With wrong side of floweret facing you, sl st in any sc on 2nd rnd, then crochet 13″-long chain for tie. Break off. Sl st in sc on opposite edge of same rnd and crochet 2nd tie in same manner. Tie in bow at back of neck.

JULIET MESH CAP AND SCARF*

The mesh stitch is easy, the gold metallic yarn is glamorous.

MATERIALS: Bucilla Spotlight (83% polyester/17% nylon yarn), 3 (0.7–oz, 130–yd) balls gold; aluminum crochet hook size H (or international hook size 5.00 mm) **or the size that will give you the correct gauge.**

GAUGE: 3 sp = 1.″

CAP

Starting at center, ch 6. Join with sl st to form ring. **1st rnd:** Ch 3, work 11 dc in ring; join with sl st to ch 3 (12 dc, counting ch 3 as 1 dc). **2nd rnd:** Ch 3, dc in same place as sl st, 2 dc in each dc around; join (24 dc). **3rd rnd:** Ch 3, 2 dc in next dc, * dc in next dc, 2 dc in next dc. Repeat from * around (36 dc); join. **4th rnd:** Ch 4, * dc in next dc, ch 1. Repeat from * around; (36 sp); join. Repeat 4th rnd until cap measures about 5″ from center.

Border: 1st rnd: Ch 1, sc in next sp, * sc in next dc, sc in next sp. Repeat from * around; join with sl st in ch 1. **2nd rnd:** Ch 1, sc in each sc around; join. Repeat last rnd twice more. Break off.

SCARF

Starting at 1 end, ch 24. **1st row:** Dc in 6th ch from hook, (ch 1, skip next ch, dc in next ch) 9 times (10 sp); ch 4, turn. **2nd row:** Skip 1st dc and ch-1 sp, dc in next dc, (ch 1, dc in next dc) 8 times; ch 1, skip next ch, dc in next ch; ch 4, turn. Repeat 2nd row until piece measures 56″. Break off. Knot each end as shown.

"THE MAZE" HANDBAG**

Despite the name, you'll be able to copy this design without losing your way thanks to explicit, stitch-by-stitch directions.

SIZE: 9½" high × 9" wide.

MATERIALS: Knitting worsted, 2 ounces each: olive green, royal blue, yellow, Kelly green, light blue and orange; aluminum crochet hook size F (or international size 4.00 mm) **or the size that will give you the correct gauge;** 12" × 22" piece each of nonwoven interfacing and fabric for lining; four 1" plastic rings; 24" length of ½" cord for handles; 9" zipper; tapestry needle.

GAUGE: 4 sc × 1".

Note: We recommend this bag for experienced crocheters. Bag is worked in free-form rows to form one piece which we divided into sections for identification.

Enlarge diagram, (see "How to Enlarge Patterns," page 14); working sections in alphabetical order. Always work with right side facing you. Join new color at beg of previous row and, unless otherwise specified, in the following manner: Insert hook on 1st (or specified) st and make a sl knot on hook with new color, draw sl knot through st, ch 1, then work in sc.

FRONT: Section A: Starting at 1 on diagram with

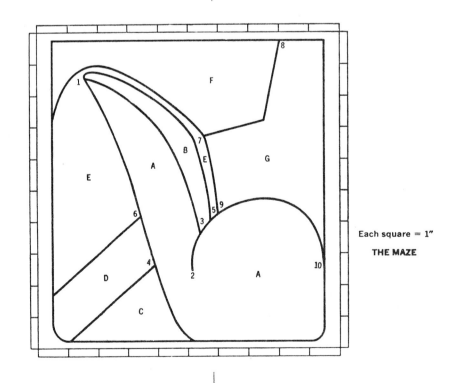

Each square = 1"

THE MAZE

olive, ch 44 loosely to measure about 10″. **1st row:** Sc in 2nd ch from hook and in each ch across (43 sc). Break off. **2nd row:** Attach royal to 1st sc, ch 25; sc in 2nd ch from hook and in each of next 23 ch; working in 1st row, sc in 1st olive sc where royal was attached, sc in next 2 sc, skip next sc, (sc in each of next 3 sc, skip next sc) twice; sc in next 16 sc, (2 sc in next sc, sc in each of next 5 sc) twice (3 sc remain unworked). Break off. **3rd row:** Attach yellow to 1st sc, ch 32, place marker on 6th ch from beg; sc in 2nd ch from hook and in next 30 ch, sc in 1st royal sc where yellow was attached, sc in next 2 sc, skip next sc, (sc in each of next 3 sc, skip next sc) 6 times; sc in each of next 32 sc (3 sc remain unworked). Break off. **4th row:** Attach Kelly, sc in 1st sc, (sc in each of next 3 sc, skip next sc) 11 times; sc in next 24 sc, 2 sc in next sc, sc in each of next 6 sc, 2 sc in next sc, sc in each of next 4 sc (3 sc remain unworked). Break off. **5th row:** Attach light blue, (sc in each of next 5 sc, skip next sc) 7 times; sc in next 26 sc (2 sc remain unworked). Break off. **6th row:** Attach orange, (sc in each of next 6 sc, skip next sc) 4 times; sc in next 24 sc, 2 sc in next sc, sc in each of next 5 sc (2 sc remain unworked). Break off. **7th row:** Attach olive, (sc in each of next 7 sc, skip next sc) 4 times; (sc in next 7 sc, 2 sc in next sc) twice; sc in next 4 sc (2 sc remain unworked). Break off.

8th row: Starting at 2 on diagram, make lp on hook with royal and, working along ends of rows, work 1 sc over first sc on 3rd, 4th, 5th and 6th rows, then work 2 sc in 1st sc on 7th row, sc in next sc, skip next sc, (sc in each of next 3 sc, skip next sc) 3 times; sc in each of next 4 sc, skip next sc, sc in each of next 5 sc. Fold work over with right sides held together, then sl st first 2 royal sts of 8th row to next 2 olive sts. Break off. Next 2 rows fill in opening just worked. **9th row:** With yellow, sc in 3rd royal sc (this is first free sc) and 4th and 5th sc of 8th row, 2 sc in next sc, (sc in next sc, skip next sc) 3 times; (sc in each of next 3 sc, skip next sc) twice; sc in each of next 2 sc. Break off, leaving long end. Fold work over with right sides held together, then sl st 1st 3 yellow sts of 9th row to corresponding 3 royal sts. Break off. **10th row:** With Kelly, sc in 4th sc on 9th row, sc in each of next 3 sc, skip next sc, (sc in next sc, skip next sc) twice, sc in each of next 5 sc. Break off, leaving long end. Fold work, right sides together, then sl st first 5 sts on 10th row to next 5 sts, working through front lps. Break off.

Section B: 1st row: Starting at 3 on diagram, skip 1st 4 free olive sc, with yellow, sc in next free olive sc on 7th row (Section A) and in each of next 6 sc, 2 sc in next sc, sc in each of next 5 sc, 2 sc in next sc, sc in each of last 6 sc; working along ends of rows, sc in each of next 2 unworked sc on next 3 rows of Section A, then sc in each of next 2 unworked yellow sc of 3rd row, insert hook at base of next yellow sc and work sc tightly. Break off. **2nd row:** With royal, sc in each st across 1st row, draw up a lp in each of 3 unworked sc on 2nd row (Section A), y o hook and draw through all 4 lps on hook. Break off. **3rd row:** With olive, sc in 2nd sc of last row and in each of next 7 sc, 2 sc in next sc, sc in each of next 10 sc, 2 sc in next sc, sc in each remaining st across, working 3 sc over joined sc; then sc in each of 3 unworked sc on 1st row. Break off.

Section C: Place marker on 27th foundation ch of Section A (4 on diagram). **1st row:** With orange, sc in marked sc, ch 17; sc in 2nd ch from hook and in each of next 15 ch; skip marked sc, sc in each of next 14 foundation ch (2 ch remain unworked). Break off. Work short rows for center section as follows: **2nd row:** Skip 1st 15 sc of 1st row. With light blue sc in each of next 2 sc (leaving 13 sc unworked). Break off. **3rd row:** Place marker in 2nd free sc from 1st sc of last row. With Kelly, sc in marked sc of 1st row, skip 1 sc of 1st row, sc in each sc of previous row, skip next sc of 1st row, sc in next sc. Break off. **4th row:** With yellow, work as for 3rd row. **5th row:** With royal, work as for 3rd row. **6th row:** With olive, work as for 3rd row but do not break off, then sc in each st of 1st row to within last st. (There are 8 sc in center section.) Break off. **7th row:** With royal, sc in each of 1st 7 unworked sc of 1st row, skip next olive sc, sc in each of next 8 sc of center section (mark 1st sc and last sc of center section for corners), skip next olive sc, sc in each sc of last row to within last sc. Break off. **8th row:** With yellow, sc in 2nd sc and in each sc to corner, skip corner sc, sc in each sc to next corner, skip next corner sc, sc in each sc across. Break off. **9th row:** With Kelly, repeat 8th row. **10th row:** With light blue, repeat 8th row. **11th row:** With orange, sc in 1st sc, * skip next sc, sc in next sc. Repeat from * across. Break off.

Section D: 1st row: Starting at 4 on diagram with light blue, sl st in next free foundation ch of 1st row (Section A); working across foundation ch of Section C, sc in each ch across 1st row to within last sc, 2 sc in last sc. Break off. **2nd row:** With Kelly, sl st in next free ch (Section A), sc in each sc of previous row. Break off. **3rd–5th rows:** Repeat 2nd row with yellow, royal and olive.

Section E: 1st row: Starting at 5 on diagram with orange, sc in each olive sc across 3rd row of Section B, then work (sc, ch 1 and sc) in corner; working along foundation ch of 1st row of Section A, sc in each olive ch across (6 on diagram); then, working across olive sc of Section D, skip 1st sc, sc in each sc across. Break off. **2nd row:** Starting at beg of last row and marking 19th sc (for beg of Section F), with light blue, sc in 2nd sc and in each sc to corner, (sc, ch 1 and sc) in corner ch-1 sp, sc in each of next 2 sc, 2 sc in next sc. (Mark last sc worked for 1st st of next row.) Sc in each sc to within 1 sc of next corner (6 on diagram), skip next 2 sc, sc in each sc across. Break off. Work short rows as follows: **3rd row:** With Kelly sc in marked sc, * sc in each sc to within 1 sc of corner, skip next 2 sc, sc in each sc to within last sc. Break off. **4th row:** With yellow, sc in 2nd sc, repeat from * on 3rd row. **5th row:** With royal, work as for 4th row, ending sc in last sc. Break off. **6th row:** With olive, sc in 2nd sc, sc in each sc to corner, skip corner sc, sc in each sc to within last sc. Break off. **7th row:** With orange, repeat 6th row, ending sc in last sc. Break off. **8th row:** With light blue, work as for last row. **9th row:** With Kelly, sc in 2nd sc, sc in each sc across, skipping 2 sc at corner. Break off. **10th row:** With yellow, repeat last row. Break off. **11th row:** With yellow, working in back lp of st, sc in 1st st, * skip 1 st, sc in next st. Repeat from * across. Break off. **12th row:** With light blue, sc in same blue sc as 1st Kelly sc of 3rd row of Section E, then, working along ends of rows, sc evenly along next 5 rows; sl st to 1st sc of next row. Break off.

Section F: Attach Kelly to marked sc on Section E (7 on diagram), ch 18. Break off. **1st row:** Attach light blue to last ch st of ch just made (8 on diagram), sc in each of 1st 7 ch, skip next ch, sc in each of next 9 ch, sl st in marked sc. Break off. **2nd row:** With orange, sc in each of 1st 6 sc on 1st row, skip next sc, sc in each of next 9 sc, sl st in next sc on Section E. Break off. **3rd row:** With olive, sc in each of 1st 6 sc, skip next sc, sc in each of next 8 sc, sl st in next sc on Section E. Break off. **4th row:** With royal, sc in each of 1st 5 sc, skip next sc, sc in each of next 8 sc, sc in sl st, then sl st in next sc on Section E. Break off. **5th row:** With yellow, sc in each of 1st 5 sc, skip next sc, sc in each of next 8 sc, skip sl st and next sc, sc in each sc on Section E to corner, work (sc, ch 1 and sc) in corner sp, sc in each sc or ends of rows across (13 sc). Break off. **6th row:** With Kelly, sc in each of 1st 4 sc, skip corner sc, sc in each of next 7 sc, skip next sc, sc in each sc to next corner, (sc, ch 1 and sc) in corner ch, sc in each of next 11 sc. Break off. **7th row:** With light blue, sc in 1st 4 sc, skip corner sc, sc in each of next 6 sc, skip next corner sc, sc in each sc to within ch-1 corner sp, ch 1, skip corner sp, (sc in each of next 3 sc, skip next sc) twice, sc in next sc (3 sc unworked). Break off. **8th row:** With orange, sc in each of 1st 2 sc, skip next sc, sc in each of next 6 sc, skip corner sc, sc in each of next 11 sc, sl st in next sc. Break off. Skip all scs after sl st and continue with orange, sc in ch-1 corner sp and in each of next 6 sc. Break off. Place marker on 2nd sc. **9th row:** Starting at beg of last row with olive, sc in each of 1st 2 sc, skip corner sc, sc in each of next 5 sc, skip next corner sc, sc in each of next 8 sc, sl st in next sc. Break off. With olive, sc in marked sc and in each of next 3 sc. Break off. **10th row:** With royal, sc in 1st sc, skip corner sc, sc in each of next 4 sc, skip next corner sc, sc in each of next 5 sc, sl st in

next sc. Break off. **11th row:** With yellow, sc in 1st 2 sc, skip next sc, sc in each of next 4 sc, sl st in next sc. Break off.

Section G: 1st row: Starting at 9 on diagram with Kelly, sc in 1st st of 11th row (Section E) and in each free sc to within corner, skip corner sc; working along opposite side of foundation ch of Section F, sc in each of next 8 ch, 2 sc in next ch, sc in each of next 8 ch. Break off. **2nd row:** With yellow, sc in each sc to corner, skip corner sc, sc in each sc across. Break off. **3rd row:** Starting at marked ch on 3rd row of Section A (10 on diagram) and working along opposite side of ch, attach royal with sc in marked ch on 3rd row and sc in each of next 17 ch, leaving opening (between 2 and 5 on diagram); sc in 1st sc on 2nd row (Section G), skip next sc, sc in each sc to corner, sl st in next sc. Break off.

4th row: With right sides of Section A and B held together, with yellow sl st opening closed (between 2 and 5 on diagram). **4th row:** With olive, * sc in each of 4th and 5th scs, 2 sc in next sc, sc in each of next 5 sc *, sc in each sc to within 1 sc of corner, skip next 2 sc, sc in each sc across, sl st in next free sc on 2nd row. Break off. **5th row:** With orange, repeat from * to * on 4th row, sc in each sc to corner, skip corner sc, sc in each sc across, sl st in next sc on 2nd row. Break off. **6th row:** With light blue, sc in 2nd sc and in each of next 4 sc, 2 sc in next sc, sc in each sc to within 1 sc of corner, skip next 2 sc, sc in each sc across, sl st in next sc on 2nd row. Break off. **7th row:** With Kelly, sc in 2nd sc, 2 sc in next sc, sc in each sc to corner, skip corner sc, sc in each sc across, sl st in next sc on 2nd row. Break off. **8th row:** With yellow, sc in 2nd sc and in each sc to corner, sl st in next free sc on 7th row. Break off. **9th row:** With royal, sc in each sc across, sl st in next free sc on 7th row. **10th through 13th rows:** Repeat 8th and 9th rows twice more with olive, orange, light blue and Kelly. **14th row:** With yellow sc in 1st sc and in each sc to corner, skip corner sc, sc in each sc across 7th row, sl st to next free sc on 2nd row. Break off. **15th row:** With royal, sc in each sc to corner, skip corner sc, sc in next sc, skip next sc, sc in each sc to corner, skip next corner, sc in each sc across on 2nd row. Break off. **16th row:** With olive, sc in each sc to corner, skip corner sc and next sc, sc in next corner and in each sc across. Break off. **17th row:** With orange, sc in each sc to corner, skip next 2 sc, sc in each sc across. Break off. **18th row:** With light blue, sc in each sc to corner, skip corner sc, sc in each sc across. Break off. **19th row:** With Kelly, repeat 18th row. **20th row:** With yellow, sc in each sc to corner, sc in corner sc, skip next sc, sc in each sc across. Break off. **21st row:** With royal, repeat 18th row. **22nd row:** Working in back lp of sts, sc in 1st sc, * skip next sc, sc in next sc. Repeat from * across, sl st in last st, then fold work in half with right sides held together and, working

see page 73

◀ see page 25

see page 67 ▼

see page 73 ▼

see page 46 ▼

see page 15 ▼

see page 48 ▼

see page 42 ▼

see page 69 ▲

see page 74 ▲

see page 19 ▲

see page 33 ▶

see page 34 ▼

see page 63 ▲

see page 68 ▶

see page 169 ▼

see page 58 ▲

see page 172 ▲   ▼ see page 50   see page 39 ▼   see page 97▲

see page 155 ▲

see page 153 ▲

▼ see page 164

see page 151 ▲

see page 154 ▲   see page 156 ▼

see page 106 ▲

see page 108 ▲

▼ see page 113

see page 170 ▼

see page 100 ▼

see page 119 ▼

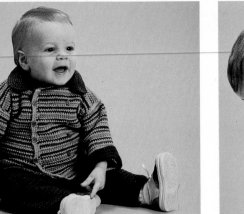

see page 105 ▼

see page 125 ▼

see page 114 ▼

see page 115 ▼

see page 166 ▼

see page 127 ▼

see page 112 ▼

see page 110 ▼

see page 123 ►

see page 122 ▼

see page 124 ▼

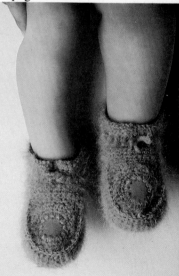

see page 122 ▼

see page 101 ▲

see page 49 ▲

see page 71 ▲

see page 17 ▲

see page 16 ▲

see page 118 ▲

see page 129 ▼

see page 162 ▲

see page 162 ▲

see page 75 ▼

see page 166 ▼

see page 163 ▲

see page 147 ▲

see page 139 ▲

see page 146 ▲

◀ see page 149

▶ see page 138

see page 144 ▲

see page 143 ▲

see page 157 ▼

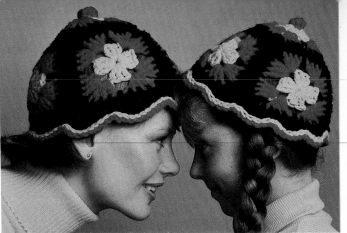

see page 121 ▲

see page 37 ▼

see page 98 ▲

▲ see page 41

▲ see page 22   ▼ see page 44

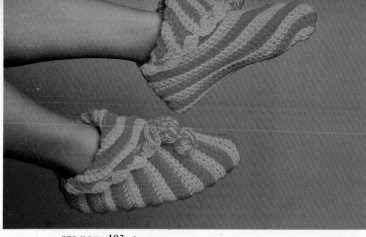

see page 103 ▲

see page 171 ▼

see page 171 ▲

see page 78 ▲   see page 72 ▼

see page 77 ▼

see page 133

through back lps only, sl st last row together. Break off.

BACK: Work as for front.

FINISHING: Following diagram for measurements (½″ seam allowance included), block front and back. Work 1 row machine stitching along seam line around outer edges.

Placket and Facing: Turn upper edge of front to inside and, with right side of front facing you, with royal, work one row h dc evenly spaced over edge of fold at seam allowance line. Break off. **Facing:** Hold work with wrong side facing you. With royal and working through lp below top ch of sts on last row, sc in each st across; ch 1, turn. Work 1 more row sc. Break off. Fold facing to inside. Work placket and facing on back in same manner. With right sides together, with royal, sew front to back. Turn right side out.

Following diagram, cut 2 pieces each of lining fabric and interfacing. Baste interfacing to wrong sides of fabric. With right sides facing, sew lining pieces together, leaving top straight edge open.

Tabs (make 4): With royal, ch 5. **1st row:** Sc in 2nd ch from hook and in each ch across; ch 1, turn. **3rd row:** Sc in each sc across; ch 1, turn. Repeat 3rd row 5 times more. **Edging:** Sc in each sc and row around, working 3 sc at each corner and 3 sc in center ch of starting ch. Break off.

Rings (make 4): With royal, make lp on hook. Sc closely around ring (going through ring). Join with sl st. Break off.

Handles (make 2): With royal, ch 6. Join with sl st to form ring. **1st rnd:** Work 6 sc in ring. **2nd rnd:** Sc in each sc around. Insert 12″ length of cord in ring. Repeat 2nd rnd, working around cord, until handle measures 13″. Break off.

Following photograph for placement, with tapestry needle and royal, sew tabs in place. Sew rings to tabs, insert ends of handle through rings and sew in place.

Insert lining in bag. Turn top edges under ½″ and, with sewing thread, whipstitch to wrong side of zipper. Sew zipper to facings.

Zipper Tab: With royal, sl st in hole in zipper tab, ch 9, sl st in 2nd ch from hook and in each ch across. Break off.

POCKETED SCARF

This clever accessory is worked vertically in rows; the pockets are made separately and sewn on.

SIZE: 8½″ × 70″.

MATERIALS: Knitting-worsted-weight yarn, 5 oz each blue (color B) and red (color R); aluminum crochet hook size K (or international hook size 7.00 mm) **or the size that will give you the correct gauge.**

GAUGE: 3 sts = 1″.

Note: To Change Colors: With color in use, work last dc until 2 lps remain on hook; with new color, y o and draw through 2 lps on hook; continue with new color. When working with 2 colors, work over color not in use.

SCARF: Starting at a long edge with B, ch 208 to measure about 70″. **1st row (right side):** Dc in 4th ch from hook, dc in each remaining ch across (206 dc, counting turning ch 3 as 1 dc); ch 3, turn. **2nd row:** Skip 1st dc (directly below ch 3), dc in each dc across, dc in top of turning ch. Break off B, attach R; ch 3, turn. Repeating 2nd row, work in stripe pattern of (2 rows R, 2 rows B) 3 times. Break off.

POCKETS (make 2): With B, ch 26. Attach R. **1st row:** With B, dc in 4th ch from hook and in each of next 2 ch; with R, dc in each of next 4 ch; * with B, dc in each of next 4 ch; with R, dc in each of next 4 ch. Repeat from * once more (24 dc, counting turning ch 3 as 1 dc); ch 3, turn. **2nd row:** With R, skip 1st dc, dc in each of next 3 dc; with B, dc in each of next 4 dc; * with R, dc in each of next 4 dc; with B, dc in each of next 4 dc. Repeat from * once more; with R, ch 3, turn. **3rd row:** Repeat 2nd row, ending with B; ch 3, turn. **4th row:** With B, skip 1st dc, dc in each of next 3 dc; with R, dc in each of next 4 dc; * with B, dc in each of next 4 dc; with R, dc in each of next 4 dc. Repeat from * once more; with B, ch 3, turn. **5th row:** Repeat 4th row, ending with R; ch 3, turn. **6th row:** Repeat 2nd row. **7th row:** Repeat 2nd row, ending with B; ch 3, turn. **8th row:** Repeat 4th row. Repeat 5th through 8th rows once, then 5th and 6th rows once more. Break off.

FINISHING: Pin 1 pocket to each end of scarf. With B, sl st through both thicknesses around 3 outer edges of pocket; then, working across pocket thickness only, sl st across top edge. Break off.

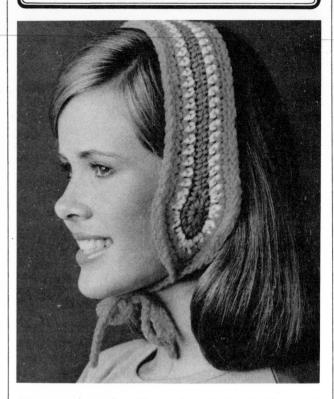

EAR WARMER

Use scrap yarn for this quick-to-do band; it's mostly single crochet with chain-stitch ties.

SIZES: Child's [adult's].

MATERIALS: Knitting-worsted-weight yarn, ½ ounce each green (color G), white (color W) and orange (color O); aluminum crochet hook size J (or international hook size 6.00 mm) **or the size that will give you the correct gauge.**

GAUGE: 3 sts = 1".

Starting at center with G, ch 38 [42] to measure 12½" [14"]. **1st rnd:** Work 8 sc in 2nd ch from hook, sc in each ch to within last ch, work 8 sc in last ch; working along opposite side of chain, sc in each ch across; sl st in turning ch 1. **2nd rnd:** With G, ch 1, sc in each sc around, increasing 3 sc as evenly spaced as possible across 8 sts at each end; join. Break off G. **3rd rnd:** With W, sc in each sc around, increasing 8 sc across 11 sc at each end; join. Break off W. **4th rnd:** With O, sc in each sc around, increasing 3 sc at each end; join. **5th rnd:** Ch 1, sc in each sc around, increasing 3 sc at each end; join. **6th rnd:** Sl st in each sc around; join. Break off.

Ties (make 2): With O, sl st at end of piece, ch 38, sl st in 2nd ch from hook and in each ch across, sl st at base of chain. Break off. Repeat at other end.

RAINBOW SNEAKERS

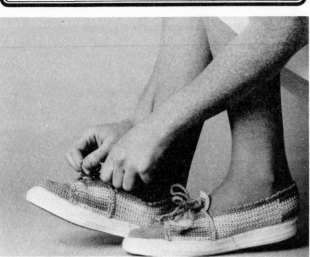

Snip away the sneaker uppers, leaving just a rim of fabric. Next, blanket stitch all around and work single crochet into the stitches. Edges are scalloped, laces chain-stitched.

SIZES: Directions will fit any women's size.

MATERIALS: 1 pair white sneakers; J. & P. Coats Knit-Cro-Sheen, 1 (175-yd.) ball each watermelon No. 122, mid rose No. 46-A, dark yellow No. 43, robinette No. 76, parakeet No. 132-A, tango No. 135-C and small amount white No. 1; aluminum crochet hook size B (or international hook size 2.00 mm) **or the size that will give you the correct gauge;** large-eye crewel needle.

GAUGE: 6 sc = 1".

Note: Work with 2 strands of thread throughout.

TO PREPARE SNEAKERS: Cut away fabric tops, leaving ¼" canvas above upper edge of rubber soles. With white, work blanket stitch (see Stitch Diagram, page 14) along ¼" edge of canvas, being careful to work 6 sts to the inch. Be sure that each sneaker has the same number of sts.

LEFT SNEAKER

Toe and Tongue: Mark center st on toe of canvas base. With toe pointing toward you, count off 16 sts to the right of center st and mark 16th st. Remove center st marker. With watermelon, form lp on hook. **1st row:** Sc in marked st and in each of next 32 sc around toe; ch 1, turn. **2nd row:** Sc in each st across; ch 1, turn. **3rd row:** Sc in each of next 10 sts; draw up lp in each of next 2 sts, y o and draw through all 3 lps on hook (1 sc dec); sc in each of next 9 sts, dec 1 sc, sc in each of next 10 sts; ch 1, turn. **4th row:** Sc in each of next 14 sts, dec 1 sc, sc

in each of next 15 sts; ch 1, turn. **5th row:** Sc in each of next 10 sts, (dec 1 sc, sc in each of next 3 sts) twice; dec 1 sc, sc in each of next 8 sts; ch 1, turn. **6th row:** Work 2 sc in 1st st, sc in each of next 6 sts, (dec 1 sc, sc in next st) 3 times; dec 1 sc, sc in each of next 8 sts, 2 sc in last st; ch 1, turn. **7th row:** Work 2 sc in 1st st, sc in each of next 8 sts; * (y o and draw up lp in next st) twice, y o and draw through all 5 lps on hook (1 h dc dec). Repeat from * 3 times more; sc in each of next 7 sts, 2 sc in last st; ch 1, turn. **8th row:** Work 2 sc in 1st st, sc in each of next 4 sts, dec 1 h dc; * (y o and draw up lp in next st, y o and draw through 2 lps on hook) twice, y o and draw through all 3 lps on hook (1 dc dec). Repeat from * 3 times more; dec 1 h dc, sc in each of next 5 sts, 2 sc in last st; ch 1, turn. **9th row:** Work 2 sc in 1st st, sc in each of next 5 sts, (dec 1 dc) 4 times; sc in each of next 4 sts, 2 sc in last st; ch 1, turn. **10th row:** Work 2 sc in 1st st, sc in each of next 3 sts, h dc in each of next 2 sts, (dec 1 dc) twice; h dc in next st, sc in each of next 6 sts; ch 1, turn. **11th row:** Sc in each of next 5 sts, h dc in next st, (dec 1 dc) twice; h dc in next st, sc in each of next 5 sts; ch 1, turn. **12th row:** Sc in each of next 4 sts, h dc in next st, (dec 1 dc) twice; h dc in next st, sc in each of next 4 sts (12 sts); ch 1, turn. Repeat 2nd row 8 times. **Next row:** Dec 1 sc, sc in each st across; ch 1, turn. Repeat last row 5 times more, omitting last ch 1 (6 sts). Break off.

Edging: With robinette, form lp on hook, **1st row:** With right side facing you; sl st in next blanket st on canvas base on one side of toe and tongue, sc along edge of toe and tongue, sl st in blanket st on base on other side of sneaker; ch 1, turn. **2nd row:** (Dec 1 sc) 4 times; sc in each st to within last 8 sts, (dec 1 sc) 4 times; sl st in same place as 1st sl st of edging. Break off.

Striped Instep Sections: Mark off next 15 blanket sts along each side of canvas base. **Right side—1st row:** With robinette, sc in each marked st along inner edge of sneaker; ch 1, turn. **2nd row:** Sc in each sc across; break off robinette, attach tango; ch 1, turn. **3rd through 10th rows:** Working even in sc, work 2 rows each with tango, parakeet, dark yellow and robinette. Break off robinette, attach tango; ch 1, turn. **Next row:** Sc in each of next 5 sts, h dc in each of next 5 sts, dc in each of next 5 sts; ch 1, turn. **Following row:** Sc in each st across. Break off. Right section completed.

LEFT SIDE—1st row: With robinette, sc in each marked st along outer edge of sneaker. Work as for right section through 10th row. Break off robinette, attach tango; ch 3, turn. **Next row:** Skip 1st st, dc in each of next 4 sts, h dc in each of next 5 sts, sc in each of next 5 sts; ch 1, turn. **Following row:** Sc in each st across. Break off. Left section completed.

Edging: With parakeet, form lp on hook. **1st row:** With right side facing you, work sc along one side edge of an instep section, work 2 sc in corner, * ch 2 for lacing hole, skip next st, sc in each of next 3 sc. Repeat from * twice more; ch 2 for lacing hole, skip next st, 2 sc in corner, work sc along other side edge; ch 1, turn. **2nd row:** Sc in each sc and work 2 sc in each lacing hole across. Break off. Work edging on other instep section in same manner.

Striped Heel: Mark off 22 blanket sts along heel edge of canvas base. **1st row (right side):** With robinette, sc in each marked st (22 sc); ch 1, turn. **2nd row:** Sc in each sc across; break off robinette, attach tango; ch 1, turn. Working even in sc, work 2 rows each tango, parakeet, dark yellow, robinette and tango. Break off.

Sides: With mid rose, work sc in each remaining unworked blanket st along outer edge of sneaker; ch 1, turn. Work 9 more rows even in sc. Break off. Work across unworked blanket sts on inner edge of sneaker in same manner.

Finishing: With mid rose, sew sides to heel. Lap instep sections over sides and over toes and with double strand of parakeet, sew in place, leaving tongue section free.

Edging—1st row: With right side of work facing you, using watermelon, sc evenly along upper edge of sides and heel, decreasing 9 sts as evenly spaced as possible; turn. **2nd row:** * Ch 3, sl st in next st. Repeat from * across. Break off.

Laces (make 2): With 4 strands of watermelon held together, crochet a 25″ chain. Lace shoe. Make a knot at each end of lace.

RIGHT SNEAKER

Toe and Tongue: Work as for left sneaker through 3rd row. **4th row:** Sc in each of next 15 sts, dec 1 sc, sc in each of next 14 sts; ch 1, turn. **5th row:** Sc in each of next 8 sts, (dec 1 sc, sc in each of next 3 sts) twice; dec 1 sc, sc in each of next 10 sts; ch 1, turn. **6th row:** Work 2 sc in 1st st, sc in each of next 8 sts, (dec 1 sc in next st) 3 times; dec 1 sc, sc in each of next 6 sts, 2 sc in next sc; ch 1, turn. **7th row:** Work 2 sc in 1st st, sc in each of next 7 sts, (dec 1 h dc) 4 times; sc in each of next 8 sts, 2 sc in last st; ch 1, turn. **8th row:** Work 2 sc in 1st st, sc in each of next 5 sts, dec 1 h dc, (dec 1 dc) 4 times; dec 1 h dc, sc in each of next 4 sts, 2 sc in last st; ch 1, turn. **9th row:** Work 2 sc in 1st st, sc in each of next 4 sts, (dec 1 dc) 4 times; sc in each of next 5 sts, 2 sc in last st; ch 1, turn. **10th row:** Sc in each of next 6 sts, h dc in next st, (dec 1 dc) twice; h dc in each of next 2 sts, sc in each of next 3 sts, 2 sc in last st; ch 1, turn. Complete as for left sneaker.

Work remaining sections and finish as for left sneaker.

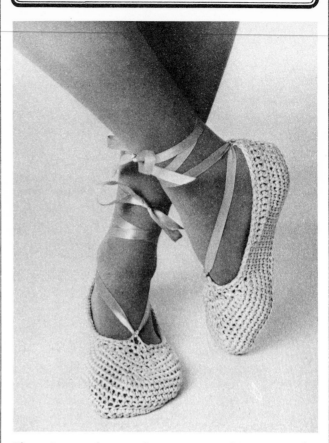

"BALLET" SLIPPERS

Charming at-home footwear combining single-, double- and half double-crochet stitches.

SIZE: Will fit adult size 8—8½ as written. See Note below to adjust size.

MATERIALS: Joseph Galler's RBC Parisian Cotton (knit and crochet cord), 4 (1-oz—120yd) balls pink; aluminum crochet hook size G (or international size 4.50 mm) **or the size that will give you the correct gauge;** 3 yd ⅜″-wide satin ribbon.

GAUGE: 4 sc = 1″; 5 rows sc = 1″.

Note: To adjust slipper size, for each size add or subtract 2 st on foundation ch of sole.

Work with cord triple throughout.

SOLE: Starting at center bottom, ch 28 for foundation. **1st rnd:** Starting at heel, sc in 2nd ch from hook and in each of next 11 ch, h dc in next ch, dc in each ch to last ch; working around end of foundation, work 5 dc in last ch (toe); working along opposite edge of foundation, dc in each st where dc was worked, h dc in next st, sc in next 12 st, work 4 sc over end of ch; do not join, but continue in rnds and mark beg of each rnd. **2nd**

rnd: Sc in each st around, working as many increases around heel and toe as necessary to keep piece flat (to inc, work 2 st in 1 st). Repeat last rnd once more.

4th rnd: Continuing to inc around heel and toe, work sc along half of 1 side of sole, h dc in next sc, dc along remainder of side to toe, dc around toe; complete to match other side. **5th rnd:** Sc in each st around, increasing at heel and toe as before.

6th rnd: Sc in back lp of each sc around (ridge formed to mark edge of sole).

TOP: 1st rnd: Sc in each sc around. Repeat last rnd twice more. **4th rnd:** Repeat last rnd, decreasing 1 st at toe (to dec, draw up lp in each of 2 st, y o and draw through all 3 lp on hook). **5th rnd:** Mark center on each side edge of slipper. Ch 3, dc in each st to 1st marker, h dc in next st, sc in each st to within 4 st of center front,

dec 2 st, sc to next marker, h dc in next st, dc to end; join with sl st in top of ch 3. Break off. Remove markers.

To Shape Vamp: Mark beg and end of 7″ along center front of slipper on last rnd. (You will be working in rows over these sts to shape vamp.) **1st row:** With wrong side facing you, sc in st at 1st marker, sc in each st to within center 2 st, dec 1 st, sc in next marker; ch 1, turn. **2nd row:** Dec 1 sc, sc to center, dec 1 sc, sc to end and dec 1 sc; ch 1, turn. Repeat last row twice more or as many times as necessary to make vamp lie flat on foot. **Last rnd:** Sc in each st around; join. Break off. Make other slipper in same manner.

Cut ribbon in half. Knot center of 1 piece through center st on edge of vamp. Run 1 end through center st at heel. Run other end through same st in opposite direction. Tie ribbon ends around ankle.

POPCORN HOT SOCKS, LOOPY FOOT WARMERS

The puffy socks are high enough to warm the ankles; the warmers are crocheted with three strands of variegated yarn worked together.

Popcorn Hot Socks

SIZE: Woman's medium.

MATERIALS: Knitting-worsted-weight yarn, 7 oz pink (color P), 3 oz turquoise (color T); 1 (100-yd) ball Coats & Clark's Speed-Cro-Sheen to reinforce sole; aluminum crochet hook size I (or international hook size 5.50 mm) **or the size that will give you the correct gauge.**

GAUGE: 3 sc = 1″.

SOLE: Starting at heel with 1 strand each P, T and Speed-Cro-Sheen held together, ch 6. **1st row:** Sc in 2nd ch from hook and in each ch across (5 sc); ch 1, turn. **2nd row:** 2 sc in 1st sc, sc in each sc across (6 sc); ch 1, turn. **3rd row:** Repeat 2nd row (7 sc). **4th row:** Sc in each sc across; ch 1, turn. Repeat 4th row 5 times more. **10th row:** Sc in each sc across, increasing 1 sc at center of row; ch 1, turn. Repeat 4th row once. **12th row:** 2 sc in 1st sc, sc in each sc to within last sc, 2 sc in last sc (10 sc); ch 1, turn. Repeat 4th row 6 times. **19th row:** Sc in each sc across, decreasing 1 sc at center of row as follows: Draw up lp in each of next 2 sc, y o and pull through all 3 lps on hook (1 sc dec—9sc); ch 1, turn. **20th row:** Repeat 4th row. **21st row:** Repeat 19th row. **22nd row:** Repeat 4th row. **23rd row:** Dec 1 sc at beg and end of row (6 sc).

TOP: Starting at upper edge with T, ch 32 to measure 10″. **1st row (right side):** Sc in 2nd ch from

hook and in each ch across (31 sc). Break off T; do not turn work. **2nd row (right side):** With P, form lp on hook. Starting at beg of last row with P, sc in each of 1st 2 sc, * work popcorn in next sc as follows: (Y o, insert hook in sc and draw lp through, y o and pull through 2 lps on hook) 5 times, y o and pull through all 6 lps on hook, ch 1 tightly (popcorn made); sc in each of next 2 sc. Repeat from * across (10 popcorns). Break off P; do not turn work. **3rd row (right side):** Starting at beg of last row with T, sc in each of 1st 2 sc, * sc in top of popcorn, sc in each of next 2 sc. Repeat from * across (31 sc). Break off T. Repeat 2nd and 3rd rows 4 times more (front opening completed).

To Join for Back of Heel and Instep: 1st rnd: With P, sl st in 1st st on last row and, working in rnds instead of rows, repeat 2nd and 3rd rows twice more, joining and breaking off at the end of each rnd. Place marker on 10th st from beg and on 10th st from end of last rnd (2 sts marked, 18 sts between markers). **Instep Section: 1st row:** With right side facing you, with P, sc in marked sc to right, (popcorn in next sc, sc in each of next 2 sc) twice; popcorn in next sc, (draw up lp in each of next 2 sts, y o and draw through all 3 lps on hook) twice; (popcorn in next sc, sc in each of next 2 sc) twice; popcorn in next sc, sc in next marked sc (6 popcorns). Break off. **2nd row:** Starting at beg of last row with T, sc in 1st sc, sc in top of next popcorn, (sc in each of next 2 sc, sc in top of popcorn) 5 times; sc in last sc. Break off. Repeat last 2 rows 8 times more. Break off.

FINISHING: Sew top to sole, easing top at tip of toe.

Ties (make 2): With 1 strand each of P and T held together, sl st in edge of front opening about 1½" from top and crochet 9" ch. Break off.

Ball Trim: With 1 strand each of P and T held together, ch 2. **1st rnd:** Work 6 sc in 2nd ch from hook. **2nd rnd:** Work 2 sc in each sc around. **3rd rnd:** (Dec 1 sc) 6 times (forms cup). Break off, leaving 6" end. Stuff cup with scraps of yarn. Thread end in tapestry needle, weave through sts of last rnd, pull tight and sew to end of chain.

Loopy Foot Warmers

SIZES: Woman's small [medium–large].
MATERIALS: 3 (3½-oz) skeins ombré knitting-worsted-weight yarn; aluminum crochet hook size K (or international hook size 7.00 mm) **or the size that will give you the correct gauge.**
GAUGE: 5 sts = 2".
Starting at center of sole, with 3 strands of yarn held together, ch 15 [18–21] to measure 5" [6"–7"] or 2" less than length of foot. **1st rnd:** Work 2 sc in 2nd ch from hook, mark 1st sc worked, sc in each ch to within

last ch, work 3 sc in last ch, mark center sc of 3-sc group; working along opposite side of chain, sc in each ch across; join with sl st in turning ch. (Side of piece facing you is inside of slipper.) **2nd rnd:** Ch 1, work 3 sc in marked sc, mark center sc of 3-sc group; sc in each sc to within next marked sc, work 3 sc in marked sc, mark center sc of 3-sc group, sc in each remaining sc; join with sl st in ch 1. **3rd rnd:** Ch 1, * sc in each sc to within marked sc, work 3 sc in marked sc, mark center sc of 3-sc group. Repeat from * once more, sc in each remaining sc; join. Repeat 3rd rnd once more. **5th rnd:** Ch 1; * continuing with 3 strands held together, make 1"-long lp over index finger of left hand. Insert hook in next sc and draw a bit of lp through the st (9 strands over hook); remove finger from lp, y o and draw through all lps on hook to complete sc (lp sc made). Repeat from * around; join. Note that lps appear on side of piece away from you. Repeat 5th rnd 6 times more. Break off. With wrong sides (sides without lps) together, fold in half lengthwise. To form instep, sew edges of last row together, leaving about 5" opening for ankle. Work 1 row sc around opening.

BIG-GIRL BOOTEES

The snug cuffs have shell-stitch edging, ball-end ties; striped pattern is worked in single-crochet stitch.

SIZE: Fits sizes 6 to 9.

MATERIALS: Knitting worsted, 3 ounces each orange (color O) and scarlet (color S); aluminum crochet hook size H (or international size 5.00 mm) **or the size that will give you the correct gauge;** tapestry needle.

GAUGE: 7 sc = 2″; 7 sc rows = 2″.

Starting at sole with O, ch 39 to measure about 10½″. **1st row (right side):** Sc in 2nd ch from hook and in each ch across (38 sc). Mark 1st sc at beg of row and 14th sc for toe section. Ch 1, turn. Work in back lp of sc throughout. **2nd row:** Sc in each sc across. Drop O; attach S. With S, ch 1, turn. **3rd row:** With S, sc in each sc across; ch 1, turn. **4th row:** Repeat last row, changing to O at end of row. With O, ch 1, turn. Continue in stripe pattern as established, working 2 rows O and 2 rows S. Mark end of 14th row for end of toe section, then continue in stripe pattern until 36th row is completed, ending with S stripe. Piece should measure 10½″ in length when stretched. Break off both colors. Block piece lightly to measure 10½″ square.

SHELL EDGING: With right side of work facing you, skip 1st 14 sc of last S row for back seam. Make lp on hook with O and, working through both lps of sts, sc in each of next 2 sc, * skip next sc, 4 dc in next sc (shell made), skip next sc, sc in next sc. Repeat from * 4 times more, then work a shell in last sc for corner shell. Working along ends of rows, continue as follows: * Sc in O stripe; work a shell in S stripe. Repeat from * 4 times more; work 2 sc evenly spaced in next O stripe. There are 11 shells in all. Break off. The 4″ of work left free between last sc and next corner is for back seam.

FINISHING: With corner shell on fold and right sides together, fold square in half diagonally to form triangle and sew back seam from end of shell edging to corner at lower edge, leaving remaining edge (sole) open. **For Toe Shaping:** Fold corner of toe section in toward lower edge so that all 3 markers come together, then sew toe and sole seams. Turn slipper right side out, folding corner with shell edging to right side to form cuff.

Tie: With 1 strand each O and S make a chain about 24″ long. Do not break off. Work 12 dc in 4th ch from hook for ball trim. Join with sl st to top of ch, then * skip 1 dc, sc in next dc. Repeat from * around. Break off, leaving a long end of yarn. Thread yarn into tapestry needle and, holding chain in center of ball, gather top edge of sc row tightly around chain to form ball. Sew ends securely. Tie has ball at one end only.

Starting at center of cuff just above shell edging and working through both thicknesses, weave end of tie around cuff, ending at center front. Join O and S to end of tie without ball trim and make another ball. Tie ends into bow.

2

Fashions For Children

BABY SHIRT AND SOAKER

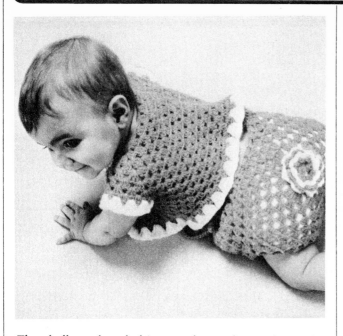

The shell-crocheted shirt matches a drawstring-waist soaker that's "bottomed off" with a big flower.

SIZE: Newborn to 6 months.

MATERIALS: Bernat Berella 3-Ply Fingering (Orlon/nylon yarn), 3 (1-ounce) skeins rose heather No. 7037 and 1 skein white No. 7042; aluminum crochet hook size G (or international size 4.50 mm) **or the size that will give you the correct gauge;** tapestry needle.

GAUGE: 3 shells = 2''; 5 pattern rows = 2''.

SHIRT

Shirt is worked in one piece. Starting at neck edge with rose heather, ch 55. **1st row:** Work 2 dc in 4th ch from hook, (skip 2 ch, 3-dc shell in next ch) twice for left front; skip 2 ch, in next ch work corner of (3-dc shell, ch 3 and 3-dc shell), skip 2 ch, 3-dc shell in next ch, skip 2 ch, work another corner in next ch for left sleeve; (skip 2 ch, 3-dc shell in next ch) 6 times for back; skip 2 ch, work corner in next ch, skip 2 ch, 3-dc shell in next ch, skip 2 ch, work corner in next ch for right sleeve; (skip 2 ch, 3-dc shell in next ch) 3 times for right front (22 shells); ch 3, turn. **2nd row:** Work shell in sp between 1st 2 shells and in each sp between all shells across, working corners as before in each ch-3 corner sp; dc in last dc of last shell (25 shells); ch 3, turn. **3rd row:** Work 2 dc in sp before 1st shell; work shell in each sp between shells, working corners as before; work shell in sp between last shell and last dc (30 shells); ch 3, turn.

Repeat 2nd row, 3rd row, then 2nd row again (41 shells at end of last row).

To Divide for Underarms: Next row: Work across in pattern to within 1st corner; * work shell in corner ch-3 sp; skip next 8 shells for sleeve (**Note:** do not work corners); work shell in next corner ch-3 sp *; work across back in pattern, repeat from * to * once, work across remainder of row in pattern; ch 3, turn (28 shells). **Following row:** Work across in pattern, working shell in sp at each underarm.

Continue in pattern until piece measures 3½'' from underarm or desired length, ending with 2nd pattern row.

FINISHING: Border: With white make 8''-long ch. Sl st in top corner of either front edge, sc evenly along front edge to within last row; in last row (between dc and 1st shell) work shell of 6 long dc (to make long dc, y o, insert hook in corner sp and draw up ½'' lp, complete dc). Continue to work border across lower edge of shirt, working 5 long-dc shell in each sp between shells and 6 long-dc shell in opposite corner; sc evenly along opposite front edge; make 8''-long ch; break off. (**Note:** Do not work neck edge.)

Sleeve Border: With white work 5 long-dc shell in each sp between shells on each sleeve.

SOAKER

PANEL (make 2): Center Section: Always work with right side facing you. Starting at center with rose heather, ch 3. Join with sl st to form ring. **1st rnd:** Ch 3, work 2 dc in ring, (ch 3, 3-dc shell in ring) 3 times; ch 3, join to 1st shell (4 shells). **2nd rnd:** Sl st in each dc to corner ch-3 sp, sl st in corner sp, ch 3; in same sp work 2 dc, ch 3 and 3-dc shell (1st corner made); * skip next shell, in next corner sp work corner of (shell, ch 3 and shell). Repeat from * twice (8 shells); join. **3rd rnd:** Sl st to corner, sl st in corner, ch 3 and complete 1st corner as for 2nd rnd, * skip next shell, shell in next sp between shells, skip next shell, work corner. Repeat from * around (12 shells); join. **4th rnd:** Sl st to corner, in corner sp work 1st corner, * work shell between shells to next corner, corner in next corner. Repeat from * around (16 shells); join.

Repeat last rnd 3 times more (28 shells at end of 7th rnd). Sl st to corner, sl st in corner, ch 3; do not break off.

Left Side: (**Note:** Work in rows only from now on.) **1st row (right side):** Complete shell in corner, work shell in each of next 6 sp between shells, dc in corner (for left leg edge—7 shells); ch 3, turn. **2nd row:** Skip 1st shell, work shell in next sp and in each sp across, dc in last dc of last shell (6 shells); ch 3, turn. **3rd row:** Starting at waist edge, work shell in 1st sp and in each sp across (6 shells), dc in last dc of last shell; ch 3, turn. Repeat last 2 rows once more (5 shells); then repeat 2nd row again (4 shells). Break off. Work right side to correspond.

Crotch Band: Turn piece so waist edge is at bottom and right side is facing you. Attach rose heather to ch-3 sp at right corner of crotch, ch 3. **1st row:** Skip 1st shell, work shell in sp between 1st 2 shells and in each sp between shells across crotch edge only; dc in next corner sp (6 shells); ch 3, turn. Repeat 2nd row of Left Side twice more. Break off.

FINISHING: With tapestry needle and rose heather sew 2 panels tog at sides and crotch.

Waistband: Make lp on hook with rose heather, y o, dc in any sp at top of soaker, * ch 1, skip ¼" edge of soaker, dc in edge. Repeat from * around, ch 1; join with sl st to 1st dc. Break off.

Drawstring: With 2 strands rose heather crochet 36" ch and weave through waistband.

Leg Bands: With rose heather sc evenly around each leg edge.

Flower: Starting at center with white, ch 4. Join with sl st to form ring. **1st petal rnd:** In ring work (sc, ch 3) 8 times; join. Drop white but do not break off. Attach rose heather to any ch-3 lp, work petal of (sc, h dc, dc, h dc and sc) in each ch-3 lp around; join to 1st petal; break off. **2nd petal rnd:** Pick up white and draw lp to back of work. Fold previous petal rnd forward, insert hook from right to left around post of 1st sc, y o, draw lp through and complete sc, ch 3, work (sc, ch 3) around post of each sc around; join. Continuing with white, work petal in each ch-3 lp around. **3rd through 5th petal rnds:** Work as for 2nd petal rnd, working 1 rnd each rose heather and white. Tack flower to soaker.

MATCHING BUNTING AND AFGHAN

The bunting starts with a circle at the bottom, continues with simple rectangles and has a single-crochet border. The afghan begins at one corner and expands—in single- and half double-crochet stitches— to any size you like.

SQUARE AFGHAN

SIZE: 32" square.

MATERIALS: Knitting-worsted-weight 4-ply yarn, 5 oz green (color G) and 3 oz each red (color R), orange (color O), yellow (color Y), blue (color B) and purple (color P); aluminum crochet hook size J (or international hook size 6.00 mm) **or the size that will give you the correct gauge.**

GAUGE: 11 sts = 4"; 5 rows = 2".

Afghan is crocheted on the bias. Starting at 1 corner with color R, ch 2. **1st row:** Work (h dc, sc and h dc) in 2nd ch from hook; ch 1, turn. **2nd row:** Work (h dc and sc) in 1st st (1st inc made); hdc in next st, (sc and h dc) in last st (2nd inc made); ch 1, turn. **3rd row:** 1st inc in 1st st; work 1 h dc, 1 sc, 1 h dc; work 2nd inc in last st; ch 1, turn. Last st worked is at lower edge; mark lower edge with pin. **4th row:** 1st inc in 1st st; 1 h dc, * 1 sc, 1 h dc. Repeat from * to last st, 2nd inc in last st; break off R, attach O and ch 1, turn.

Repeating 4th row for pattern st and changing colors at end of every 3rd row, work in stripe pattern of 3 rows each O, Y, G, B, P and R until 18 stripes are completed, or until lower edge (marked with pin) measures about 29½" from beg, ending with 3 rows of any stripe (or work until 2½" less than the desired finished size, to allow for border).

Keeping in stripe pattern as established, dec as follows: **Next row:** Draw up lp in each of 1st 2 sts, y o and draw through all 3 lps on hook (dec made); 1 sc, * 1 h dc, 1 sc. Repeat from * to last 2 sts; dec; ch 1, turn.

Repeat last row until 3 sts remain. **Last row:** Draw up lp in each of 3 remaining sts, y o and draw through all 4 lps on hook. Break off.

FINISHING: Border: 1st rnd: With G, sc evenly around entire outer edge of afghan, working 3 sc in each corner; at end of rnd, join with sl st to 1st sc. Work 3 more sc rnds, working 3 sc in each corner st and joining as before. Break off.

BABY BUNTING

SIZE: Infant to 6 months. Length from neck to lower edge is 24".

MATERIALS: Knitting-worsted-weight 4-ply yarn, 4 oz light yellow (color A), 2 oz each dark yellow (color B), peach (color C), orange (color D), red (color E), wine (color F), dark purple (color G), medium purple (color H), medium blue (color I), turquoise (color J) and dark green (color K); aluminum crochet hook size H (or international hook size 5.00 mm) **or the size that will give you the correct gauge;** snag-loop tape (we used Velcro) or large snaps for front opening.

GAUGE: 10 st = 3".

Starting at center of circle at lower edge, with color A, ch 3. Join with sl st to form ring. **1st rnd:** Work 8 sc in ring. Mark beg of rnds, but do not join rnds. **2nd rnd:** Work 2 sc in each sc (16 sc). **3rd rnd:** (Sc in next sc, 2 sc in next sc) 8 times (24 sc). **4th rnd:** (2 sc in next sc, sc in next 2 sc) 8 times (32 sc). **5th rnd:** (Sc in next 3 sc, 2 sc in next sc) 8 times (40 sc). **6th through 10th rnd:** Sc in each sc, increasing 6 sc on each rnd as evenly spaced as possible; do not inc over increases of previous rnd (70 sc). **11th rnd:** Inc 10 sc evenly around (80 sc). **12th rnd:** Sc in each sc around, marking 1st sc, 40th sc, 41st sc and 80th sc. Piece should measure about 3½" from center. Ch 1, but do not turn. With A, work 2 sc in first marked sc, sc in next 38 sc, work 2 sc in next marked sc (42 sc in all; do not work on remaining 40 sc between 2 markers—these will be used for front). Ch 1, turn.

BACK: Work back and forth in rows from now on. Working on 42 sts of last row and starting with a wrong-side row, work even in sc in stripe pattern of 2 rows each of color sequence A through K, then repeating from A through K until piece measures 18½" from 1st row of back (above circle), ending with 2nd row of any stripe.

To Shape Shoulders: 1st Shoulder: With next color work 13 sc; ch 1, turn. Work 1 row sc. Break off. Skip center 16 sts, make lp on hook with yarn and work even in sc on next 13 sts for 2 rows. Break off.

FRONT: With right side of last rnd of circle facing you, with A, work 2 sc in next marked sc, sc in next 38 sc, 2 sc in next marked sc (42 sc); ch 1, turn. Starting with a wrong-side row, work as for back in striped

pattern for about 3", ending with 2nd row of any stripe.

To Divide for Front Opening: First Side: Continue in stripe pattern and work as follows: **1st row:** Work 20 sc; ch 1, turn. **2nd row:** Work even in sc. Work even on 20 sc until piece measures same as back to shoulder shaping, ending at side edge. Repeat 1st shoulder shaping.

Second Side: Skip center 2 sts; working even on remaining 20 sts, complete to correspond to first side.

SLEEVES: Sew shoulder seams. Put a marker 4" from shoulder seam along each side edge of work to mark sleeve positions. With right side of work facing you, with A, work 32 sc evenly spaced along 8" edge between 2 markers; ch 1, turn. Working even on 32 sc, work in stripe pattern from A through K for 6". **Cuff:** * With K, draw up lp in each of next 2 sc, y o and draw through all 3 lps on hook (dec made). Repeat from * across. Work even on 16 sc for 1 row. Break off. Repeat for other sleeve.

HOOD: With right side of work facing you, with A, work 49 sc across neck edge; ch 1, turn. Starting with a wrong-side row, work even in stripe pattern as for back for about 7", ending with a completed stripe. Break off. Fold piece in half and sew top seam with matching yarn.

Front and Hood Borders: 1st row: Starting at lower end of opening with right side facing you, with K, sc evenly along right front edge, face edge of hood and along left front edge; ch 1, turn. Work 1 row even; ch 1, turn. Work 3 more rows on right front edge. Break off. Repeat same 3 rows along left front edge.

FINISHING: With K, working through both thicknesses, sl st sleeve and side seams from right side of work. Lap borders at beg of opening and sew tog. Cut pieces of snag-loop tape and sew on border, or use snaps if desired.

HOODED BABY JACKET**

This design, a combination of afghan and shell stitches, is a bit tricky to make, but worth it for that special baby.

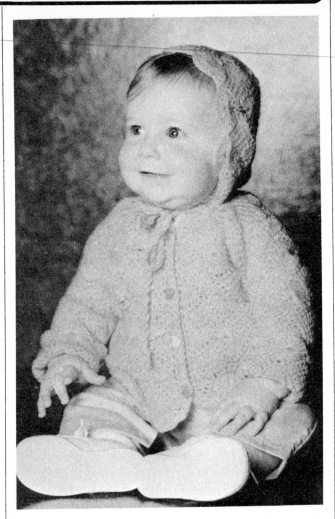

SIZE: 1 year. Jacket measures about 11″ across back at underarms and 8″ from underarm to lower edge.

MATERIALS: Bucilla Perlette (Orlon acrylic yarn), 3 (1¾-ounce) balls strawberry No. 16; aluminum crochet hooks sizes I and H (or international sizes 5.50 mm and 5.00 mm) **or the sizes that will give you the correct gauge;** 4 buttons.

GAUGE: With size I hook 2 shell patterns = 3¾″; 4 pattern rows = 2″.

BODY: Starting at lower edge with size I hook, ch 100 to measure about 22″. **1st row (wrong side—shell row):** Work 4 dc in 4th ch from hook (½ shell made), * skip 3 ch, sc in next ch, skip 3 ch, work shell of 9 dc in next ch. Repeat from * across, ending last repeat with 5 dc (½ shell) in last ch (11 whole shells, with ½ shell at beg and end of row); ch 1, turn. **2nd row (right side—afghan st** [4 rows of afghan st will be worked between shells to form a block]): Sc in first dc, * draw up lp in each of next 4 dc, draw up lp in next sc (6 lps on hook), draw up lp in next dc and draw it through 1st lp on hook to form a vertical st or bar; (y o and draw through 2 lps on hook) 5 times. This forms 6 vertical bars, and 1 lp remains on hook (first row of block made). ** Skip first vertical bar, draw up lp in each of next 5 bars (6 lps on hook); draw up lp in next dc and draw it through 1st lp on hook, (y o and draw through 2 lps on hook) 5 times (another row of vertical bars). Repeat from ** twice more. Then to bind off across block sl st in 2nd bar and in each bar across (one block made); sc in next (center) dc of shell. Repeat from * across, ending last repeat with sl st instead of sc in top of turning ch; ch 1, turn. **3rd row (sc row):** Skip 1st st, sc in each st across sawtooth edge to within last sc, sl st in last sc; ch 3, turn. **4th row (shell row):** Skip 1st st, (y o, draw up lp in next st, y o and draw through 2 lps on hook) 4 times, y o and draw through all 5 lps on hook, ch 1 tightly to form eye of ½ shell, * ch 3, sc in next st, ch 3, (y o and draw up lp in next st, y o and draw through 2 lps on hook) 9 times, y o and draw through all 10 lps on hook to fill 1 space between 2 points, ch 1 tightly to form eye of whole shell. Repeat from * across, ending

last repeat with ½ shell as follows: (Y o and draw up lp in next st, y o and draw through 2 lps on hook) 4 times, y o and draw through all 5 lps on hook, ch 1 tightly to form eye of ½ shell; ch 3, turn. **5th row (shell row):** Work 4-dc ½ shell in eye of first ½ shell, skip ch-3 lp, work sc in next sc, * skip ch-3 lp, work 9-dc shell in eye of next shell, skip ch-3 lp, work sc in next sc. Repeat from * across, ending by skipping last ch-3 lp; work 5-dc ½ shell in eye of last ½ shell; ch 1, turn.

Repeat 2nd through 5th rows for pattern until piece measures about 7½″ from beg, ending with 4th row of pattern. Edging will be worked later and will add ½″ to length.

To Divide Work: Left Front: 1st row (wrong side): Work 4-dc ½ shell in eye of first ½ shell, sc in next sc, (9-dc shell in eye of next shell, sc in next sc) twice. Mark last sc worked. Do not work across remaining sts; ch 1, turn. **2nd row (afghan st):** Skip 1st sc, sl st in each of next 4 dc of shell, sc in next dc (center dc of shell).

Repeat from * on 2nd row of pattern across row (2 block patterns); ch 1, turn.

Repeat 3rd and 4th rows of pattern once but do not ch 3 at end of 4th row. Break off, turn.

To Shape Neck: 1st row: Make lp on hook, skip ½ shell, sc in next sc, work 9-dc shell in eye of next shell, sc in next sc, work 5-dc ½ shell in eye of last ½ shell; ch 1, turn. **2nd row:** Repeat 2nd row of pattern, working 1 block only; sl st in next st, do not work remaining sts; ch 1, turn. **3rd row:** Repeat 3rd row of pattern. **4th row:** Work a 4-dc ½ shell, ch 3, sc in next sc, ch 3, work a 4-dc ½ shell; ch 1, break off.

Back: Next row: Make lp on hook. With wrong side facing you, starting at marker, skip 1 shell for underarm, sc in next sc, (9-dc shell in eye of next shell, sc in next sc) 5 times. Place 2nd marker on last sc worked. Do not work remaining sts; ch 1, turn. **Following row (afghan st):** Skip sc, sl st in each of next 4 dc of shell, sc in next dc, work in pattern across until 4th block is completed, sl st in center dc of last shell, do not work remaining sts; turn.

Work even in pattern (with 3 whole shells and ½ shell at beg and end of shell rows) until 8th row is completed. Break off.

Right Front: Next row: With wrong side of work facing you, starting at 2nd marker, skip 1 whole shell, make lp on hook and sc in next sc, (9-dc shell in eye of next shell, sc in next sc) twice; 5-dc ½ shell in eye of ½ shell; ch 1, turn. **Following row (afghan st):** Work in pattern until 2nd block is completed, sl st in center dc of next shell, do not work remaining sts; ch 1, turn. Finish to correspond to left front.

SLEEVES: Starting at cuff with size H hook, ch 36. Working as for body, work 1st row of pattern (3 whole shells with ½ shell at each end). Repeat 2nd through 5th rows of body pattern twice, then change to size I hook and continue in pattern until sleeve is about 7½" from beg, ending with 4th row of pattern; do not ch 3. Break off.

To Shape Cap: 1st row (wrong side): Turn, make lp on hook, skip ½ shell, sc in next sc, (9-dc shell in eye of shell, sc in next sc) 3 times; do not work across ½ shell; ch 1, turn. **2nd row:** Skip 1st sc, sl st in each of next 4 dc of shell, sc in center dc, work across row in pattern until 2 blocks are completed, sl st in center dc of last shell; ch 1, turn. **3rd row:** Skip sl st, sl st in each of next 5 sts, ch 3, (y o, draw up lp in next st, y o and draw through 2 lps on hook) 9 times, y o and draw through all 10 lps on hook, ch 1 tightly, ch 3, sl st in next sc. Break off.

HOOD: Starting at neck edge with size I hook, ch 52. Working as for body, work 1st row of pattern (5 whole shells with ½ shell at each end). Work even in body pattern until piece measures 6", ending with 4th row of pattern. Break off, turn.

Center Section: Make lp on hook. Skip ½ shell and 1st whole shell, sl st in eye of next whole shell, ch 3, work 4-dc ½ shell in same st as sl st, sc in next sc, 9-dc shell in eye of next shell, sc in next sc, 5-dc ½ shell in eye of next whole shell. Do not work remaining sts.

Continue in pattern on these sts only for 7 more rows. Break off. Last row worked is front edge of center section of hood.

FINISHING: Sew seams on hood. Sew shoulder and sleeve seams; sew sleeves in place. Use size H hook for all finishing.

Neckband: Work 2 rows of sc around neckline; at end of 2nd row ch 3, turn. **3rd row:** Dc in first sc, * ch 1, skip next sc, dc in each of next 2 sc. Repeat from * across. Break off.

Left Front Border: Work 4 rows sc. Break off.

Right Front Border: Work 2 rows sc. **3rd row (buttonhole row):** Work in sc, making 4 buttonholes evenly spaced as follows: For each buttonhole, ch 1, skip 1 sc. **4th row:** Work in sc, working 1 sc in each ch 1. **Last row:** Sl st loosely in each st across. Break off.

Sew neck edge of hood to last row of neckband.

Scalloped Edging: With right side facing you, work around front edge of hood as follows: Sc evenly to 1st whole shell, sc before shell, * work 9-dc shell in eye of shell, sc in next sp after shell. Repeat from * across; sc evenly to end of hood, then sl st loosely along left front edge; work scalloped edging along entire lower edge. Break off. Sew buttons in place.

Repeat scalloped edging along each sleeve edge. Turn up 1½" cuff on sleeves.

Cord: Make a Twisted Cord (see below) or crochet a 31" chain cord using 3 strands of yarn. Weave in and out of spaces on neckband. Tie a knot ½" from each end.

To Make Twisted Cord: Cut five 2-yard strands yarn. Hold together and knot at one end. Catch knotted end firmly in a drawer. Holding other end, stand so that yarn is taut. Twist yarn tightly in one direction until kinks form when tension is released slightly. Keeping yarn taut, hold center of cord with one hand and bring ends together. Starting from folded end, pinch cord at 2" intervals, releasing it as you go. It will twist neatly around itself. Make knot about ½" from each end.

PARCHEESI CARDIGAN

For a boy or girl, this sweater is worked mostly in single crochet plus some long dip stitches.

SIZES: Toddler's (1–2) [(3–4)]. Sweater measures 11½″ [12″] across back.

MATERIALS: Bucilla Win-Knit (Orlon acrylic knitting-worsted-weight yarn), 1 (4-oz) twin-pak each black No. 452 (color B), white No. 451 (color W), Spanish tile No. 431 (orange, color O), yellow No. 477 (color Y), avocado No. 437 (green, color G) and medium turquoise No. 412 (color T)—see note on materials below; aluminum crochet hook size G (or international hook size 4.50 mm) **or the size that will give you the correct gauge;** 6 small orange buttons.

Note on Materials: Only 1 oz of yarn is needed in each of the last 4 colors listed. Use leftover yarns if desired.

GAUGE: 10 sts = 3″.

Note: Back section of sleeves and back of body are worked all in 1 piece, starting at top and working down to lower edge (see diagram). Each front and front

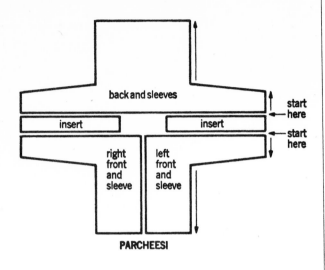

PARCHEESI

section of sleeve is worked in same manner. Shoulder inserts and front border are added later. Work in direction of arrows.

BACK AND SLEEVES SECTION: Starting at top edge with color B, ch 74 [80] to measure about 22″ [24″].

Border Pattern: 1st row: With B, sc in 2nd ch from hook and in each ch across to within last ch, insert hook in last ch and draw up B lp; attach O, draw O lp through both lps on hook, break off B (73 [79] sc). Always change colors in this manner. With O, ch 1; turn. **2nd row (right side):** With O, * sc in next sc, insert hook in next st in row below (in foundation ch) and work sc (long sc made). Repeat from * across, ending with sc in last sc; ch 1, turn. **3rd row:** With O, sc in each sc and in each long sc across, changing to Y on last st. Break off O. With Y, ch 1; turn. **4th row (right side):** With Y, sc in each of 1st 2 sc, * work long sc in next sc in row below, sc in next sc. Repeat from * across, ending last repeat with sc in each of last 2 sc; ch 1, turn. **5th row:** With Y, sc in each st across, changing to G on last st. Break off Y. With G, ch 1; turn. **6th row:** With G, sc in 1st sc, * work long sc in next sc in row below, sc in next sc. Repeat from * across; ch 1, turn. **7th row:** With G, sc in each st across, changing to T on last st. **8th and 9th rows:** With T, repeat 4th and 5th rows, changing to W on last st of 9th row. Break off T. With W, ch 1; turn. Border pattern completed.

10th row (right side): With W, sc in each st across; ch 1, turn. Work even in sc on 73 [79] sc for 2 rows more, or until piece measures 2½" from foundation chain.

Sleeve Shaping: 1st row: Sl st across 1st 6 sts, ch 1, sc in each sc across to within last 6 sts; ch 1, turn. Repeat last row once. **3rd row:** Sl st across 1st 5 [7] sts, ch 1, sc in each sc across to within last 5 [7] sts; ch 1, turn.

Continue with W and work even in sc on 39 [41] sts for 4½" [5"] more, ending with a wrong-side row. Break off W. With T, ch 1; turn.

Border Pattern: 1st through 8th row: Working 2 rows each with T, G, Y, and O, repeat 4th, 5th, 6th, and 7th rows of border pattern twice. Break off all colors. **9th row (right side):** With B, sc in each st across. Break off. **10th through 13th row:** Working only right-side rows, work 1 sc row each in W, B, W, and B. This is lower edge of back. Piece should measure about 7½" [8"] from sleeve shaping to lower edge.

RIGHT FRONT AND SLEEVE SECTION: Starting at top edge with B, ch 38 [40] to measure about 11" [12"]. Working on 37 [39] sts, work same as for Back and Sleeves Section to beg of sleeve shaping, ending with a wrong-side row. Piece should measure 2½" in all.

Sleeve Shaping: 1st row (right side): Starting at wrist edge with W, sl st across 1st 6 sts; ch 1 sc in each sc across to end of row; ch 1, turn. **2nd row:** Sc in each sc across to within last 6 sc; ch 1, turn. **3rd row:** Sl st across 1st 6 [7] sts, sc in each sc across; ch 1, turn.

Continue with W and work even in sc on 19 [20] sts for 4½" [5"], ending at side edge, and on last row inc 0 [1] sts (19 [21] sts). Break off W and work 13 rows of Border Pattern to correspond with border at lower edge of back. Break off all colors.

LEFT FRONT AND SLEEVE SECTION: Work to correspond to right side, reversing all shaping.

FINISHING: Insert for Left Shoulder: With right side of work facing you, start at sleeve edge of left front section and work 1st row of insert across edge of foundation ch as follows: **1st row:** With W, sc in each of next 28 [29] sts of foundation ch. Do not work across last 9 [10] sts—these are left free for neck. Break off W; do not turn. Working each row with right side of work facing you, work 1 row sc each with B and W alternately until 6th [8th] row is completed. (Last row worked in a B row.)

Pin last row of insert to edge of starting chain at top edge of back and sleeve section and, with B, sew both sections together.

Insert for Right Shoulder: Work as for left shoulder insert, but start at front edge as follows: **1st row:** Skip 1st 9 [10] sts for neck, with W, sc in each of next 28[29] sts, working across foundation ch to sleeve edge. Break off. Complete to correspond to left insert.

Pin last row of insert to back and sleeve section, starting at sleeve edge. Sew seams.

Neck and Front Borders: Always work with right side facing you. **1st row:** Starting at lower right front corner with W, sc evenly along right front edge, work 2 sc in corner, sc evenly across neck edge, work 2 sc in corner, sc evenly across left front edge. Break off. **2nd row:** With B, sc in each sc of last row, working 2 sc in each corner. (**Note:** For boy's sweater, work buttonholes on left front. For girl's sweater, work buttonholes on right front.) With pins, mark border for placement of 6 buttons. **3rd row:** With W, repeat last row and work a buttonhole opposite each marker as follows: **For each buttonhole** ch 1, skip 1 sc. **4th row:** With B, sc in each sc across, sc in each ch-1 sp of buttonhole and work 2 sc in each corner; also dec across back of neck as necessary for a smooth fit. Continue with B and sc along entire lower edge of sweater. Join with sl st in 1st sc. Break off. Sew on buttons.

Sleeve Border: Working in rounds, with right side of work always facing you, work 1 rnd of sc each with W, B, W, and B around wrist edge of each sleeve.

"PEPLUM" PULLOVER

The unusual "peplum" border is worked vertically; the body is one piece in a combination of single and double crochets.

SIZES: 2 [4–6]. Sweater measures 10½" [11½"–12½"] across back at underarms.

MATERIALS: Sport-weight yarn, a total of 6 [7–8] ounces in the following colors: mint green (color M), jade green (color J), dusty rose (color D), white (color W), navy (color N) and camel (color C); aluminum crochet hook size F (or international size 4.00 mm) **or the size that will give you the correct gauge.**

GAUGE: 4 sts = 1".

BODY: Body of pullover is made in one piece without side seams. Lower border, sleeves and cuffs are worked separately.

Border: (Note: Border is worked vertically.) With M, ch 9 [13–17] to measure 2¼" [3¼"–4¼"]. **1st row:** Sc in 2nd ch from hook and in each ch across (8 [12–16] sc); ch 1, turn. **2nd row:** Working in back lp only, sc in each sc across; ch 1, turn. Repeat 2nd row until border measures 21" [23"–25"] long when slightly stretched. Sl st in each sc on 1st row to form ring.

Working around 1 long edge (top edge) of border, start body of pullover as follows: **1st rnd:** Ch 1, sc in same place as sl st, work 83 [91–99] more sc evenly spaced around; join with sl st to 1st sc (84 [92–100] sc). **2nd rnd:** Ch 1, sc in same place as sl st, sc in each st around; join with sl st to 1st sc. Break off M. With J, sl st to 1st sc on last rnd. (**Note:** Always attach new color in this manner.) **3rd and 4th rnds:** Ch 3, skip 1st st, dc in each remaining st (84 [92–100] dc, counting ch 3 as 1 dc); sl st in 3rd ch of ch 3 to join. Repeat 2nd and 3rd rnds once with J, then once with D. **9th rnd:** With W repeat 2nd rnd. Repeat 3rd rnd twice with J, then repeat 3rd rnd once each with N, C and D. **15th and 16th rnds:** With D repeat 2nd rnd. **17th rnd:** With M repeat 3rd rnd. **18th rnd:** With J repeat 2nd rnd. **19th and 20th rnds:** With C repeat 3rd rnd. **21st rnd:** With N repeat 2nd rnd. Mark the 4th sc, the 39th [43rd–47th] sc, 46th [50th–54th] sc and 81st [89th–97th] sc on last rnd. Put body piece aside.

SLEEVE: Cuff: With D, ch 11. Work as for border of body (10 sc) until piece measures 6" long when stretched slightly. Sl st in each sc on 1st row to form ring.

Working around 1 long (top) edge, work sleeve as follows: **1st rnd:** Ch 1, sc in same place as sl st, continue to work 29 more sc evenly spaced around (30 sc); sl st in 1st sc to join. **2nd and 3rd rnds:** Ch 3, dc in each st; join. **4th rnd (inc rnd):** Ch 3, work 2 dc in same place as sl st, dc in each remaining dc (2 dc inc–32 dc); join.

Continue to work in dc pattern in the following color sequence: 2 rnds J, 3 C, 2 N, 1 C, 2 J, 2 W and 1 D and, **at same time,** work increases as follows: **For size 2 only,** repeat inc rnd every 4th rnd 3 times more; **for sizes [4–6] only,** repeat inc rnd on next rnd, then every [3rd–2nd] rnd [4–6] times more.

For all sizes: 18th rnd: With D, ch 1, sc in same place as sl st and in each dc around (38 [42–46] sc); join. **For sizes [4–6] only,** work 2 dc rnds with J, then 1 dc rnd with D. **For size 6 only,** work 2 more dc rnds with W, then 1 dc rnd with D. Break off. Make other sleeve in same manner. Set aside.

YOKE: 1st rnd: Pick up body piece; with M, sc in 1st marked st (move marker to this st), * sc in each st across body piece to next marked st, sc in marked st (move marker); pick up sleeve, skip 3 sts on sleeve, sc in next st and in each st across sleeve to within last 3 sts, skip last 3 sts on sleeve *, sc in next marked st on body.

Repeat from * to * once more (136 [152–168] sc); join. Break off. Mark 18th [20th–22nd] st with pin for center back. Start each of remaining yoke rnds at center back.

With M, sl st in center back st. **2nd rnd (dec rnd):** Ch 3, skip 1st sc, dc in each sc to 1st marked st; * (y o and draw up lp in next st, y o and draw through 2 lps on hook) twice, y o and draw through all 3 lps on hook (1 dc dec; move marker to this st); dc in each sc to within 1 st of next marked sc, dec 1 dc and move marker*, dc in each sc to next marked st. Repeat from * to * once more, dc in each remaining sc (4 dc dec); join. **3rd rnd (double dc dec rnd):** Ch 3, skip 1st st, dc in each st to within 1 st of 1st marked st; * (y o and draw up lp in next st, y o and draw through 2 lps on hook) 3 times, y o and draw through all 4 lps on hook (double dc dec made; move marker to this st); dc in each dc to within 1 st of next marked st, work double dc dec and move marker*, dc in each st to within 1 st of next marked st. Repeat from * to * once, dc in each remaining st (8 dc dec); join. Break off.

With N, sl st to 1st st of last rnd. **4th rnd (double sc dec rnd):** Ch 1, sc in same sp as sl st and in each st to within 1 st of 1st marked st; * draw up lp in each of next 3 sts, y o and draw through all 4 lps on hook (double sc dec made; move marker); sc in each st to within 1 st of next marked st, work double sc dec and move marker*, sc in each st to within 1 st of next marked st. Repeat from * to * once more, sc in each remaining st (8 sc dec); join. **5th rnd:** With N repeat 3rd rnd. **6th and 7th rnds:** With W repeat 4th rnd. **8th and 9th rnds:** With D repeat 4th rnd. **For sizes [4–6] only,** repeat 4th rnd [once–twice] more with D. Break off.

FINISHING: Sew underarm seams. To adjust size of neck opening, if desired, run elastic thread through last rnd of sc around neck.

STRIPED JUMPER

A good design for using up scrap yarn, it's all one piece with a center back seam and all single crochet.

SIZES: 2 [4–6]. Jumper measures about 20″ [21″–22″] around waist and 7″ [8″–9″] from waist to lower edge. Length is adjustable.

MATERIALS: Knitting worsted, 1 ounce each bright yellow (color Y), orange (color O), red (color R), peacock blue (color B) and apple green (color G); aluminum crochet hook size G (or international size 4.50 mm) **or the size that will give you the correct gauge;** two ⅜″-diameter buttons; tapestry needle.

GAUGE: 4 sc = 1″; 4 rows = 1″.

Note: Jumper is worked in one piece with center back seam.

PATTERN STITCH: Work sc in back lp only of each sc throughout unless otherwise specified.

BIB: Starting at upper edge of bib with Y, ch 22

[24–26] to measure about 5½″ [6″–6½″]. **1st row:** Sc in 2nd ch from hook and in each ch across (21 [23–25] sc); ch 1, turn. **2nd row:** Work pattern st in each sc across; break off A, attach O; ch 1, turn. Work pattern st for 2 rows each O, R, B, G, Y, O, R, B and G. Break off.

SKIRT: 1st row (right side): With Y ch 30 [31–32], sc in each sc on last row of bib; ch 31 [32–33]; turn. **2nd row:** Sc in 2nd ch from hook and in each ch to bib, work across bib in pattern st, sc in each st across other ch (81 [85–89] sc); break off Y, attach O; ch 1, turn. **Next row (inc row):** Work 2 sc in back lp of 1st sc, work pattern st across, working 2 sc in back lp of last sc (2 sc inc on row); ch 1, turn. **Following row:** Work even in pattern; break off O, attach R; ch 1, turn. Repeat last 2 rows, working * 2 rows each R, B, G, Y and O. Repeat from * once more (103 [107–111] sc). **For size 2 only** break off. **For size 4 only** continue as before for 2 rows each R and

B (111 sc). Break off. **For size 6 only** continue as before for 2 rows each R, B, G and Y (119 sc). Break off.

STRAPS (make 2): With O [B–Y] or color matching last row worked ch 6. **Note:** Work in both lps of each sc throughout. **1st row:** Sc in 2nd ch from hook and in each ch across; ch 1, turn. **2nd row:** Sc in each sc across; ch 1, turn. Repeat last row until piece measures 16″ or is long enough to fit from top of bib, over shoulder, across back to top of skirt. Break off.

FINISHING: Sew center back seam on skirt. With right side facing you, using color matching straps, work 1 row sc around upper edge of skirt and bib, working (sc, ch 1 and sc) in corners; join. Break off. Sew straps to waist edge of back of skirt. Sew buttons to corners of bib. Cross straps and, using spaces between sts for buttonholes, button to fit.

GRANNY-SQUARE PONCHO

It's a combination of two-tone and solid-color grannies finished with picot edging.

SIZES: (4–5) [(6–8)]. Poncho measures about 17″ [21″] from base of neckline to lower point.

MATERIALS: Knitting-worsted-weight yarn, 2 (4-ounce) skeins red and 1 skein green; aluminum crochet hook size H (or international size 5.00 mm) **or the size that will give you the correct gauge;** tapestry needle.

GAUGE: Each square measures 3¼″.

Following directions below, make 30 [48] squares using green through 1st rnd and red for 2nd and 3rd rnds (R-G squares). Make 6 [8] squares using green throughout (G squares).

TO MAKE SQUARE: Starting at center, ch 4. Join with sl st to form ring. **1st rnd:** Ch 3, work 2 dc in ring, (ch 1, work shell of 3 dc in ring) 3 times, ch 1; join with sl st to top of ch 3. **2nd rnd:** Sl st to 1st ch-1 sp, make 1st corner as follows: Ch 3, in same sp work 2 dc, ch 1 and 3-dc shell (1st corner completed); (ch 1, in next sp work shell, ch 1 and shell for another corner) 3 times, ch 1; join. **3rd rnd:** Sl st to corner sp, work 1st corner in corner sp, (ch 1, work shell in next sp, ch 1, work corner in next corner sp) 3 times; ch 1, work shell in next sp, ch 1; join. Break off.

JOINING SQUARES: With right sides facing and catching back lps only, whipstitch R-G squares together to form 10 [12] strips of 3 [4] squares each. Join G squares to form 2 strips of 3 [4] squares each. Join 4 [5] R-G strips, 1 G strip (shoulder band) and 1 R-G strip (joining end) to form rectangle. Make 1 more rectangle. Following diagram, sew joining end (X) of 1st rectangle (1) to side of 2nd rectangle (2). Then sew joining end (Y) of 2nd rectangle to side of 1st rectangle.

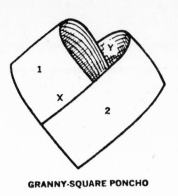

GRANNY-SQUARE PONCHO

V-SHAPED NECKLINE INSERT: 1st row: Starting at point of V with green, ch 5, tr in 4th ch from hook, ch 1, tr in next ch; ch 5, turn. **2nd row:** Work 2 tr in ch-1 sp, ch 2, work 2 tr over 1st ch st of ch-4 lp, ch 1, tr in next ch st; ch 5, turn. **3rd row:** Work 2 tr in 1st ch sp, ch 1, work 2 tr in next ch sp, ch 1, work 2 tr in 1st ch of ch-5, ch 1, tr in next ch st; ch 5, turn. **4th row:** Work 2 tr in 1st sp, ch 1, (work 3 tr in next sp, ch 1) 3 times; work 2 tr in 1st ch of ch 5, ch 1, tr in next ch st; ch 5, turn. **5th row:** Work 2 tr in 1st sp, ch 1, (work 3 tr in next sp, ch 1) 4 times; work 2 tr in 1st ch of ch 5, ch 1, tr in next ch st; ch 4, turn. **6th row:** Work 2 dc in 1st sp, ch 1, (work 3 dc in next sp, ch 1) 5 times; work 2 dc in 1st ch of ch 5, ch 1, dc in next ch st; ch 4, turn. **7th row:** Work 2 dc in 1st sp, ch 1, (work 3 dc in next sp, ch 1) 6 times; work 3 dc in 1st ch of ch 4. Break off. Make another insert in same manner. Sew an insert to each side of poncho in V at neckline, from center edge of 1 green shoulder band to center edge of other band.

COLLAR: 1st rnd: Make lp on hook with green, y o hook twice; with right side of poncho facing you, insert hook through center edge of a green shoulder band between inserts, draw up lp and complete tr; ch 1, (work 3-dc shell in next sp, ch 1) 7 times across top of V-shaped insert, tr between inserts, ch 1, (work 3-dc shell in next sp, ch 1) 7 times across 2nd insert; join to tr. **2nd rnd:** Sl st in 1st sp, ch 3, work 2 dc in same place as sl st, ch 1, (work shell in next sp, ch 1) 3 times; * in center dc of next shell work shell, ch 1 and shell; ch 1 *; (work shell in next sp, ch 1) 8 times. Repeat from * to * once, (work shell in next sp, ch 1) 4 times; join to top of ch 3. **3rd rnd:** Sl st to 1st sp, ch 3, work 2 dc in same place as sl st, ch 1, (work shell in next sp, ch 1) 3 times; * in next sp work shell, ch 1 and shell; ch 1 *; (work shell in next sp, ch 1) 9 times. Repeat from * to * once; (work shell in next sp, ch 1) 5 times; join. Break off.

EDGING: Work picot edging along lower edge of poncho as follows: Using red, work sc in any sp, * ch 4, sc in 4th ch from hook (picot made), work sc evenly for 1″ along edge of poncho. Repeat from * around, working 2 picots at each point; sl st in 1st sc to join. Break off.

HER CARDIGAN AND PULL-ON SKIRT

HIS CARDIGAN AND SHORTS*

The sweaters are easy single crochet with a minimum of shaping. The skirt and shorts have elasticized waists.

SIZES: These garments are sizes 8 months and toddler's [1–2–3–4]. Cardigans, pullovers, jacket and overalls measure 10″ [10½″–11″–11½″–12″] across back at underarms. Lengths from lower edge to shoulders and sleeve lengths vary with specific styles. All sleeves measure 7″ [7½″–8″–8½″–9″] wide before seaming. Skirt and shorts measure 9¼″ [9¾″–10″–10¾″–11″] across waistline and have elastic in waistband. Finished length from lower edge to waistline is 6½″ [7″–7½″–8″–8½″] for skirt and 8½″ [9″–9½″–10″–10½″] for shorts. Overalls are 16″ [17″–19″–21″–23″] from lower edge to underarms. Most lengths can be adjusted if desired.

YARNS: All garments were made with Coats &

Clark's Red Heart 2-ply Sport Yarn (Orlon acrylic), sold in 2-oz skeins. This yarn is machine washable and dryable. For amounts and colors, see materials under individual garments.

We tested several other brands of acrylic sport yarn (2, 3 and 4 ply) and found that some can be substituted for the Coats & Clark's. Yardages may vary slightly, however, from brand to brand.

All buttons are JHB Import.

HOOK: Size F hook (international size 4.00 mm).

Check your gauge carefully before starting, as even a small difference in gauge can make a big difference in the size of these little garments. It is advisable to make a swatch about 3" square first, block it and check your gauge, as some acrylic yarns stretch more than others. It may be necessary to change hook size to get the correct gauge. All garments are worked in single crochet.

GAUGE: 9 sc = 2"; 5 rows = 1".

TO SHAPE CROCHET: To inc 1 sc: Work 2 sc in 1 st. **To dec 1 sc:** Insert hook in next st, y o and draw up lp, insert hook in next st, y o and draw through all 3 lps on hook.

TIPS: 1. Use safety pin, paper clip or loop of contrasting-color yarn as marker. **2.** Whenever possible, leave long end of yarn when breaking off at edge of work, and use this end for joining.

BLOCKING: Before assembling garment, pin matching pieces together, right sides facing, then place on padded board. Steam lightly with steam iron or with damp cloth and dry iron. Remove pins and let garment dry thoroughly while lying flat. After assembling, a final light pressing of seams and borders may be necessary.

FINISHING: Pieces can be joined by sewing or crocheting them together from the wrong side, or by slip-stitching them together from the right side. Always use matching yarn. For cardigans and pullovers, join shoulders first. Join armhole edges of sleeves to body, centering them at shoulder seams, then join side and sleeve seams. For other pieces, see individual directions.

Her Cardigan and Pull-On Skirt

See General Directions.

MATERIALS: The 2-piece set requires 5 skeins red yarn No. 905, 1 skein dark blue No. 847; 4 silver buttons ⅝" diam; 1 yd ½"-wide elastic for skirt.

CARDIGAN

BACK: See diagram. Starting at lower edge with

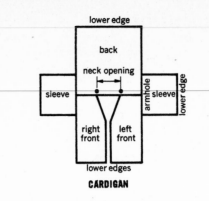

CARDIGAN

red, ch 47 [49–51–53–56]. **1st row:** Sc in 2nd ch from hook and in each ch across (46 [48–50–52–55] sc); ch 1, turn. **2nd row:** Sc in each sc across; ch 1, turn. Repeating 2nd row, work even until piece measures 9" [9¾"–10½"–11¼"–12"] from lower edge. Break off. Mark 13th [14th–14th–15th–16th] st from each end of last row (dots on diagram) to mark neck opening.

LEFT FRONT: Starting at lower edge with red, ch 24 [25–26–27–28]. Work same as for back on 23 [24–25–26–27] sc until piece measures 5½" [6"–6½"–7"–7½"] from lower edge. Mark end of row for front edge.

Neck Shaping: Dec 1 sc at beg of next row and, continuing in sc, dec 1 sc at marked edge every other row 9 [9–10–10–10] times more. Work even on 13 [14–14–15–16] sc, if necessary, until piece measures same length as back to shoulder. Break off.

RIGHT FRONT: Work as for left front.

SLEEVES: Starting at lower edge with red, ch 33 [35–37–40–42]. Work same as for back on 32 [34–36–39–41] sc until piece measures 5½" [6½"–7½"–8½"–9½"] or desired length. Break off. Mark center of last row on sleeve.

FINISHING: Sew or crochet pieces together as follows: Join shoulder seams. Matching center of last row of sleeve to shoulder seam, pin and join sleeve at armhole edge; join side and sleeve seams.

Border: 1st row: With right side facing you, starting at lower right front corner with blue, sc evenly along right front edge, right neck edge, back of neck, along left front neck edge and left front edge; ch 1, turn. Mark right border for girl's (or left border for boy's) cardigan for placement of 3 [3–4–4–4] buttonholes, the 1st ¾" from lower edge, the last at beg of V-neck shaping, the others evenly spaced between. **2nd row:** Sc in each sc of last row, working 3 sc in each corner at V of neck, and working a buttonhole at each marker as follows: Ch 2, skip 2 sc, work to next marker. **3rd row:** Sc in each sc across, working 2 sc in each ch-2 sp and ending ch 1, turn. **4th row:** Sc in each sc across. Break off.

Sew buttons opposite buttonholes.

PULL-ON SKIRT

BACK: See diagram. Starting at lower edge with red, ch 64 [67–70–73–76]. Working in sc as for cardigan,

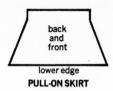

back
and
front

lower edge
PULL-ON SKIRT

work even on 63 [66–69–72–75] sc for 5½″ [6″–6½″–7″–7½″]. **Next row (dec row):** * Dec 1 sc over next 2 sc, sc in next st. Repeat from * across. Working on 42 [44–46–48–50] sc of waistband, work even for 2″ more. Break off. Skirt will be 1″ shorter when waistband is hemmed.

FRONT: Work as for back.

FINISHING: Sew or crochet pieces together as follows: Join side seams. Cut elastic 2″ less than waistline measurement and fasten ends together securely. Fold half of waistband to wrong side over elastic and sew in place.

His Cardigan and Shorts

See General Directions.

MATERIALS: Same as for Her Cardigan and Skirt, reversing yarn colors.

CARDIGAN

Follow directions for Her Cardigan, reversing buttonholes.

SHORTS

LEG (make 2): See diagram. Starting at top edge

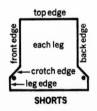

top edge

front edge

each leg

back edge

crotch edge
leg edge
SHORTS

with blue, ch 43 [45–47–48–51]. Working in sc throughout as for cardigan, work even on 42 [44–46–47–50] sc for 2½″. Put marker in center of last row. **Next row:** Work across, increasing 1 sc at marker. Repeat inc above marker every 1″ 3 [3–3–4–4] times more. Work even on 46 [48–50–52–55] sc until leg

measures 6½″ [7″–7½″–8″–8½″] from top edge. **Next row:** Inc 1 sc at beg and end of row. Repeat last row 4 [4–5–5–5] times more (56 [58–62–64–67] sc). Place marker at beg and end of last row for end of crotch (dots on diagram).

Work even for 2″. Break off. Piece should measure 9½″ [10″–10½″–11″–11½″] from beg. Finished piece will be 1″ shorter when top edge is hemmed.

FINISHING: Starting at top edge, join front and back seams, then join crotch and leg seams below markers. Cut elastic 2″ less than waistline measurement and fasten ends securely. Fold 1″ of top edge of shorts to wrong side over elastic and sew in place.

TINY TUNIC*

Very little shaping is needed and it's all single-crochet stitch with worked-in bold stripes.

See General Directions.

MATERIALS: 3 [3–3–3–4] skeins yarn color new camel No. 328, 1 skein each wood (dark) brown No. 360, medium brown No. 354 and pantile (rust) brown No. 283.

BACK: See diagram. Always change colors on a

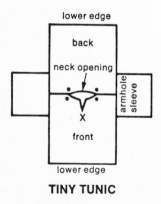

lower edge

back

neck opening

armhole
sleeve

X

front

lower edge

TINY TUNIC

right-side row. Mark 1st row worked for right side of work. Using camel, work in sc pattern as for Her

Cardigan for 2 rows. Drop camel, attach dark brown and, continuing in pattern, work 2 rows dark brown, 4 rows rust and 2 rows medium brown (8-row stripe completed). With camel, continue in pattern until back measures 5½″ [6″–6½″–7″–7½″] from lower edge, ending with a wrong-side row.

Stripe Pattern for Yoke: Continue in sc pattern and work as needed in the following stripe pattern until piece measures 9″ [9¾″–10½″–11¼″–12″] from lower edge: 4 rows dark brown, 6 rows camel, repeat 8-row stripe pattern, then work 4 rows camel, 2 rows dark brown, 4 rows camel, 2 rows rust, 4 rows camel, 2 rows medium brown; then, if necessary, complete back with camel. Break off. Mark 12th [13th–13th–14th–14th] st from each end on last row (dots on diagram) for neck opening.

FRONT: Work as for back until first 4-row dark brown stripe of yoke is completed, and on last row on size 4 only, dec 1 st (46 [48–50–52–54] sc).

For All Sizes: To Divide for Front Opening: Continue in sc pattern and, with camel, work across 1st 23 [24–25–26–27] sc. Do not work across remaining sts; ch 1, turn.

Working on sts of one side only, complete yoke in same stripe pattern as for back yoke. Mark sts same as for back for neck opening. Work sts on other side to correspond.

SLEEVES: Using camel, work same as for sleeves on Her Cardigan, but work in same color and st pattern as for back of tunic until 10th row is completed (end of 8-row stripe). With camel only, continue in sc until sleeve is 3½″ [4½″–5½″–6½″–7½″] from beg, or 2″ less than desired length, ending with a wrong-side row.

Continue in sc, working 8-row stripe pattern, then work 2 rows camel, 2 rows dark brown. Break off.

FINISHING: See General Directions. **Trim: 1st row:** With right side facing you, starting at front opening, using camel and crochet hook, sc evenly along front opening, work 3 sc in corner, sc evenly across neck edge, work corner, sc across front edge; turn. **2nd row:** Sl st in each sc across. Break off.

Tie: Using 2 strands camel, crochet 20″ chain. Break off. Lace tie through knitted edge halfway up center opening. Knot each end of tie and make bow.

DOUBLE-BREASTED JACKET AND OVERALLS

The jacket has worked-in stripes accented with solid-color collar and cuffs; overalls pull on and button at the shoulders.

See General Directions.

MATERIALS: The 2-piece set requires 3 [3–3–4–4] skeins paddy green yarn No. 686, 2 skeins baby aqua No. 510 and 1 skein each apply green No. 648 and sapphire blue No. 516; ten ½"-diameter green buttons (8 for jacket, 2 for overalls).

JACKET

BACK: See diagram. Starting at lower edge of hem with aqua, ch 47 [49–51–53–56]. **1st row:** Sc in 2nd

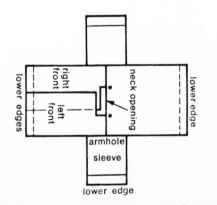

ch from hook and in each ch across (46 [48–50–52–55] sc); drop aqua, attach paddy green; ch 1, turn. **2nd row:** Sc in each sc across. Break off green; do not turn. **3rd row:** Starting at beg of last row, pick up aqua and sc in each sc across, drop aqua, attach apple green; ch 1,

turn. **4th row:** Sc in each sc across. Break off green; do not turn. **5th row:** Starting at beg of last row, pick up aqua and sc in each sc across, drop aqua, attach blue; ch 1, turn. **6th row:** Sc in each sc across. Break off blue; do not turn. **7th row:** Starting at beg of last row with aqua, sc in each sc across, drop aqua, attach paddy green; ch 1, turn.

Repeating 2nd through 7th rows for color pattern, work even until piece measures 11" [11¾"–12½"–13¼"–14"] from beg (includes a 1" hem). Break off. Mark top edge same as for Her Cardigan.

LEFT FRONT: Starting at lower edge of hem with aqua, ch 31 [33–34–36–38]. Working on 30 [32–33–35–37] sc, work as for back until piece is 2" less than back to shoulder, ending at side edge.

Neck Shaping: Next row: Continue in stripe pattern, sc in each sc to within last 17 [18–19–20–21] sc; turn. Work even on 13 [14–14–15–16] sc for 2" more. Break off.

RIGHT FRONT: Work to correspond to left front, reversing neck shaping.

SLEEVES: Work as for sleeves on Her Cardigan, working the first 1½" with paddy green for border, then follow stripe pattern until sleeve is completed.

COLLAR: Starting at neck edge with paddy green, ch 51 [52–53–54–55]. Working on 50 [51–52–53–54] sc, work even for 1½". Break off.

FINISHING: See General Directions. Sew 1" hem at edge of jacket.

Collar Border: With paddy green, work 3 rows sc on outside edges of collar (not across neck edge), rounding out corners. Break off. Centering collar and leaving about 2½" at each front neck edge free, ,then sew collar in place.

Front Border: 1st row: With right side facing you, starting at left front for boy's jacket (or right front for girl's), with aqua, sc evenly along front edge; ch 1, turn. Mark border for placement of 4 buttonholes, the 1st 3" from lower edge, the 4th 1½" below neck edge, the others evenly spaced between. **2nd row:** Sc in each sc of last row, working a buttonhole at each marker as follows: Ch 1, skip 1 sc, work to next marker. Break off. Work 2 rows with aqua along other front edge.

Sew 4 buttons opposite buttonholes, and 4 more buttons about 3" from buttonholes on outside front for decoration.

OVERALLS

Note: Overalls are paddy green and trimmed with aqua. They have center front and back seams and buttons on each shoulder.

FIRST LEG: See diagram. Starting at lower edge, ch 39 [41–41–43–44]. Working on 38 [40–40–42–43] sc, work even for 1" [1½"–2"–2"–2½"]. Inc 1 sc at beg and end of next row, then repeat this inc row every ½" 9 [9–10–10–11] times more. Work even on 58 [60–62–64–67] sc until piece measures 6½"[7"–8"–9"–10"] from beg. Adjust leg length here if desired.

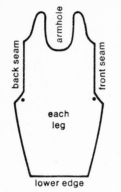

Crotch Shaping: Dec 1 sc at beg and end of next 6 rows. Work even on 46 [48–50–52–55] sc until piece measures 16" [17"–19"–21"–23"] from beg, or desired length to underarm. Mark end of last row for front seam.

To Shape Top Section: First Strap: Work across first 17 [18–19–20–21] sc (mark next 12 [12–12–12–13] sts for underarm); ch 1, turn. * Dec 1 sc at beg of next row (armhole edge), work to end of row. Repeat this dec at armhole edge every row for next 3 rows, ending at armhole edge.

To Shape Neck: Next row: Sc to within last 3 [4–4–4–5] sc (neck shaping at front edge); ch 1, turn. **Following row:** Dec 1 st at neck edge, work to end of row. Keeping armhole edge even, repeat dec at neck edge on next 2 rows (7 [7–8–9–9] sts).

Keeping armhole edge even, repeat dec at neck edge every 3rd row until 2 sts remain. Work even, if necessary, on 2 sts until top section measures 4½" [4½"–5½"–5½"–5½"] from beg of armhole shaping. Break off.

Second Strap: Skip 12 [12–12–12–13] marked underarm sc, attach yarn and work to end of row. Mark this edge for back seam. Work even in sc on 17 [18–19–20–21] sc for 1 row, ending at armhole edge. Repeat from * (at end of 1st row) on 1st strap to end.

SECOND LEG: Work as for 1st leg (pieces are reversible).

FINISHING: See General Directions. Join front and back crotch seams to marker, then join leg seams.

Edging: With right side facing you, using aqua, work 1 rnd sc evenly around all top edges; join and break off.

Sew 1 button to top edge of each back strap and button through sts on front straps.

MIDDY SWEATER

A nautical stripe is worked in the sailor collar and sleeve ends and a crocheted chain forms the tie.

See General Directions.

MATERIALS: 3 [3–3–4–4] skeins white yarn, 1 skein royal blue No. 845.

BACK: See diagrams. Using white, work as for Her Cardigan, but mark 15th [16th–16th–17th–18th] st from each end on last row (dots on diagrams) for neck opening.

FRONT: With white, work as for back until piece measures 5½" [6"–6½"–7"–7½"] from lower edge.

Neck Opening: First Side: Continue in sc and work across 1st 21 [22–23–24–25] sts; ch 1, turn. Working on one side only, dec 1 sc at neck edge every 3rd row 6 [6–7–7–7] times. Work even, if necessary, on 15 [16–16–17–18] sc until piece measures same length as back to shoulder. Break off.

Second Side: Skip next 4 [4–4–4–5] sts at center front (X on diagram); with white, sc in each sc to end of row. Complete as for first side.

SLEEVES: Using white, work as for Her Cardigan, but make sleeves ½" shorter, as border will be added later.

MIDDY

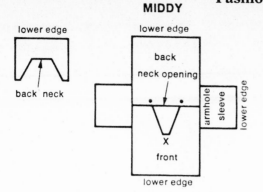

COLLAR: Starting at lower edge of back of collar, with white ch 32 [32–35–35–38]. Working on 31 [31–34–34–37] sc, work even for 3″ [3″–3¼″– 3½″–3½″].

Neck Opening: First Side: Work across 1st 7 [7–8–8–9] sts; ch 1, turn. Working on one side only, dec 1 st at beg of next row (neck edge), work to end of row. Repeat dec at neck edge every 4th row 4 [4–5–5–6] times more (2 sts remain). Break off.

Second Side: Skip center 17 [17–18–18–19] sc for back of neck; with white, sc in each st to end of row; ch 1, turn. **Next row:** Dec 1 sc at end of row (neck edge). Complete to correspond to first side.

FINISHING: See General Directions.

Border for Collar: Work across 3 outside edges of collar, do not work across shaped edge. **1st row:** With right side facing you, using blue, sc evenly across 3 edges of collar, working 3 sc in each corner; ch 1, turn. **2nd row:** Sc in each sc across. Break off blue, attach white; ch 1, turn. **3rd row:** Repeat 2nd row. Break off.

Sleeve Border: Work 2 rnds blue, 2 rnds white.

Tie: With 2 strands blue, crochet 30″ chain. Break off. Knot each end.

Small Loop: With white, crochet 2″ chain. Break off.

Sew collar in place. Sew loop below front edges of collar. Place tie under collar and draw both ends through loop. Make double knot in tie. Tack tie at back under collar.

MOTHER-DAUGHTER HATS

Each has five granny squares—four around and one on top—a button at the crown and scallops at the edge.

SIZES: Child's hat will stretch to fit 18″ head. Mother's hat will stretch to fit 21″ head.

MATERIALS: Knitting worsted, 1 ounce each gold (color G), wine (color W) and black (color B) for each hat; tapestry needle. **For Child's Size:** Aluminum crochet hook size H (or international hook size 5.00 mm). **For Mother's Size:** Aluminum crochet hook size J (or international size 6.00 mm) **or the sizes that will give you the correct gauge.**

GAUGE: Child's: Each square = 4″. **Mother's:** Each square = 4¾″.

Note: Directions are basically the same for both sizes (the size hook used makes the difference). Any changes for Mother's size are in brackets.

SQUARE (make 5): Starting at center with color G and size H [J] hook, ch 4. Join with sl st to form ring.

Right side of work should always face you.

Important: To get gauge on 1st and 2nd rnds only, always draw up 1st lp ¾″ [1″] for each dc.

1st rnd: With G ch 3, work 2 dc in ring, (ch 3, 3 dc in ring) 3 times, ch 3; join with sl st to top of ch 3. Break off. **2nd rnd:** With W sl st in any ch-3 sp; ch 3, in same sp work 2 dc, ch 3 and 3 dc (1st corner); * ch 1, in next corner sp work 3 dc, ch 3 and 3 dc (another corner). Repeat from * twice more; ch 1; join as before. Break off. **3rd rnd:** With B make lp on hook and work 3 dc in any ch-3 corner sp; h dc in each dc and each ch-1 sp around, working 3 dc in each remaining corner; join with sl st to top of 1st dc. Break off. Square should measure 4″ [4¾″] across.

To Assemble: Hold 2 squares together with right sides facing. With B sew together along 1 edge through both lps of sts. Join 2 more squares to 1st 2 to form strip, then join ends of strip to form ring. Join 5th square to top of ring to form hat. Turn hat right side out.

Border: 1st rnd: With right side of hat facing you, using B and working around lower edge of hat, work 1 rnd of 45 h dc. **2nd rnd:** * Sc in each of next 3 h dc, work 3 dc in each of next 2 h dc. Repeat from * around (9 scallops); sl st in 1st sc. Break off. Holding W on wrong side of work, work 1 rnd sl st loosely on right side of work near top edge of scallop rnd. Break off. With G work another rnd of sl st just above 1st one. Break off.

Button Trim: With W and size H [J] hook ch 7. Work 4 h dc in 3rd ch from hook and in each remaining ch. Break off. Roll chain edge into a tight ball and sew in place on top of hat.

PASTEL PIXIE BOOTEES

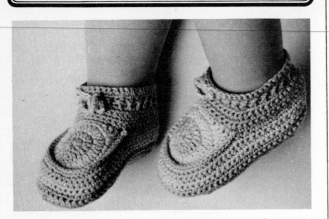

Every bootee is a quickie. Uppers are single and double crochet attached to soles of double felt.

SIZE: Length of sole is 4¾″. Fits one-year-old child.

MATERIALS: J. & P. Coats Knit-Cro-Sheen (cotton yarn), 1 (175-yard) ball each robinette (light blue) No. 76 (color B), beauty pink No. 65 (color P), chartreuse green No. 49 (color G) and dark lavender No. 37 (color L); 12″ square bright pink felt; steel crochet hook No. 4 **or the size that will give you the correct gauge;** leather punch for ¹/₁₆″-diameter holes.

GAUGE: 6 sc = 1″; 8 rows = 1″.

Note: Use thread held double throughout.

SOLE: Enlarge sole pattern, (see To Enlarge Patterns, page 14), and cut paper pattern (do not add seams). For each bootee cut 2 felt pieces from sole pattern. Baste pairs together. With leather punch make 63 holes evenly spaced around each sole ¼″ from edge.

SIDES: 1st rnd (right side): Make lp on hook with B and, starting at center hole at heel of sole, sc in each hole (63 sc); sl st in 1st sc to join; ch 1, turn. **2nd rnd:** Sc in each sc around; join; ch 1, turn.

Repeating 2nd rnd for pattern, work 1 more rnd with B, then 2 rnds each P and G (mark 1st sc on last rnd with pin for center back). Omit turning ch on last rnd. Break off.

INSTEP: Starting at center with B, ch 5. Join with sl st to form ring. **1st rnd (right side):** Ch 2, work 9 dc in ring (10 dc, counting ch 2 as 1 dc); sl st in top of ch 2 to join. **2nd rnd:** Ch 2, dc in same sp, work 2 dc in each dc around (20 dc); join. Break off. **3rd rnd:** Make lp on hook with P and work 2 dc in each dc around (40 dc); join. **4th rnd:** Ch 1, sc in each of next 19 dc, 2 h dc in next dc, 2 dc in next dc, 2 tr in next dc (mark 1st tr), dc in next dc, h dc in next dc, sc in each of next 4 dc, h dc in next

dc, dc in next dc, 2 tr in next dc (mark 2nd tr), 2 dc in next dc, 2 h dc in next dc, sc in each of remaining 6 dc; join. Break off.

To Join Instep to Sides: Make lp on hook with B and, holding pieces with wrong sides facing, skip 13 sts to left of center back pin, insert hook in next st and through 1st marked tr on instep, y o and pull up lp, y o and pull through both lps on hook. Continue joining in each st to next marker (36 sts), then work sc in each of remaining 27 sc on side piece; sl st in 1st st to join. Break off.

ANKLE BAND: 1st rnd (right side): Starting at center back with L, sc in each side-section sc to instep, sc in each of next 10 sts across instep, sc in each remaining sc on side section (37 sc); sl st in 1st sc to join. **2nd rnd:** Ch 1, turn; sc in each st around; join. Repeat 2nd rnd 3 times more. Ch 3, turn. **Next rnd (beading rnd):** Work dc in each sc around; join. Repeat 2nd rnd twice. Break off.

TIE: With G crochet 12″ chain. Weave through beading rnd of Ankle Band. Tie in bow at front of bootee. Knot ends and cut off excess.

BOLD BOOTEES

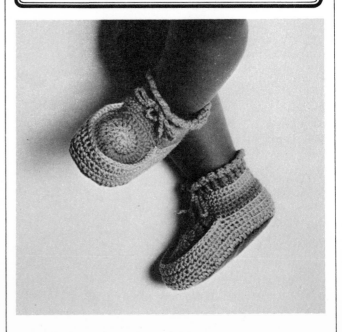

SIZE: Length of sole is 4¾″. Fits one-year-old child.

MATERIALS: J. & P. Coats Knit-Cro-Sheen (cotton yarn), 1 (175-yard) ball each parakeet (bright blue) No. 132-A (color B) and watermelon (bright pink) No 122 (color P); Coats & Clark's Red Heart Wintuk Sock and Sweater Yarn, small amount apple green No. 648 (color G); 12″ square emerald green felt; steel crochet hook No. 4 **or the size that will give you the correct gauge;** leather punch for ¹/₁₆″-diameter holes.

GAUGE: 6 sc = 1″; 8 rows = 1″.

Note: Use strands doubled throughout.

SOLE: Work as for Pastel Pixie Bootees.
SIDES: Using B, work as for Pastel Pixie Bootees.
INSTEP: Using B for 1st rnd, P for 2nd rnd and G for 3rd and 4th rnds, work as for Pastel Pixie Bootees.

To Join Top to Sides: With B work as for Pastel Pixie Bootees.

ANKLE BAND: Using G, work as for first 2 rnds of Pastel Pixie Bootees. Then repeat 2nd rnd 5 times more, working 2 rnds P and 3 rnds B. Using G, repeat beading rnd, then repeat 2nd rnd once more. Break off. **Scalloped Edging (wrong side):** With P sl st in center back sc, * work 3 dc in next sc, sl st in next sc. Repeat from * around; join. Break off.

TIE: With P work as for Pastel Pixie Bootees.

JOLLY GREEN GIANT BOOTEES

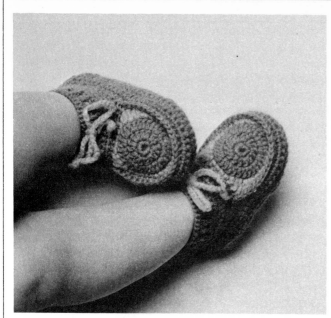

SIZE: Length of sole is 4¾″. Fits one-year-old child.

MATERIALS: Coats & Clark's Red Heart Wintuk Sock and Sweater Yarn, 1 (2-ounce) skein shamrock green No. 645 and small amount vibrant orange No. 251; 12″ square yellow-orange felt; steel crochet hook size 2 **or the size that will give you the correct gauge;** leather punch for ¹/₁₆″-diameter holes.

GAUGE: 11 sc = 2″; 6 rows = 1″.

Note: Use yarn held double throughout.

SOLE: Work as for Pastel Pixie Bootees.
SIDES: Working with green throughout, work as for Pastel Pixie Bootees for 5 rnds, marking 1st sc on last rnd with pin for center back.
INSTEP: Starting at center, with green ch 5. Join with sl st to form ring. **1st rnd (right side):** Ch 1, work 7 sc in ring (8 sc, counting ch 1 as 1 sc); sl st in ch 1 to join. **2nd rnd:** Ch 2, work 2 dc in each sc around (16 dc, counting ch 2 as 1 dc); join. **3rd rnd:** Ch 2, work 2 dc in each dc around (32 dc); join. Break off. **4th rnd:** Make lp on hook with orange and sc in any dc, sc in each of next 14 dc, 2 h dc in next dc, 2 dc in next dc, 2 tr in next dc (mark 1st tr), dc in next dc, h dc in next dc, sc in each of next 3 dc, h dc in next dc, dc in next dc, 2 tr in next dc (mark 2nd tr), 2 dc in next dc, 2 h dc in next dc, sc in each of remaining 4 dc; join. Break off.

To Join Instep to Sides: With green work as for Pastel Pixie Bootees skipping 16 sts to left of center back pin and working 29 joining sts and 34 sc in remaining sts of side piece; join. Break off.

ANKLE BAND: Work as for Pastel Pixie Bootees working 1st rnd as wrong side rnd and working across 9 instep sts (43 sc).

TIE: With orange, work as for Pastel Pixie Bootees.

ELF BOOTEES

piece (do not add seams). For each bootee, cut 2 pieces each of felt for sole, front upper and side upper pieces. Baste matching shapes together. Using double strand of blue and running stitch, center and sew sole edge of front upper to toe end of sole, turning ¼" of sole under for seam (see diagram). Pin sole edge (between dots) of side upper piece to heel end of sole in same manner, overlapping X edge of front upper ¼". Sew pinned edges and overlapped X edges. Work a few straight stitches to join center back seam.

With leather punch make 33 holes evenly spaced ⅜" from ankle-band edge around side upper.

ANKLE BAND: 1st rnd (right side): With right side of bootee facing you, using 1 strand blue, insert hook in 1st hole to left of center back seam and work sc, work sc in each hole around (33 sc); sl st in 1st sc to join; ch 1, turn. **2nd rnd:** Sc in each sc around; join; ch 1, turn.

Repeating 2nd rnd for band, work 1 more rnd with blue, then work (3 rnds white, 3 rnds blue) twice, then 3 rnds white, 1 rnd blue. Do not break off. Ch 1, turn.

Next row (scalloped edging): Skip 1st sc, * work 3 dc in next sc, sl st in next sc. Repeat from * around; join. Break off.

SIZE: Length of finished sole is about 4".

MATERIALS: Coats & Clark's Red Heart Wintuk Sock and Sweater Yarn, small amounts each royal blue No. 845 and white No. 1; ¼ yard 36"-wide red felt; steel crochet hook No. **4 or the size that will give you the correct gauge;** leather punch for ¹/₁₆"-diameter holes; upholstery needle.

GAUGE: 6 sc = 1"; 8 rows = 1".

FELT BOOTEE: Enlarge pattern, (see "How to Enlarge Patterns," page 14), and cut pattern for each

Cross Section of Elf Boots

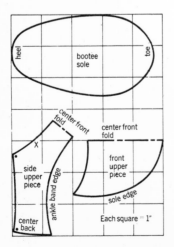

Each square = 1"

FURRY BOOTEES

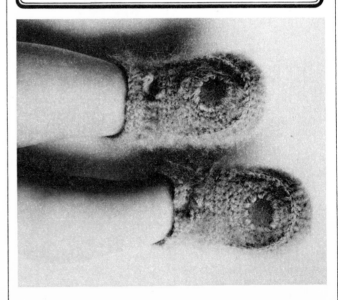

SIZE: Length of sole is 4¾". Fits one-year-old child.

MATERIALS: Medium-weight mohair yarn, 1 ball lilac; Coats & Clark's Red Heart Wintuk Sock and Sweater Yarn, small amount vibrant orange No. 251; 12" square orange felt; steel crochet hook size No. **2 or**

124

the size that will give you the correct gauge; leather punch for $1/16$″-diameter holes.

GAUGE: 5 sc = 1″; 7 rows = 1″.

SOLE: Work as for Pastel Pixie Bootees.

SIDES: With lilac work as for Pastel Pixie Bootees for 6 rows, marking 1st sc on last rnd with pin for center back.

INSTEP: From felt cut two $1¼$″-diameter circles and baste together. Punch 12 holes evenly spaced around circle ¼″ from edge. **1st rnd (right side):** With lilac work 2 sc in each hole around (24 sc); sl st in 1st sc to join. **2nd rnd:** Ch 1, work sc in each sc around; join. **3rd rnd:** Ch 1, sc in 1st sc, * 2 sc in next sc, sc in next sc. Repeat from * around, ending with 2 sc in last sc (36 sc); join. **4th rnd:** Ch 1, turn; sc in each of first 15 sc, 2 h dc in next sc, 2 dc in next sc, 2 tr in next sc (mark 1st tr), dc in next sc, h dc in next sc, sc in each of next 3 sc, h dc in next sc, dc in next sc, 2 tr in next sc (mark 2nd tr), 2 dc in next sc, 2 h dc in next sc, sc in each remaining 7 sc; join. Break off.

To Join Instep to Sides: Using lilac throughout, work as for Pastel Pixie Bootees skipping 14 sts to left of center back pin and working 33 joining sts and 30 sc in remaining sts on side piece.

ANKLE BAND: Using lilac throughout, work as for Pastel Pixie Bootees working across 9 instep sts (39 sc).

TIE: With orange work as for Pastel Bootees.

CHILD'S MOCCASINS

Snug, stay-on slippers with soles are done mostly in single crochet using leftover yarn.

SIZES: Directions are for moccasins to fit a 3- to 4-year-old child. Adjustments can be made for sizes 6 months, 1 to 2 years, 5 to 6 years, and 7 to 8 years.

MATERIALS: Knitting-worsted-weight yarn, 1 oz each red (color R), green (color G) and blue (color B); steel crochet hook No. 3 and aluminum crochet hook size F (or international size 4.00 mm) **or the size that will give you the correct gauge;** chamois skin (real or synthetic), piece of leather, suede or felt for soles; leather punch.

GAUGE: With size F hook, 5 sc = 1″; 5 rows = 1″.

Note: Follow these directions for size 3 to 4 years. For other sizes make adjustments by following individual instructions.

SOLE: Use our pattern, or draw outline of sole of child's shoe (see "Sole" under "To Adjust Moccasin for Other Sizes").

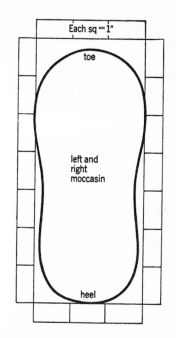

Each sq = 1″

toe

left and right moccasin

heel

If using our pattern, enlarge it (see "How to Enlarge Patterns," page 14) and cut out 2 soles. (**Note:** If using thin felt, make soles double, cutting and basting pairs together.) Using smallest punch of leather punch, cut holes all around about ¼″ apart and ¼″ in from edge.

FOOT 1st rnd: Using color G, make lp on No. 3 hook. Starting at center back, work sc in each hole; join with sl st to 1st sc, ch 1. Change to size F hook for remainder of moccasin. **2nd rnd:** Sc in each sc around; join to ch 1. **3rd rnd:** Ch 1, repeat 2nd rnd. Break off. **4th rnd:** Working in back lp of each st, with R, sc around; join, ch 1. **5th rnd (dec rnd):** Sc around, decreasing 5 sts evenly spaced around toe area (to dec 1 sc, draw up lp in each of next 2 sc, y o and draw through all 3 lps on hook); join. Break off. **6th rnd:** With B, repeat 4th rnd. **7th rnd (dec rnd):** Repeat 5th rnd. Break off. **8th rnd:** With R, repeat 4th rnd. **9th rnd (dec rnd):** Repeat 5th rnd. Break off.

ANKLE: Mark st on last rnd directly above center back heel. Count number of sts on last rnd; divide rnd in half with marked st at center of one half. This is ankle section (remaining half is instep section). **1st row:** Starting at one end of ankle section, with B, work sc in back lp of each sc along ankle section; ch 1, turn. **2nd row:** Sc across; ch 1, turn. Repeat 2nd row twice more, ending last row with ch 4; turn. **5th row (beading):** *Skip next sc, dc in next sc, ch 1. Repeat from * across, ending with dc in last st; ch 1, turn. **6th row:** Sc across. Break off.

TO CLOSE INSTEP: 1st row: With B, work sc in back lp of each of center 2 sts of instep section (at toe); turn. (**Note:** Always work in 1 lp only of each instep sc so that ridge forms on right side.) **2nd row:** Skip 1st B sc, sc in next B sc, sc in 1 lp of next instep sc; turn. Repeat last row until joining measures 1½". **Next row (1st inc row):** Skip 1st B sc, work 2 sc in next B sc, sc in 1 lp of next instep sc; turn. * **Following row:** Skip 1st B sc, sc in each B sc, sc in 1 lp of next instep sc; turn. * Repeat last row until 4 R sc remain on each side of instep. **Next row (2nd inc row):** Skip 1st B sc, 2 sc in each of next 2 B sc, sc in 1 lp of next instep sc; turn. Repeat from * to * until all instep sts are used. Ch 1, turn. Closure completed. Do not break off, but continue for tongue.

TONGUE: 1st row: Sc in each sc, increasing 2 sc evenly spaced (7 sc); ch 1, turn. **2nd row:** Sc across; ch 1, turn. Repeat last row until tongue is same height as ankle section. Break off.

EDGING: With G, sc evenly around all edges of ankle section and tongue; join. Break off.

TIE: With R, crochet 22" chain. Break off. Weave chain through beading row at ankle. Make tassel with 3 strands R and tie one to each end of chain.

Make other moccasin in same manner.

TO ADJUST MOCCASIN FOR OTHER SIZES

SOLE: Trace sole of child's shoe or have child stand on sheet of paper and draw outline of both feet. If one foot is slightly larger than other, choose larger pattern. Then, following general shape of our pattern, modify your outline so that 1 pattern will fit both feet as ours does. Or make separate left- and right-foot patterns.

6-MONTH-SIZE MOCCASIN: Use 2 colors (G and R). **Foot:** Refer to directions, making following changes: Work 6 rnds instead of 9. **1st and 2nd rnds:** Use G. **3rd rnd:** Use R. **4th rnd:** Use R and dec 4 sts around toe area. **5th rnd:** Use G. **6th rnd:** Use G and dec 4 sts around toe area.

Ankle: Follow directions, working 5 rows instead of 6 with R and working beading on 4th row.

To Close Instep: With R, follow directions.

Tongue: With R, follow directions.

Edging and Ties: With G, follow directions.

1- TO 2-YEAR-SIZE MOCCASIN: Use 2 colors (G and R). **Foot:** Refer to directions, making following changes: Work 8 rnds instead of 9. **1st through 5th rnd:** Follow directions. **6th rnd:** Use R. **7th rnd:** Use G and dec 6 sts around toe area. **8th rnd:** Use G.

Ankle: Follow directions, working 5 rows instead of 6 with R and working beading on 4th row.

To Close Instep: With R, follow directions.

Tongue: With R, follow directions.

Edging and Ties: With G, follow directions.

5- TO 6-YEAR-SIZE MOCCASIN: Foot: Follow directions.

Ankle: Follow directions, working 7 rows instead of 6 and working beading on 6th row.

To Close Instep: Follow directions until 6 R sc remain on each side of instep, then work 2nd inc row and continue as directed.

Tongue: Follow directions, but inc to 8 sts instead of 7.

Edging and Ties: Follow directions.

7- TO 8-YEAR-SIZE MOCCASIN: Foot: Follow directions, adding a 10th rnd of sc with R.

Ankle: Follow directions, working 7 rows instead of 6 and working beading on 6th row.

To Close Instep: Follow directions, but inc to 6 sts instead of 5 on 2nd inc row.

Tongue: Follow directions, but inc to 8 sts instead of 7.

Edging and Ties: Follow directions.

SCARF AND MITTEN SET

The fringed scarf goes quickly in double crochet; mittens are a combination of single and double crochet.

SIZES: Scarf is 5″ x 60″, not including fringe. Mittens will fit child (3 to 4) [(5 to 6)]. Both mittens are made the same.

MATERIALS: Bucilla Winsom (Orlon-acrylic knitting-worsted-weight yarn), 1 (2-oz) skein each royal blue No. 292, scarlet No. 309 and white No. 1 (see Note below); aluminum crochet hook size H (or international hook size 5.00 mm) **or the size that will give you the correct gauge.**

Note: You can make a 2nd scarf and mitten set with the remaining Winsom yarn by using either white or scarlet as the main color.

GAUGE: 7 sts = 2″.

SCARF

With scarlet, ch 20. **1st row:** Dc in 4th ch from hook and in each ch across (18 dc, counting turning ch as 1 dc). Break off scarlet; turn. **2nd row:** With white, make lp on hook and work dc in each dc across, dc in top of turning ch (18 dc). Break off white, turn. Repeating 2d row for pattern, work 1 row each scarlet, white and scarlet. **6th row:** With blue, repeat 2nd row but do not break off at end of row; ch 3, turn. **7th row:** Skip 1st dc (directly below ch 3), dc in each dc across; ch 3, turn. **8th row:** Skip 1st dc, dc in each dc and in top of turning ch; ch 3, turn.

Repeat 8th row until scarf measures 54″ from beg, omitting ch 3 at end of last row. Break off blue; turn. Work 5 dc rows more, working 1 row each scarlet, white, scarlet, white and scarlet.

Fringe: Cut scarlet yarn in 6″ lengths. Hold 3 strands tog and fold in half. Draw folded end through a st at 1 end of scarf, draw loose ends through fold and pull tight. Continue across each end of scarf.

MITTENS

With scarlet, starting at fingertips, ch 2. **1st rnd:** Work 6 sc in 2nd ch from hook. Do not join rnds; put a marker in work at end of each rnd. **2nd rnd:** Work 2 sc in each sc around (12 sc). **3rd rnd:** * Sc in next sc, work 2 sc in next sc. Repeat from * around (18 sc). **4th rnd:** (Sc in each of next 8 sc, inc in next sc) twice (20 sc). **5th rnd:** Sc in each sc around. Repeat 5th rnd until mitten measures 3″ [3½″] from beg.

Thumb Opening: Next rnd: Ch 3, skip next 3 sc, sc in each remaining 17 sc. **Following rnd:** Sc in each of 3 ch st, sc in each sc around. Work even on 20 sc for 2 [3] rnds more.

Cuff: 1st rnd: Ch 3, dc in same sc at base of ch 3 (1st inc), work 2 dc in next sc (2nd inc), dc in each sc around; join with sl st to top of ch 3. **2nd rnd:** Ch 3, dc in each dc around; join as for last rnd. **3rd rnd:** Working from left to right, work 1 rnd of reverse sc around cuff. Join and break off.

Thumb: With scarlet, work 8 sc around opening. Work even in sc for 4 [5] rnds more. **Dec rnd:** (Draw up a lp in each of next 2 sc, y o and draw through all 3 lp on hook) 4 times; sl st in 1st st. Break off. Sew opening closed.

BABY HELMET AND MITTENS

The hat's earflap secures under baby's ear with a snag-loop fastening; the mittens—double, half double and single crochet—fit either hand.

SIZE: Fits 6 months to 1 year.

MATERIALS: Bucilla Winsom acrylic yarn, 1 (2-ounce) skein each burgundy No. 8, scarlet No. 309, deep rose No. 42 and tapestry green No. 104; aluminum crochet hook size G (or international size 4.50 mm) **or the size that will give you the correct gauge;** Velcro fastener or snap; one ½"-diameter button; tapestry needle.

GAUGE: Hat: 8 sts = 1"; 6 rnds h dc = 2". **Mittens:** 4 sc = 1"; 4 rows = 1".

HAT

Starting at center of crown with burgundy, ch 6; join with sl st to form ring. **1st rnd:** Ch 3, work 2 dc in each ch around (11 dc, counting ch 3 as 1 dc); join with sl st to top of ch 3. **2nd rnd:** Ch 3, dc in sl st, work 2 dc in each dc around (22 dc); join. **3rd rnd:** Ch 3, * 2 dc in next dc, dc in next dc. Repeat from * 9 times more, 2 dc in last dc (33 dc); join. **4th rnd:** Ch 3, * dc in each of next 2 dc, 2 dc in next dc. Repeat from * 9 times more, dc in each of next 2 dc (43 dc); join. **5th rnd:** Ch 3, * dc in each of next 3 dc, 2 dc in next dc. Repeat from * 9 times more; dc in each of last 2 dc (53 dc); join. **6th rnd:** Ch 3, * dc in each of next 4 dc, 2 dc in next dc. Repeat from * 9 times more; dc in each of last 2 dc (63 dc). Break off burgundy; join with scarlet. **7th rnd:** Ch 2, h dc in sl st, h dc in next dc and in each dc around (64 h dc, counting ch 2 as 1 h dc); join. **8th rnd:** Ch 2, h dc in next h dc and in each h dc around (64 h dc); join. Work as for 8th rnd, working 4 more rnds scarlet, 2 rnds rose and 2 rnds green. Drop green but do not break off.

Earflaps and Strap: Right Flap: Skip next 8 h dc, with burgundy sl st in next h dc. **1st row (right side):** Ch 2, h dc in each of next 11 h dc (12 h dc, counting ch 2 as 1 h dc); ch 2, turn. **2nd row (wrong side):** Skip 1st h dc (directly below ch 2), h dc in each h dc across to within last h dc (1 h dc dec); ch 2, turn. Repeat last row 6 times more (5 h dc at end of 8th row); do not break off. **Chin Strap:** Continuing with burgundy, crochet 4½" chain; dc in 4th ch from hook and in each ch across; join with sl st to 1st h dc of last row of flap. Break off burgundy. **Left Flap:** Skip 23 h dc (for front of hat) on last row of hat, attach burgundy and work as for right flap, breaking off after 8th row.

Finishing: Pick up green, work 1 row sc evenly around lower edge of hat, earflaps and chin strap; join to 1st sc; break off. Tack 1 side of Velcro fastener or snap to right side of chin strap and the other to wrong side of left earflap. Following photograph, tack button for decoration to right side of left earflap.

MITTENS

Starting at wrist edge with deep rose, ch 20; join with sc to form ring. Work in rnds. **1st rnd:** Sc in each ch around (20 sc). Do not join but continue in rnds, marking beg of each rnd. **2nd rnd:** Sc in each sc around. **3rd rnd:** Work 2 sc in 1st sc, sc in each sc around to within last sc, work 2 sc in last sc (22 sc). Repeat last rnd once more (24 sc). Repeat 2nd rnd once, working to within last sc, draw up lp in last sc, break off rose; draw lp of scarlet through both rose lps on hook. Work in rows from now on.

1st row (right side): With scarlet sc in each of next 23 sc (skip last sc); ch 1, turn. **2nd row (wrong side):** Sc in 23 sc across; ch 1, turn. **3rd row:** Dec 1 sc as follows: Draw up lp in each of 1st 2 sc, y o and draw through all 3 lps on hook; sc in each sc across (22 sc); ch 1, turn. Repeat last row 3 times more (19 sc), working ch 1 with burgundy at end of last row; turn. Break off scarlet. **7th row:** Sc in each sc across. Work in rnds from now on. Do not turn but work 1st st of next rnd in 1st st of last row, leaving opening for thumb. **1st through 5th rnds:** Sc in each sc around.

To Shape Tip: Lay mitten flat with beg of rnds at 1 side edge; mark both side edges. **6th through 9th rnds:** Dec 1 sc, sc in each sc across to marker, dec 1 sc, sc to end of rnd (11 sc at end of 9th rnd). Break off, leaving 6″ strand. Sew tip.

Thumb: 1st rnd: Working around thumb opening with right side facing you, using green, work sc in end st of last row of scarlet, work 5 more sc along edge of scarlet band, sc in skipped sc on last rnd of rose (base of thumb), 6 sc along opposite edge of scarlet band (13 sc). Continue in rnds. **2nd rnd:** Sc in each of 1st 4 sc, (dec 1 sc) twice; sc in each next 5 sc (11 sc). **3rd rnd:** Sc in each of 1st 3 sc, (dec 1 sc) twice; sc in each of next 4 sc (9 sc). **4th rnd:** Sc in each sc around. **5th rnd:** Sc in each of next 3 sc, dec 1 sc, sc in each of next 4 sc (8 sc). **6th rnd:** Sc in each of next 3 sc, dec 1 sc, sc in each of next 3 sc (7 sc). Break off, drawing strand through remaining sts and pulling tight.

Make other mitten in same manner; they fit either hand.

CUDDLY TOYS

A winsome threesome—chick-in-egg, sailor duck and baby bunny—are single crochet with touches of embroidery, polyester- fiberfill stuffing.

MATERIALS: All animals shown were made with knitting-worsted-weight yarn and small amounts of sport-weight yarn. For stuffing, you can use Dacron® polyester stuffing or any of your leftover yarns. If your yarns are machine-washable, be sure the stuffing is too.

Note: See materials listed under toy before starting.

Crochet Tips: Tip 1: When working in rounds, the right side of work should always be facing you. Unless otherwise specified, do not join rounds, but work around in spiral fashion and mark beginning of each new round with a safety pin, paper clip or length of yarn in a contrasting color. Move marker from round to round as you work.

Tip 2: If you are making more than one animal, label small sections to simplify assembly.

Tip 3: Stuff all sections firmly before last decrease round.

Tip 4: Finishing: Upon completion of a section, leave a long end of yarn for sewing. Sew pieces together with matching yarn.

To inc 1 sc: Work 2 sc in 1 st.

To dec 1 sc: Insert hook in next st, y o and draw up lp; insert hook in next st, y o and draw up lp (3 lps on hook), y o and draw through all 3 lps on hook.

CHICK AND EGG

Note: Chicks are the same for both eggs. Eggs are both worked the same way, but colors and trim are different.

SIZE: Egg is 4½" tall, chick (inside egg) is 3½" tall. See General Directions.

MATERIALS: Yarns: For Each Chick: Knitting-worsted-weight yarn, 1 oz light yellow, small amounts blue and orange. **For Egg with Pink Ties:** Knitting-worsted-weight yarn, 1 oz off-white, small amount pink; sport-weight yarn, small amounts deep yellow and green. **For Egg with Yellow Ties:** Knitting-worsted-weight yarn, 1 oz off-white, small amount deep yellow; sport-weight yarn, small amounts green and light orange.

Crochet Hooks: Aluminum crochet hooks size D and size E for chick, size E for egg (or international sizes 3.00 mm and 3.50 mm) **or the sizes that will give you the correct gauges;** tapestry needle; stuffing.

GAUGES: With size D hook, 5 sc = 1"; with size E hook, 9 sc = 2".

EGG

Note: Use size E hook throughout.

BOTTOM HALF: Starting at center of lower edge with white, ch 3. Join with sl st in 3rd ch from hook to form ring. **1st rnd:** Work 8 sc in ring. **2nd rnd:** * Sc in next sc, inc in next sc. Repeat from * around (12 sc). **3rd rnd:** Repeat last rnd (18 sc). **4th rnd:** Sc in each sc around, increasing 1 sc in every 3rd sc. Work even on 24 sc for 1 rnd. **6th rnd:** Sc in each sc around; increasing in every 4th sc. Work even on 30 sc for next 2 rnds. **9th rnd:** Sc in each sc around, increasing in every 10th sc. Work even on 33 sc for next 3 rnds (12 rnds in all). At end of last rnd, sl st in next sc and break off.

Trim: Make lp on hook with pink (or deep yellow). Working below both top lps on each st on last rnd, sl st in each sc around (two lps forming chain edge of sc will show above sl sts). Join with sl st in 1st sl st; then ch 32 for tie. Break off. Put piece aside.

TOP HALF: Work same as for bottom half through 2nd rnd (12 sc). **3rd rnd:** Sc in each sc around, increasing in every 3rd sc (16 sc). **4th rnd:** Sc in each sc around, increasing in every 4th sc (20 sc). **5th rnd:** Repeat last rnd. Work even on 25 sc for next 2 rnds. **8th rnd:** Sc in each sc around, increasing in every 5th sc. Work even on 30 sc for 1 rnd. **10th rnd:** Sc in each sc around, increasing in every 10th sc. Work even on 33 sc for next 3 rnds (12 rnds in all). At end of last rnd, sl st in next sc and break off.

Trim: 1st rnd: Work 1 rnd sl st with pink (or deep yellow) same as for bottom half; join with sl st in 1st sl st (do not ch for tie); ch 1; **2nd rnd:** Working in top lp only of sl st, sc in each sl st around. Join with sl st in 1st sc; then ch 32 for tie. Break off.

FINISHING: Embroidery for Egg with Pink Ties, Zigzag Trim: Work same embroidery on both halves of egg. Skip 1st 2 rnds of sc below pink trim, work across next 2 rnds as follows: With deep yellow and chain st (see Special Stitch Diagrams, page 14), embroider zigzag pattern all around egg. With green, work French knots above and below zigzag pattern. With pink, below zigzag trim work 1 rnd ch st, skip 1 rnd, then work another rnd ch st.

Joining: Keeping ties at center front, hold both sections of egg tog, and with white, sew 5 sts at center back tog.

Embroidery for Egg with Yellow Ties: Work same embroidery on both halves of egg. **Flower Trim:** Skip 1st rnd of sc below yellow trim, work across next 2 rnds as follows: With orange, work 4-petal flowers in lazy daisy st all around egg, spacing sts about 1 sc apart. With deep yellow, work French knot in center of each flower. With green, work straight st for stem below each flower, and work 1 green lazy daisy on each stem for leaf.

With yellow, working above and below next sc rnd, work a small zigzag ch st. Skip next sc rnd below zigzag, and work 1 rnd ch st with yellow.

Joining: Work same joining as for egg with pink ties.

CHICK

Starting at top of head, with size D hook and light yellow, work same as for bottom half of egg through 2nd rnd (12 sc).

Change to size E hook and work even on 12 sc for 1 rnd. **4th rnd:** Sc in each sc around, increasing in every 4th sc. Work even on 15 sc for next 2 rnds. **7th rnd:** Change to size D hook and work even in sc. **8th rnd:** Dec 5 sc evenly around (10 sc). Stuff head.

9th rnd: Sc in each sc around for neck. **10th rnd:** Sc in each sc around, increasing in every other sc. Change to size E hook and work even on 15 sc for 1 rnd. **12th rnd:** Sc in each sc around, increasing 1 sc in every 3rd sc (20 sc). **13th rnd:** Sc in each sc around, increasing in every 5th sc. Work even on 24 sc for next 2 rnds.

Change to size D hook and work even for 1 rnd. Stuff body. **17th rnd:** Sc in each sc around, decreasing 6 sc evenly spaced (18 sc). **18th rnd:** Sc in each sc around, decreasing 3 sc (15 sc). **19th rnd:** Sc in each sc around, decreasing 5 sc (10 sc). Stuff body again. **20th rnd:** Repeat last rnd (5 sc). This is tip of tail. Stuff tail. **21st rnd:** Dec 1 sc over 1st 2 sc. Break off. Sew opening closed.

WING (make 2): With size D hook and light yellow, ch 7 for back edge of wing. **1st row:** Sc in 2nd ch from hook and in each remaining ch; ch 1, turn (6 sc). **2nd row:** Skip 1st sc, sc in each sc across (1 sc dec); ch 1, turn. Repeat 2nd row 4 times more. Break off.

LEG (make 2): With size D hook and orange, ch 9. Sl st in 2nd ch from hook and in each of next 2 ch for 1st claw, leaving 5 ch sts free for leg, (ch 4, sl st in 2nd ch from hook and in each of next 2 ch) twice for next 2 claws; then sl st in each of next 5 ch sts for leg. Break off.

BEAK: With size D hook and orange, ch 3. Work 5 sc in 3rd ch from hook. Join with sl st to ch 2. Break off.

FINISHING: Sew back edge of each wing to each side of body, about 1 rnd below neck. Sew legs to front of lower section of body. Sew beak to front of head.

Eyes: Embroider eyes with blue straight sts.

Place completed chick inside egg, tie ends into a bow.

SAILOR DUCK

SIZE: 7″ tall (without hat).

See General Directions.

MATERIALS: Knitting-worsted-weight yarn, 2 ozs. light yellow; 2-ply or sport-weight yarn, small amounts orange, medium blue and white; aluminum crochet hooks size D and size E (or international sizes 3.00 mm and 3.50 mm) **or the sizes that will give you the correct gauges;** tapestry needle; stuffing.

GAUGES: With knitting worsted and size D hook, 5 sc = 1″; with size E hook, 9 sc = 2″.

HEAD, BODY AND TAIL: Starting at top of head, with size D hook and yellow, ch 3. Join with sl st in 3rd ch from hook to form ring. **1st rnd:** Work 7 sc in ring. **2nd rnd:** Sc in 1st sc (inc in next sc, sc in next sc) 3 times (10 sc). **3rd rnd:** (Sc in next sc, inc in next sc) 5 times (15 sc). **4th rnd:** (Sc in each of next 2 sc, inc in next sc) 5 times (20 sc).

Change to size E hook and work even on 20 sc for 5 rnds. **10th rnd (dec rnd):** (Sc in each of next 3 sc, dec 1 sc) 4 times (16 sc). **11th rnd (dec rnd):** Change to size D hook. (Sc in each of next 2 sc, dec 1 sc) 4 times (12 sc). Work even on 12 sc for 2 rnds for neck. Stuff head.

Change to size E hook and work even on 12 sc for 1 rnd. **15th rnd (inc rnd):** Sc in each sc around, increasing 1 sc in every 3rd sc (16 sc). **16th rnd (inc rnd):** Sc in each sc around, increasing 1 sc in every 4th sc (20 sc). **17th rnd (inc rnd):** Repeat last rnd (25 sc). Work even on 25 sc for 2 rnds.

Change to size D hook and work even on 25 sc for 2 rnds more for waistline. **22nd rnd (inc rnd):** Sc in each sc around, increasing 1 sc in every 5th sc (30 sc). Change to size E hook and work even on 30 sc for 4 rnds. **1st short row:** Sc in each of 1st 12 sc, sl st in next st; turn.

2nd short row: Skip sl st, sc in each of next 12 sc of last row, sl st in next sc, turn. **27th rnd:** Skipping both sl st's, sc in each sc around (28 sc). **28th rnd (dec rnd):** Dec 5 sc evenly around (23 sc). **29th rnd:** Sc in 1st sc, (dec 1 sc over next 2 sc) 11 times. Work even on 12 sc for 1 rnd. Stuff body.

Change to size D hook and work even on 12 sc for 3 rnds more. **34th rnd (dec rnd):** (Dec 1 sc over next 2 sc) 6 times. Stuff tail. **35th rnd:** Repeat dec of 34th rnd 3 times (3 sts). Break off. Sew opening closed.

FOOT (make 2): With size D hook and orange, make lower section and upper section as follows:

Lower Section: Starting at back edge, ch 6. **1st row:** Sc in 2nd ch and in each ch across (5 sc); ch 1, turn. **2nd and 3rd rows:** Sc in each sc across; ch 1, turn. **4th row:** Sc in each of 1st 2 sc, inc in next sc, sc in each of next 2 sc; ch 1, turn. **5th row:** Sc across, increasing 1 sc in 3rd sc (7 sc); ch 1, turn. Work even on 7 sc for 3 rows more, ending at front edge (8 rows in all). Break off.

Upper Section: Starting at back edge, ch 5. **1st row:** Sc in 2nd ch from hook and in each ch across (4 sc); ch 1, turn. Working in rows of sc, inc 1 sc in center st of each of next 3 rows. Work even on 7 sc for 2 rows more, ending at front edge (6 rows in all). Break off.

Joining: Leaving 1st 2 rows at back edge of lower section free, place upper section on top of lower section with front edges together. With orange yarn, sew side edges and front edge, leaving back edge open. Stuff foot lightly, then sew opening closed.

LEG (make 2): Starting at lower edge with size D hook and orange, ch 8. Join with sl st to form ring. Work 7 sc in ring, then working in rnds, sc in each sc around for 1½″. Break off orange, attach yellow. **Next rnd:** With yellow, sc around, increasing 1 sc in every other st. Work even on 13 sc for 1 rnd. Break off. Sew lower edge of leg to back of foot. Stuff leg.

BILL: With size D hook and orange, starting at back edge, ch 5. **1st row:** Sc in 2nd ch from hook and in each ch across; ch 1, turn. Work even on 4 sc for 1 row, then inc 1 sc in center of 3rd row. Work even on 5 sc for 1 row. Break off. Make another piece in same manner. Sew back edges of both pieces together, then sew back edge to front of head.

CHEEK (make 2): Working same as for head, work through 2nd rnd. Break off. Stuffing cheeks lightly, sew them to face, on each side of bill.

WING (make 2): With size E hook and yellow, ch 10. Sc in 2nd ch from hook and in each of next 7 ch, work 5 sc in last ch. Working across opposite edge of foundation ch, sc in each st across, working 3 sc in last st. Then, working across sts of 1st side, sc in each of next 9 sc, sl st in next st and break off. Sew wings to body.

SAILOR COLLAR: With size D hook and blue, ch

26 loosely to measure 4½". Join with sl st to form ring. Joining is at center front of collar. **1st rnd (right side):** Ch 1, work 2 sc in same ch as sl st for 1st front inc, sc in each of next 8 ch, work 3 sc in next ch for corner inc, sc in each of next 6 ch for back, work corner inc in next ch, sc in each of next 8 ch, 2 sc in last ch for 2nd front inc. Do not join.

2nd rnd: Work 2 sc in 1st sc, (sc in each sc to center sc of corner, mark center sc, work 3 sc in next sc) twice; sc in each sc to within last sc, 2 sc in next sc. Join with sl st in 1st sc. Break off. **Short rows:** Working across sts of back only between markers of 2nd rnd, work even in sc for 3 rows. Break off. **3rd rnd:** Make lp on hook with blue, and starting at center front with right side of work facing you, work 2 sc in 1st sc, sc in each sc or row to corner, work corner as before, sc across sts of back, work corner, sc in each row or sc to within last sc of front, 2 sc in next sc. Join and break off.

Trim: With tapestry needle and white, embroider 1 row of chain st (see Special Stitch Diagrams, page 14) between 2nd and 3rd rnds of collar.

Tie: With size D hook and white, crochet 3" chain. Tie knot in center of tie. Place collar on duck and tack at center front. Tack tie at front of collar.

Hat: Use size E hook and blue. Starting at center, ch 3. Join with sl st to form ring. **1st rnd:** Work 6 sc in ring. Working in sc, on next 2 rnds inc 1 st in every st. Change to size D hook, and working in back lp only of each st, work even on 24 sc for 1 rnd. Work in both lps from now on. **Next rnd:** * Dec 1 sc over next 2 sc, sc in next sc. Repeat from * around. Work even on 16 sc for 3 rnds, ending last rnd with sl st in next sc. Break off.

Hatband and Tie: With size D hook and white, crochet 6" chain. Break off. Sew center section of chain above last rnd on hat, leaving 1" ends free.

FINISHING: Sew hat on head. Sew legs to body.

Eyes: With tapestry needle and blue, embroider eyes in satin st.

If duck is not for a young child, you can use pipe cleaners or covered wire to make legs and wings firm.

BABY BUNNY

SIZE: 7" tall.
See General Directions.

MATERIALS: Knitting-worsted-weight yarn, 2 ozs. beige, small amounts white, blue and baby pink; aluminum crochet hooks size D and size E (or international sizes 3.00 mm and 3.50 mm) **or the sizes that will give you the correct gauges;** tapestry needle; stuffing.

GAUGES: With size D hook 5 sc = 1"; with size E hook, 9 sc = 2".

HEAD, BODY AND TAIL: Starting at center of nose, with size D hook and beige, ch 3. Join with sl st in 3rd ch from hook to form ring. **1st rnd:** Work 8 sc in ring. **2nd rnd:** * Sc in next sc, 2 sc in next sc. Repeat from * around (12 sc). **3rd rnd:** * Sc in each of next 2 sc, 2 sc in next sc. Repeat from * around (16 sc).

Change to size E hook and work even on 16 sc for next 2 rnds. **6th and 7th rnds:** Sc in each sc around, increasing 1 sc every 4th sc. Work even on 25 sc for 2 rnds. Ch 1, turn at end of last rnd. For back of head, work short rows as follows: **1st row:** Sc in each of next 15 sts; ch 1, turn. Mark the 10 unworked sts for center front of neck. **2nd row:** Sc in each of 1st 5 sc, skip next sc, sc in each of next 3 sc, skip next sc, sc in each of next 5 sc; ch 1, turn. **3rd row:** Sc in each of 1st 4 sc, skip next sc, sc in each of next 3 sc, skip next sc, sc in each of next 4 sc; ch 1, turn. **4th row:** Sc in each of 1st 3 sc (skip next sc, sc in each of next 3 sc) twice; ch 1, turn. **5th row:** Sc in each of next 2 sc (skip next sc, sc in next sc) twice; skip next sc, sc in each of last 2 sc; ch 1, turn. **6th row:** Sc in 1st sc, (skip next sc, sc in next sc) twice; sc in last sc, turn. Join with sl st to 1st sc of this row; ch 1, turn.

Work in rnds from now on. Work next rnd along ends of rows of back of head, and across 10 free sts left for center front of neck, as follows: **10th rnd:** Sc in end of each of next 6 rows of back of head, sc in next free sc (1st of 10 sc); (inc in next sc, sc in next sc) 4 times; sc in last sc of 10 neck sc, sc in end of each of next 6 rows of back of head, ending at center back of neck. Mark center back for beg of rnds from now on. Work even on 26 sc for 1 rnd. **12th rnd (dec and inc rnd):** Sc in 1st sc, (skip next sc, sc in next sc) twice; sc in each of next 4 sc, (inc in next sc, sc in each of next 2 sc) 4 times; sc in next sc, (skip next sc, sc in next sc) twice. Work even on 26 sc for 1 rnd. **14th rnd:** Sc in each sc around and inc 2 sc, evenly spaced, across front of neck. Work even on 28 sc for 6 rnds. **21st rnd:** Dec 4 sc evenly around. Work even on 24 sc for 2 rnds. **24th rnd:** Inc 4 sc evenly around. Work even on 28 sc for 1 rnd. Stuff head and body. **26th and 27th rnds:** Dec 5 sc evenly around. **28th rnd:** * Dec 1 sc over next 2 sc. Repeat from * around (9 sc). Dec 1 sc over next 2 sc, sl st in next sc (8 sc). Break off beige, attach white for tail; ch 1, turn.

Tail: Wrong side of work is now facing you. **1st rnd:** Change to size D hook and work 2 lp sts in each sc of last rnd as follows: Insert hook in next sc, wind yarn twice around index finger of left hand, insert hook under both lps on finger and draw a bit of both lps through st, remove finger, y o hook and draw through all 3 lps on hook (1 lp st made). Make another lp st in same sc, then work 2 lp sts in each sc around. **2nd rnd:** Sc in each lp st around (16 sc). **3rd rnd:** Work 1 lp st in each sc around. **4th rnd:** (Dec 1 sc over next 2 sc) 8 times. Stuff tail. **5th rnd:** (Work 1 lp st, skip 1 st) 4 times. Break off. Sew opening closed.

EAR (make 2): Back of Ear: With size E hook and beige, ch 10. **1st rnd:** Sc in 2nd ch from hook and in each of next 7 ch, work 3 sc in last ch. Working across opposite edge of foundation chain, sc in each st across, working 2 sc in last st. **2nd rnd:** Sc in each sc around, increasing 2 sc in each end st; join with sl st in next st. Break off.

Front of Ear: Using size D hook and pink, work same as for back of ear. **Trim:** With tapestry needle and white, embroider 1 row of chain st (see Special Stitch Diagrams, page 14) between 1st and 2nd rnds. With beige, sew front ear to back ear, stuffing lightly before closing seam.

HIND LEG (make 2): With size D hook and beige, ch 3. Join with sl st to form ring. **1st rnd:** Work 8 sc in ring. **2nd rnd:** Sc in each sc around, increasing 2 sc evenly spaced. Work even on 10 sc for 5 rnds. At end of last rnd, sl st in next st; ch 1, turn.

Work in rows from now on as follows: **1st row:** Skip sl st, sc in each of next 8 sc, sl st in next sc; ch 1, turn. **2nd row:** Skip sl st, sc in each of next 7 sc, sl st in next sc; ch 1, turn. **3rd row:** Skip sl st, sc in each of next 6 sc, sl st in next sc; ch 1, turn. **4th row:** Skip sl st, sc in each of next 6 sc; ch 1, turn. **5th row:** Sc in each of next 5 sc, sl st in next sc; ch 1, turn. **6th row:** Skip sl st, sc in each of next 4 sc, sl st in next sc; ch 1, turn. **7th row:** Skip sl st, sc in each of next 4 sc; ch 1, turn. **8th row:** Sc in each of next 4 sc. Break off.

Stuffing leg as you go, sew open section of each leg to lower edge of front of body.

FRONT PAW (make 2): Work same as for Hind Leg through 1st rnd (8 sc). Work even on 8 sc for 3 rnds. Stuff paw. **Next rnd:** (Dec 1 sc over next 2 sc) 4 times; sl st in next sc. Break off, leaving end for sewing. Sew last rnd of each paw to upper front of body.

FINISHING: Sew ears to head.

Muzzle: With size D hook and white, ch 2. Work 6 sc in 2nd ch from hook; join with sl st in 1st sc. Break off. Make another piece in same manner. Stuff the 2 muzzle sections and sew in place on face. With pink, embroider nose (in satin st just above muzzle). With pink, embroider a straight st between the muzzle sections and 2 straight sts below muzzle for mouth.

Eyes: With blue and white yarn, embroider eyes in satin st. With white, work straight sts on ends of both paws and hind legs.

Whiskers: Cut 2″ strands of white yarn. Dip in melted wax to stiffen if desired, then draw through cheeks with needle.

Tie: With size E hook and pink, crochet 14″ chain. Tie around neck.

CHRISTENING DRESS**

You need expertise to undertake this heirloom dress and matching bonnet in dainty filet crochet. Narrow ribbons close the dress in back.

SIZE: Width of dress around at underarm about 23″; width of skirt about 44″; sleeve width about 9½″; sleeve length to underarm about 6½″; length of dress from shoulder to hem about 31″; depth of cap 5½″.

MATERIALS: D.M.C. Cordonnet Special, No. 30, 20 balls; steel crochet hook No. 10 **or the size that will**

133

give you the correct gauge; about 3 yards of narrow ribbon.

GAUGE: 5 spaces (dc, ch 2) = 1"; 5 rows = 1".

Note: To enlarge size of dress, use larger hook and/or heavier cotton. To make dress smaller, use smaller hook. To shorten skirt work fewer rows at its waistline edge.

Filet Ground (space): Ch a multiple of 3 sts plus 5. **Row 1:** Dc in 8th ch from hook for starting space, * ch 2, skip 2 ch of starting ch, dc in next ch; repeat from * across, turn. **Row 2:** Ch 5 (counts as first dc, ch 2), * dc in next dc, ch 2; repeat from * ending dc in 5th of turning ch, turn. **Row 3:** Ch 5, * dc in next dc, ch 2; repeat from * ending dc in 3rd of turning ch. Repeat Row 3 for ground.

Filled In Space or Blocks: * Dc in next dc, 2 dc in next ch-2 sp; repeat from * for desired number of blocks. A space on chart = □; a filled in space or block on chart = ⊠.

To Follow Charts: Read charts from right hand to left for Row 1 and all odd numbered rows. Even numbered rows are read from left to right.

Note: To avoid counting a large number of ch sts, a piece can be started as follows: Use 2 balls of cotton. With one, chain a number of sts, drop lp from hook (a bobby pin is convenient to prevent lp from raveling); with 2nd ball, place a sl knot lp on hook, dc in first ch st worked, * ch 2, skip next 2 ch, dc in next ch; repeat from * until desired number of spaces have been worked; if there are not enough ch sts, continue them with the first ball of thread, then work more spaces with the 2nd ball. When necessary spaces have been made, fasten off first ball of thread, turn. On the next row, work as for Row 3 of ground (filling in blocks as per chart) until the end of the row; the last dc will be worked in the first dc of first row instead of a turning ch, turn, etc.

To Increase One Space at Beg of Row: Ch 5 (counts as first dc, ch 2 of row), dc in last dc of previous row, ch 2, dc in next dc and continue as in Row 3 above.

To Increase One Space at End of Row: Work to last dc, (dc in last dc, ch 2, dc again in last dc), turn.

Increases of several spaces at a time are described in the bodice instructions.

To Dec One Space at Beg of Row: Ch 2 (instead of 5), y o hook, work first half of dc in next dc, y o, and draw through 3 lps on hook.

To Dec One Space at End of Row: Work to within 2 spaces of end of row, ch 2, y o, work first half of dc in next to last dc, y o, work first half of dc in last dc, y o hook and draw through 3 lps on hook, turn.

To Dec More Than One Space or Block at Beg of Row: Sl st to desired dc, ch 5, in that dc and proceed as for Row 3 above.

To Dec Several Spaces or Blocks at End of Row:

Work across to last desired dc, turn. On next Row, ch 5, and continue as for Row 3 above.

BODICE: Starting at the waistline of the front, ch 176. Work as for Row 1 of filet ground for 57 spaces, turn. Continue with Row 2 and follow the chart for design and armhole shaping, until 15 rows have been worked in all, turn. Mark the center 7 spaces for neck. On the next row work over to the first mark, turn. Now working on the right hand side of neck only, continue to follow the chart for shaping neck edge. Work even until there are 26 rows in all, ending at the neck edge; ch 34 for right-hand half of back, turn. Dc in 8th ch from hook, ch 2, skip 2 ch, dc in next and continue in filet across the entire row—23 spaces. Continue in filet ground without design blocks to work half of the back, shape the armhole to correspond to the front and keep the center back edge even. At the end of the 48th row (back edge) drop thread. Attach a separate ball of thread to turning ch at armhole edge and ch 15. Cut thread. Pick up thread at end of 48th row and work across next row, working 5 spaces across the 15 ch sts.

Shape Armhole: Ch 15, and attach in turning ch at armhole edge. Pick up thread at opposite end and work across row, working 5 spaces across the 15 ch sts. Work even for 3 more rows, end off. For the left side, join thread at the other end of the center neck sts, ch 5, dc in next dc, and continue to work left side of neck and back to correspond to right reversing shaping. At the end of the 48th row (arm edge), ch 18 for armhole, turn. Dc in 8th ch from hook, skip 2 ch, dc in next ch, continue across in filet. Complete left side to correspond to right.

SLEEVES: Ch 152; dc in 8th ch from hook, and continue with Row 1 of filet for 49 spaces. Now follow chart for spaces and block pattern and shaping of the sleeve cap.

SKIRT: The skirt is worked in one piece from waistline to hem starting and ending at the center back edges. Ch 395; starting at the waist, dc in 8th ch from hook and continue in filet ground for 130 spaces. On Row 2, starting at the hem edge, follow the chart for pattern blocks and scalloped edge. The star motif (20 spaces and blocks) A-B is repeated 3 times more across the row (see photo). Continue to follow the chart until the center row of skirt, C, is worked; now work 2nd half of skirt to correspond to first, reversing the design on the chart.

FINISHING: With right side of bodice facing, join thread to the bottom of the left center back edge. Along the back opening work 3 sc in each space up to the last before the neck; work 5 dc in last space to turn corner. Around neck edge work (2 sc, ch 3, sl st in first ch [picot]) in each space; work 5 sc to turn corner in last

CHARTS FOR CHRISTENING GOWN

Cap Front

Hem Edge-Skirt

space, then 3 sc in each space along right back edge, end off.

Overcast the sides of front and back together. Join thread to an armhole at a side seam. With right side of work facing, ch 5 (counts as dc, ch 2), dc in next dc, 2 dc in next ch-2 space, dc in next dc, ch 2; repeat from * around armhole for alternate spaces and blocks ending with sl st in 3rd of starting ch. **Next Row:** * 3 sc in next sp, picot 1 sc in each of next 3 dc picot; repeat from * around armhole ending with sl st in first sc, end off. Work other armhole in the same way. With right side of work facing, join thread to end dc at the wrist edge of each sleeve. Work (3 sc, picot) in each space across. Overcast the sleeve seams together; set sleeves into armholes under the picot edges; with back stitch, top stitch sleeves in place.

With right side of skirt facing, starting at the waistline, work 3 sc in each space along the back opening until the last space is reached. In the last space work 5 sc to turn corner of hem, then continue across hem edge in the same way, working 3 sc in each space, 5 sc in each corner space of the scallops; work other

back opening edge as for the first, end off. Gather in the top of the skirt to fit the waist edge of the bodice, setting it under the picot edge. With back stitch, top stitch the skirt to the bodice.

Lace ribbon around the neck, leaving ends long enough to tie in a bow at the back. Repeat around each wrist of the sleeves, tying in the center of the sleeve. Sew 2 ends of ribbon to the waistline at the back to close the robe with a bow.

BONNET: For the back, ch 98; starting at bottom dc in 8th ch from hook and following chart continue in filet blocks and spaces for 31 spaces in all. Continue to follow the chart for pattern and shaping.

For the front strip of the cap ch 89, dc in 8th ch from hook and continue in filet over 22 spaces following the chart for pattern blocks and scalloped face edge.

FINISHING: Sew front strip of cap to the back around its sides and top. Work 3 sc in each space around edges of the bonnet, as for the robe, with 5 sc in the corner spaces of scallops. Lace ribbon around the neck edge to tie in under the chin.

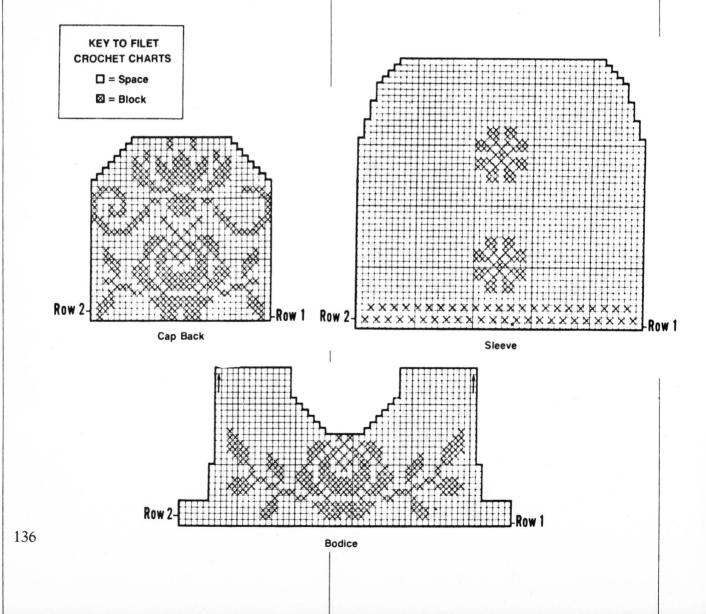

KEY TO FILET CROCHET CHARTS

□ = Space

☒ = Block

Cap Back

Sleeve

Bodice

3

Around-the-House Accessories

JEWEL OF AN AFGHAN

Each unit is a combination of single-, double- and treble-crochet stitches; the jewel-bright circles are joined as you work.

SIZE: About 45″ × 62″. Size can be adjusted by adding or omitting rows of circles.

MATERIALS: Knitting worsted, 6 (4-ounce) skeins black, 1 skein each bright green, white, light yellow, bright yellow, bright pink, blue and aqua; aluminum crochet hook size H (or international size 5.00 mm) **or the size that will give you the correct gauge;** tapestry needle.

GAUGE: Each circle measures about 5¼″. Afghan is composed of 142 circles, joined as you go.

FIRST ROW: 1st CIRCLE: Starting at center with black, ch 6. Join with sl st to form ring. **1st rnd:** Ch 1, work 12 sc in ring; join with sl st to 1st sc. Break off.

2nd rnd: Make lp on hook with another color; y o and work dc in any sc, work another dc in same sc, work 2 dc in each sc around (24 dc); join to 1st dc. Break off. Circle should measure about 2½″.

3rd rnd: Make lp on hook with black; work sc in each dc around; join to 1st sc. Break off.

4th rnd: Make lp on hook with 3rd color and make cl as follows: Y o and draw up lp in any sc, y o and draw through 2 lps on hook, y o and draw up lp in same sc, (y o and draw through 2 lps on hook) twice, y o and draw up lp in same sc again, y o and draw through 2 lps on hook, y o and draw through remaining 3 lps on hook (cl made); * ch 4, skip next sc, y o and draw up lp in next sc, complete cl. Repeat from * 10 times more (12 cl), ch 4, join to top of 1st cl. Break off.

5th rnd: Make lp on hook with black; work 3 sc over any ch-4 lp and, working in front of lp and not over it, work tr in skipped sc (between 2 cl) directly below on 3rd rnd, work 2 sc over same ch-4 lp, * work 3 sc over next ch-4 lp, tr in next sc below, 2 sc over same lp. Repeat from * around (12 tr); join to 1st sc. Break off.

2nd CIRCLE: Work as for 1st circle through 4th rnd, using black for 1st and 3rd rnds and 2 different colors for 2nd and 4th rnds.

JEWEL OF AN AFGHAN

5th rnd (joining rnd): With black repeat 5th rnd on 1st circle until 9 tr have been made, work 2 sc over same lp, 3 sc over next lp, work tr, join with sl st to a tr on 1st circle, (2 sc over same lp on 2nd circle, 3 sc over next lp, tr, join to next tr on 1st circle) twice; 2 sc over same lp on 2nd circle; join to beg of rnd. Break off.

Make and join 3rd circle to 2nd to form strip (See Diagram). Continue adding circles to strip until there are 9 circles in all.

SECOND ROW: 10th CIRCLE: Work as for 1st circle through 4th rnd. **5th rnd (joining rnd):** With black work as before until 9 tr have been made, work 2 sc over same lp on 10th circle, 3 sc over next lp, tr; following diagram, join next 3 tr to 1st circle as before at the 3 dots; join to beg of rnd. Break off.

11th CIRCLE: Work as before through 4th rnd. **5th rnd (joining rnd):** With black work as before until 5 tr have been made, work 2 sc over same lp on 11th circle, 3 sc over next lp, tr; following diagram, join next 3 tr to 10th circle at the 2 X's and next dot (joining of circles 1 and 10). Continuing around, join next 4 tr to 1st and 2nd circles at tiny squares; join to beg of rnd. Break off.

Make and join 8 more circles to complete 2nd row. There are 9 circles on 3rd row; join them to 2nd row, starting with 1st circle joined to 10th and 11th circles. Make and join 12 more rows of circles, with 10 on 4th row, 9 on 5th, 10 on 6th and so on.

STAINED-GLASS AFGHAN AND PILLOWS

These beauties require advance planning, but the actual work is all basic afghan stitch and you can use up leftover yarn.

SIZE: Afghan measures about 60″ × 80″ without fringe; each pillow measures about 15″ × 20″.

MATERIALS: Sport-weight yarn, an assortment of colors plus black and red for borders (see below for amounts); afghan hook size G (or international size 4.50 mm) **or the size that will give you the correct gauge.**

GAUGE: 5 sts = 1″; 4 rows = 1″.

Note: Wind a bobbin of yarn for each color change. Never carry any yarn across back of work.

You can use any brand or brands of sport-weight or sock-and-sweater weight yarn, but **all the yarn must be of equal thickness** and you must get the correct gauge.

The colors marked on our charts are for color families. For example, where the chart lists "B," you can use shades of blue such as navy, aqua, royal blue or turquoise. You can use our color scheme or invent your

own. Always work black where indicated, to produce the "stained glass-leading" effect and use the same shade of red for all borders.

To determine how much yarn of each color you will need, first plan your color scheme. Next find the approximate number of square inches of each color (one square inch = 5 sts × 4 rows). For each square inch you will need one yard of yarn. Sport-weight yarn is usually packaged in 2-ounce skeins of approximately 200 to 300 yards. For the afghan you will need a total of 44 ounces of yarn.

TO WORK AFGHAN STITCH: For each afghan and pillow block work as follows: With black ch 75. **1st row:** Keeping all lps on hook, draw up lp in 2nd ch from hook and in each ch across (75 lps on hook); for second half of row work as follows: Y o, draw yarn through 1st lp on hook, * y o, draw yarn through next 2 lps on hook. Repeat from * across until 1 lp remains on hook. A row of vertical bars is formed. Do not turn; always work with same (right) side facing you. **2nd row:** Insert hook under 2nd vertical bar and draw up a lp; keeping all lps

Afghan Layout Diagram

1	2	3	4
5	6	7	8
9	10	11	12
13	14	15	16

Color Key

■	black	H	grays	R	reds	
B	blues	L	purples, lavender	T	browns, beige	
F	golds	O	oranges	W	white	
G	greens	P	pinks	Y	yellows	

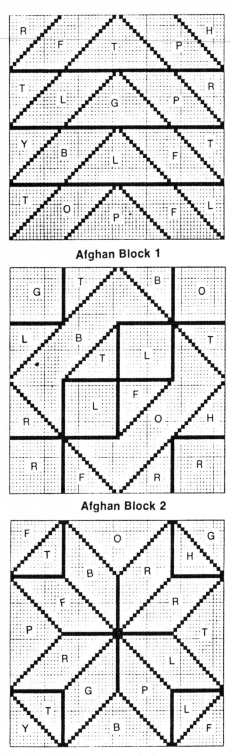

Afghan Block 1

Afghan Block 2

Afghan Block 3

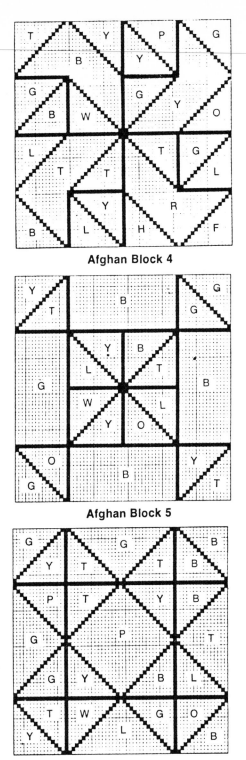

Afghan Block 4

Afghan Block 5

Afghan Block 6

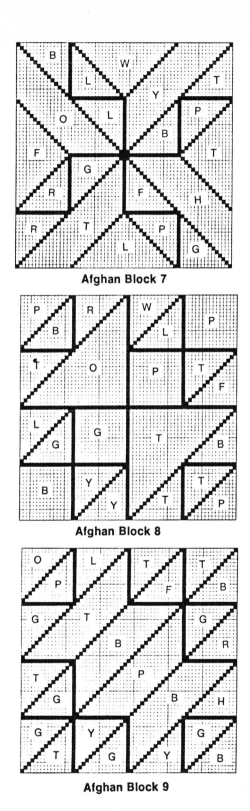

Afghan Block 7

Afghan Block 8

Afghan Block 9

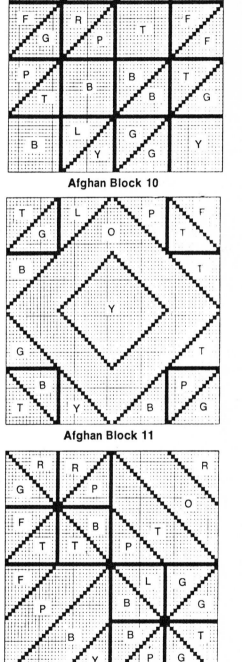

Afghan Block 10

Afghan Block 11

Afghan Block 12

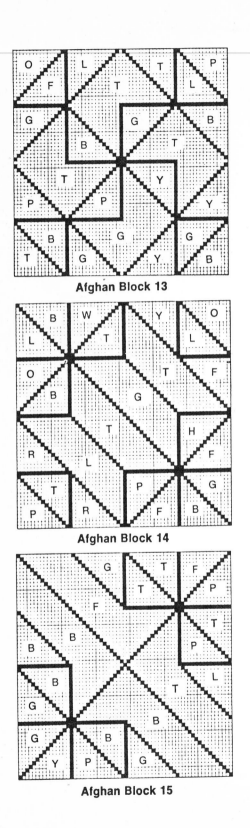

Afghan Block 13

Afghan Block 14

Afghan Block 15

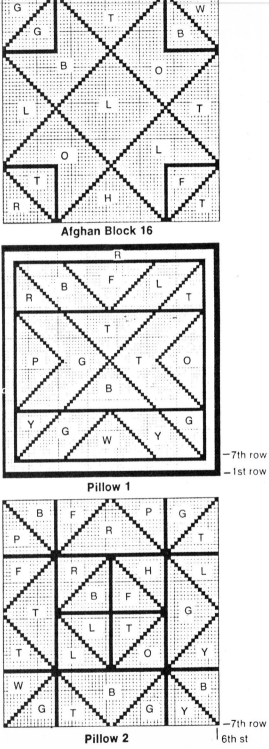

Afghan Block 16

Pillow 1

—7th row
—1st row

Pillow 2

—7th row
6th st

on hook, draw up lp in each bar across; for 2nd half of row work as for 2nd half of 1st row.

Repeating 2nd row for afghan stitch, from now on follow charts. Each square on charts equals 1 st. The 1st lp (or st) on hook is not indicated on charts. Work charts from right to left when picking up lps. The border pattern shown on chart for Pillow No. 1 should be worked on all blocks. For each block, follow pillow chart through 6th row, then on 7th row work the 1st 5 border sts of same chart (6 lps on hook), then follow 1st row of afghan chart you are making, then work border over remaining 6 sts. When afghan chart has been completed, finish with 6 border rows.

To Change Colors: For the 1st half of row pick up the designated number of lps of 1st color (in addition to the 1st lp), drop 1st color. Leaving 1″ end to be woven into work later, pick up next color by drawing up lp in next bar and in as many more bars as specified. Work 2nd half of row, working off lps with matching colors.

Last row: Sl st in each st across. Break off.

AFGHAN: Work 16 blocks following charts. Join blocks by working sl sts with black (a ridge will form on right side), following diagram for placement. With right side facing you and using black, work 1 rnd sc evenly along edges of afghan.

Fringe: Work 150 tassels evenly spaced along each narrow edge as follows: For each tassel cut three 15″-lengths of black. Holding lengths together, fold in half. Draw folded end through a st from right to wrong side of afghan and draw ends through fold. Tighten.

PILLOWS: For each pillow make 2 blocks following chart. With wrong sides facing and using black, sl st together along 3 sides. Insert inner pillow (see below) and sl st remaining side.

To Make Inner Pillow: Cut 2 pieces of muslin to size of finished block, adding ½″ all around for seam allowance. Stitch together along 3 sides. Turn and stuff with Dacron polyester. Blind-stitch last side.

RAINBOW AFGHAN*

Worked in shell-stitch pattern, this is an easy project that fairly glows in twelve different colors.

SIZE: 44″ × 58″.

MATERIALS: Spinnerin 4-Ply (Orlon-acrylic knitting worsted), 1 (4-ounce) skein each cream No. 3204, yellow No. 3242, light orange No. 3241, dark orange No. 3270, light red No. 3253, wine No. 3273, purple No. 3236, blue No. 3232, turquoise No. 3216, dark green No. 3222, medium green No. 3225, light green No. 3224; aluminum crochet hook size J (or international size 6.00 mm) **or the size that will give you the correct gauge.**

GAUGE: 4 shells = 7½″; 12 color rows = 7″.

Starting at one end with cream, ch 139. **1st row:** Work 2 dc in 4th ch from hook, * skip next 2 ch, sc in next ch, skip next 2 ch, work shell of 5 dc in next ch.

143

Repeat from * across, ending last repeat with sc in last ch. Break off. With yellow work sl st in last sc; ch 3, turn. **2nd row:** Work 2 dc in same sc as sl st, * sc in center dc of next shell, work 5-dc shell in next sc. Repeat from * across ending with sc in turning ch 3. Break off. With light orange work sl st in last sc; ch 3, turn.

Repeating 2nd row for pattern and changing colors every row, work 1 row each of light orange, dark orange, light red, wine, purple, blue, turquoise, dark green, medium green, light green, cream and yellow. Repeat this color sequence 7 times more, ending last repeat with cream.

BORDER: 1st rnd: Using purple, start at any corner and sl st evenly along edge of main section; sl st to join; ch 1, do not turn. **2nd rnd:** Inserting hook in top lp of each sl st and **through** edge of afghan, sc in each sl st around, working 3 sc in each corner; join. Break off.

RISING SUN AFGHAN

A magnificent design in colors as subtle as the dawn itself; all double crochet and chain-ones worked in stripes.

GAUGE: 5 V sts = 4''; 2 rows = 1''.

FIRST SHELL STRIP: Shell 1: Starting at center of straight edge with color C, ch 7. **1st row (right side):** In 5th ch from hook work dc, ch 1 and dc (V st made); skip next ch st, in last ch st work dc, ch 1, 2 dc, ch 1, 2 dc, ch 1 and dc (3 V sts in 1 st). Working back along other edge of starting ch, skip next ch, in next ch work a V st of dc, ch 1 and dc (this last V st is worked in same st as 1st V st, but is on opposite side of starting ch), dc at base

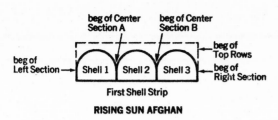

beg of Center Section A   beg of Center Section B

beg of Top Rows

beg of Left Section → | Shell 1 | Shell 2 | Shell 3 |

beg of Right Section

First Shell Strip

RISING SUN AFGHAN

of turning ch; ch 3, turn (5 V sts made).

Note: Work V sts in ch-1 sp of V st below; to increase, work in sp between V sts. Always work dc in turning ch at end of each row.

2nd row: Work V st in 1st V st, (in next V st work dc, ch 1, 2 dc, ch 1 and dc) 3 times; V st in last V st, dc in top of turning ch (3 V sts inc; total of 8 V sts); ch 3, turn. **3rd row:** * V st in each of next 2 V sts, V st in next sp between V sts. Repeat from * twice more; V st in each of last 2 V sts, dc in top of turning ch; ch 3, turn (3 V sts inc; total of 11 V sts). **4th row:** V st in each of next 3 V sts, V st in next sp, V st in each of next 2 V sts, work 2 V sts in next V st, V st in each of next 2 V sts, V st in next sp, V st in each of last 3 V sts, dc in top of turning ch (14 V sts). Break off C; attach O and ch 3, turn. **5th row:** With O, work V st in each V st across, dc in top of turning ch; ch 3, turn (14 V sts). **6th, 7th and 8th rows:** V st in each V st across, increasing 3 V sts as evenly spaced as possible; dc in top of turning ch. At end of last row, break off O, attach R and ch 3, turn. **9th row:** With R, V st in each V st across (23 V sts). **10th, 11th and 12th rows:** With R, work as for 6th row. At end of 12th row break off R, attach P and ch 3, turn. **13th row:** With P, V st in each V st across (32 V sts). **14th and 15th rows:** With P, V st in each V st across, increasing 3 V sts as before; dc in top of turning ch. **16th row:** With P, V st in each V st across (38 V sts). **17th row (mark this side for right side):** With P, work V sts across, increasing 4 V sts as before (42 V sts). Do not ch 3 at end of row. Break off. Mark 5th V st from beg of row. Put piece aside.

Shell 2: Work same as for Shell 1 through 16th row (38 V sts). Do not break off. With P, ch 3, turn. **17th row (joining row):** Working on Shell 2, work V st in each of 1st 7 V sts (marking 5th V st), V st in sp before next V st, (V st in each of next 8 V sts, V st in next sp) 3 times; V st in each of next 2 V sts. Leave the last 5 V sts unworked. Join to Shell 1 as follows: Dc in next V st on Shell 2, sc in marked V st on Shell 1, dc in same V st on Shell 2, * dc in next V st on Shell 2, sc in next V st on Shell 1, dc in same V st on Shell 2. Repeat from * until all 5 free V sts are joined, ending with dc in top of turning ch on Shell 2 sc in top of turning ch on Shell 1 (42 V sts on row). Break off.

Shell 3: Work as for Shell 2, joining Shell 3 to Shell 2 in same manner.

Background Mesh (outlined in broken lines on diagram): **Right Section:** Work as follows along side edge of Shell 3 (see diagram). **1st row:** With right side of work facing you, with B, sc in marked V st on Shell 3; ch 1, dc in next V st on shell (leave the 4 V sts below free); ch 4, turn (1 sp made). **2nd row:** Skip 1st dc and ch 1, dc in sc, ch 1, sc in next V st on shell, ch 2, sc in next V st on shell; ch 4, turn (1 sp inc; total of 2 sp). **3rd row:** Skip 1st sc and ch 2, dc in next sc, ch 1, dc in next dc, ch 1, dc in turning sp; ch 4, turn (1 sp inc; total of 3 sp). **4th row:** Skip 1st dc and ch 1, (dc in next dc, ch 1) twice; dc in next sc, ch 1, sc in next V st on shell, ch 2, sc in next V st on shell; ch 1, turn (1 sp inc; total of 4 sp). **5th row:** Skip 1st sc and ch 2, dc in next sc, work (ch 1, dc in next dc) in each dc across, ending ch 1, dc in turning sp; ch 4, turn (1 sp inc; total of 5 sp). **6th row:** Skip 1st dc and ch 1, dc in next dc, work (ch 1, dc in next dc) across, ending ch 1, dc in next sc, ch 1, sc in next V st on shell, ch 2, sc in next V st on shell; ch 1, turn (1 sp inc; total of 6 sp).

Repeat 5th and 6th rows until 11 rows have been completed (11 sp on last row). **12th row:** Work as for 6th row, but omit last ch 2, sc and ch 1 (12 sp); turn. Break off.

Left Section: Work along side edge of Shell 1 (see diagram). **1st row:** With wrong side of work facing you and leaving the 1st 4 V sts of last row free, with B, sc in 5th V st, ch 1, dc in next V st on shell; ch 4, turn (1 sp made).

Starting with 2nd row, work through 12th row in same manner as for Right Section.

Center Section A: Work as follows between Shells 1 and 2 (see diagram). **1st row:** With right side of work facing you, with B, sc in 1st free V st on Shell 2 above joining, ch 1, dc in joining st between shells, ch 1, sc in 1st free V st on Shell 1 above joining, ch 2, sc in next V st on Shell 1; ch 1, turn (2 sp). **2nd row:** Skip 1st sc and ch 2, dc in next sc, ch 1, dc in next dc, ch 1, dc in next sc, ch 1, sc in next V st on shell, ch 2, sc in next V st on shell; ch 1, turn (4 sp). **3rd row:** Skip 1st sc and ch 2, dc in next sc, work (ch 1, dc in next dc) in each dc across, ending ch 1, dc in next sc, ch 1, sc in next V st on shell, ch 2, sc in next V st on shell; ch 1, turn (2 sp inc; total of 6 sp). Repeat 3rd row 9 times more (24 sp on 12th row). Break off.

Work Center Section B in same manner between Shells 2 and 3 as shown on diagram.

Top Rows: 1st row: Attach B with sl st in corner sp at top of Right Section (see diagram); ch 4, dc in next dc, work (ch 1, dc in next dc) across Right Section (11 sp), then ch 1, dc in next sc, ch 1, * dc in same V st as sc was worked into, ch 1, dc in next free V st, work (ch 1, dc in next V st) across top of shell, ch 1, dc in same V st as sc was worked into, ch 1, dc in sc, continue to work ch 1 and dc spaces across last row of Center Section, ch 1. Repeat from * across, ending last repeat with 12 spaces across Left Section; ch 4, turn. **2nd row:** Work (ch 1, dc in next dc) across, ending ch 1, dc in last sp. Break off. First strip completed. Make 3 more strips in same manner.

FINISHING: Join strips of afghan as follows: Pin top edge of 1st strip to lower edge of 2nd strip. You will be joining the spaces on last row of 1st strip to the ends of rows on shells of lower edge of 2nd strip.

Joining: With B, sc in corner sp of 1st strip, ch 1, sc in corner sp of 2nd strip, * ch 1, sc in next sp of 1st strip, ch 1, sc in next sp of 2nd strip. Repeat from * across, adjusting joinings if necessary. Break off. Join 3rd and 4th strips to completed piece in same manner.

Border: With B, sc in any corner sp, then (ch 2, skip about ½" of edge of work, sc in next st or sp) around entire piece, increasing at corners when necessary. Break off.

Tassel Fringe: Make fringe along both long edges of afghan as follows: Cut B yarn into 12" lengths. Hold 9 strands tog and fold in half. Draw folded end through 1 corner, draw ends through loop and pull tight to form tassel. Cut P, O, R and C into 16" lengths. Holding tog 11 strands in assorted colors, make tassel about 2½" from 1st one. Alternate 1 color B tassel with 1 multicolor tassel across both edges.

SHE LOVES ME, SHE LOVES ME NOT AFGHAN

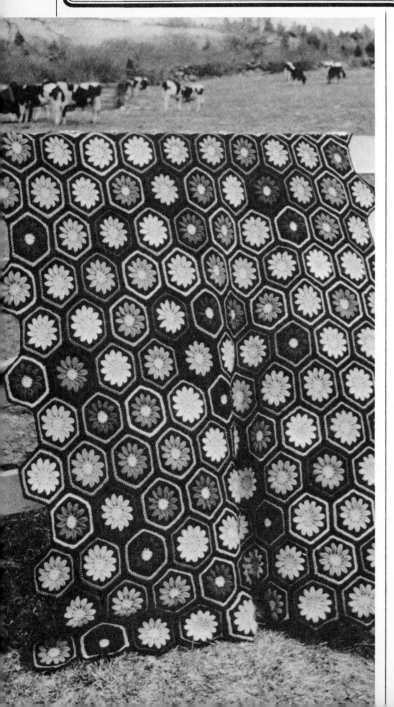

The hexagon shapes are mostly single crochet; centers are always yellow, while the petals bloom in myriad colors.

SIZE: 66" × 76".

MATERIALS: Knitting worsted, 48 ounces black for background. If you use leftover knitting worsted for the colors, you will need about 1½ ounces each of the following 24 colors: baby pink, medium pink, dark pink, baby blue, medium blue, royal blue, navy blue, gold, antique gold, dark gold, baby green, almond green, Kelly green, dusty rose, magenta, lilac, orange, dark yellow, beige, purple, peach, light brown, rust, turquoise. For hexagon centers only: 2 ounces each light yellow and medium yellow (see note below); aluminum crochet hook size G (or international size 4.50 mm) **or the size that will give you the correct gauge;** tapestry needle.

Note: You will need about 1¼ yards sport-weight yarn for center and the following amounts of knitting worsted for remainder of each hexagon: 8½ yards of one color for petal rnd, 4½ yards of another color for contrasting rnd and 20 yards black for background.

GAUGE: Each hexagon measures 6½" across center from corner to opposite corner.

HEXAGON: Always work with right side of work facing you. Use sport yarn for centers only. Make some centers with 1 shade of yellow and the rest with the other shade.

Make 158 hexagons in the following manner, varying colors for petal and contrasting rnds. Use black for all other rnds except yellow centers.

CENTER: With yellow sport yarn ch 7. Join with sl st to form ring. **1st rnd:** Ch 1, work 2 sc in each of next 6 ch sts. Join with sl st in ch 1 (12 sc). Break off. Use knitting worsted for remainder of hexagon.

2nd rnd (petal rnd): Make lp on hook and sc in any center sc, * ch 7, work sc in 2nd ch from hook, h dc in next ch, dc in each of next 2 ch, h dc in next ch, sc in last ch, work sc in next center sc. Repeat from * until 12 petals are completed, ending last petal with sl st in 1st sc. Break off.

3rd rnd: Make lp on hook with black and work dc in sc between any 2 petals of petal rnd, * ch 2, push petal forward and dc in next sc between petals. Repeat from * around, ch 2; join with sl st in top of 1st dc (12 sps made behind petals).

4th rnd: Push petals forward and work as follows: With black ch 3, * work 3 dc in next ch-2 sp, dc in next dc. Repeat from * around, ending with 3 dc in last ch sp; join with sl st in top of ch 3 (48 dc, counting ch 3 as 1 dc).

5th rnd: With black ch 1, sc in same st as sl st, sc in next dc, * insert hook in sc at tip of next petal and into next dc at same time; complete sc, attaching petal to background; sc in each of next 3 dc. Repeat from * around, ending last repeat with sc in dc after last petal (48 sc); join with sl st in 1st sc.

6th rnd: With black ch 3, work 2 dc in same st as sl st (corner made), * sc in each of next 7 sc, 3 dc in next sc (another corner made). Repeat from * around, ending sc in each of last 7 sc; join with sl st to top of ch 3 (6 corners). Break off.

7th rnd (contrasting rnd): With 1 of the contrasting colors make lp on hook. Work 3 sc in center dc of each corner and work 1 sc in each remaining st around (9 sc between corners); join and break off.

8th rnd: With black make lp on hook. Work 3 sc in center sc of each corner and 1 sc in each remaining sc around (11 sc between corners); join and break off.

Make 157 more hexagons.

FINISHING: Hold 2 hexagons with right sides together. Thread tapestry needle with black yarn and, catching back lp only of sts, whipstitch hexagons together across 1 edge from corner to corner. Break off. Continue to join hexagons in same manner, making 8 strips of 11 hexagons each and 7 strips of 10 hexagons each; then sew strips together, using diagram as guide (4 strips shown).

SHE LOVES ME,
SHE LOVES ME NOT
AFGHAN

GALAXY AFGHAN

Crochet circles and portions of circles for the center panel, then make striped bands for both sides using single- and double-crochet stitches.

SIZE: About 48″ × 67″.

MATERIALS: Brunswick Fore-'n-Aft Sport Yarn (Wintuk Orlon acrylic), 10 (1.75 oz.) balls each black No. 6060, cream (ecru) No. 60000 and dark coffee (brown) No. 60293; aluminum crochet hook size G (or international size 4.50 mm) **or the size that will give you the correct gauge.**

GAUGE: 4 sc or dc = 1″.

Afghan is composed of circles, circle sections and side panels which are made separately, then joined.

CIRCLE (make 7): With brown, starting at center, ch 6. Join with sl st to form ring. **1st rnd:** Ch 3, work 19 dc in ring (20 dc, counting ch 3 as 1 dc); join with sl st to top of ch 3. Ch 1, turn. **2nd rnd:** Sc in sl st, work sc in each dc around (20 sc); join with sl st to 1st sc; ch 3, turn. (**Note:** Piece will cup at this point but will flatten out at completion of next rnd.) **3rd rnd:** Dc in sl st, work 2 dc in each sc around (40 dc); join. Ch 3, turn. **4th rnd:** Dc in sl st, dc in each of next 3 dc, *2 dc in next dc, dc in each of next 3 dc. Repeat from * around (50 dc); join. Break off and turn. Piece should measure 4″ in diameter.

5th rnd: With white, make lp on hook; y o and

work dc in any dc on last rnd (always work 1st dc in new color in this manner), work another dc in same st, dc in each of next 4 dc, * 2 dc in next dc, dc in each of next 4 dc. Repeat from * around (60 dc); join to 1st dc. Ch 1, turn. **6th rnd:** Repeat 2nd rnd (60 sc); join. Break off and turn.

7th rnd: With black, work 2 dc in any sc, dc in each of next 5 sc, * 2 dc in next sc, dc in each of next 5 sc. Repeat from * around (70 dc); join. Ch 1, turn. **8th rnd:** Sc in sl st, sc in each of next 2 dc, 2 sc in next dc, * sc in each of next 6 dc, 2 sc in next dc. Repeat from * around ending with sc in each of last 3 dc (80 sc); join. Break off and turn. Piece should measure 6¾" in diameter. **9th rnd:** With white, make lp on hook; work as for 7th rnd, working 4 dc, instead of 5, between increases (96 dc); join. Ch 1, turn. **10th rnd:** Repeat 2nd rnd (96 sc); join. Break off and turn.

11th rnd: With black, work 2 dc in any sc, dc in each of next 5 sc, * 2 dc in next sc, dc in each of next 4 sc. Repeat from * around (115 dc); join. Ch 1, turn. **12th rnd (right side):** 2 sc in sl st, sc in next 22 dc, * 2 sc in next dc, sc in next 22 dc. Repeat from * around (120 sc); join and break off. Completed circle should measure 9½" in diameter.

CIRCLE SECTION A (make 12): With brown, starting at dot on diagram, ch 5. **1st row:** Dc in 4th ch from hook, dc in next ch (3 dc, counting ch 3 as 1 dc); ch 1, turn. **2nd row:** Sc in each dc (3 sc); ch 3, turn. **3rd row:** Dc in each of 1st 2 sc, 2 dc in next sc (5 dc); ch 1, turn. **4th row:** Sc in each dc across (5 sc); ch 3, turn. **5th row:** Dc in each sc across, working 2 dc in last sc (7 dc); ch 1, turn. **6th row:** Sc in each dc across (7 sc); ch 3, turn. **7th row:** Dc in 1st sc, work 2 dc in each sc across (14 dc); ch 3, turn. **8th row:** Dc in 1st dc, dc in each of next 4 dc, 2 dc in next dc, dc in each of next 2 dc, 2 dc in next dc, dc in each of next 4 dc, 2 dc in last dc (18 dc). Break off and turn.

9th row: With white, work 2 dc in 1st dc, dc in each dc across, working 2 dc in last dc (20 dc); ch 1, turn. **10th row:** Sc in each dc across (20 sc). Break off and turn.

11th row: With black, work 2 dc in 1st sc, dc in each of next 5 sc, 2 dc in next sc, dc in each of next 6 sc, 2 dc in next sc, dc in each of next 5 sc, 2 dc in last sc (24 dc); ch 1, turn. **12th row:** Work 2 sc in 1st dc, sc in each of next 8 dc, 2 sc in next dc, dc in next 4 dc, 2 dc in next sc, dc in next 8 dc, 2 dc in last sc (28 sc). Break off and turn.

13th row: With white, work 2 dc in 1st sc, (dc in next 8 sc, 2 dc in next sc) 3 times (32 dc); ch 1, turn. **14th row:** Sc in each dc across (32 sc). Break off and turn.

15th row: With black, work 2 dc in 1st sc, (dc in each of next 5 sc, 2 dc in next sc) twice; dc in each of next 6 sc, 2 dc in next sc, (dc in each of next 5 sc, 2 dc in next sc) twice (38 dc); ch 1, turn. **16th row (right side):** Work 2 sc in 1st dc, sc in next 15 dc, 2 sc in next dc, sc

in each of next 4 dc, 2 sc in next dc, sc in next 15 dc, 2 sc in last dc (42 sc). Break off. Completed piece should measure 5¾" from 1st row to center st of last row.

CIRCLE SECTION B (make 26): With brown, starting at X on diagram, ch 8. **1st row:** Dc in 4th ch from hook and in each of next 3 ch, 2 dc in last ch (7 dc, counting ch 3 as 1 dc); ch 1, turn. Repeat 6th through 16th rows of Circle Section A. Completed piece should measure 4½" from 1st row to center st of last row.

CIRCLE SECTION C (make 4): With brown, starting at Y on diagram, ch 5. Repeat 1st through 3rd rows of Circle Section A. **4th row:** Sc in each dc across (5 sc); ch 3, turn. **5th row:** Dc in 1st sc, (dc in next sc, 2 dc in next sc) twice (8 dc); ch 3, turn. **6th row:** Mark beg of this row as curved edge next to circle. Skip 1st dc directly below ch 3, dc in next dc and in each dc across, working 2 dc in last dc (9 dc). Break off and turn.

7th row: With white, work 2 dc in 1st dc, dc in each dc across (10 dc); ch 1, turn. **8th row:** Sc in each dc across (10 sc). Break off and turn.

9th row: With black, work 2 dc in 1st dc, dc in each sc across, working 2 dc in last sc (12 dc); ch 1, turn. **10th row:** Sc in each of 1st 4 dc, 2 sc in next dc, sc in each of next 2 dc, 2 sc in next dc, sc in each of next 4 dc (14 sc). Break off and turn.

11th row: With white, repeat 9th row (16 dc); ch 1, turn. **12th row:** Repeat 8th row (16 sc). Break off and turn.

13th row: With black, work 2 dc in 1st dc, dc in next 7 sc, 2 dc in next sc, dc in next 6 sc, 2 dc in last sc (19 dc); ch 1, turn. **14th row (right side):** Work 2 sc in 1st dc, sc in each dc across, working 2 sc in last dc (21 sc). Break off. Completed piece should measure 5¾" from 1st row to center st of last row.

CIRCLE SECTION D (make 4): With brown, starting at Z on diagram, ch 6. **1st row:** Dc in 4th ch from hook, dc in next ch, 2 dc in next ch (5 dc, counting ch 3 as 1 dc); ch 1, turn.

Repeat 4th through 14th rows of Circle Section C. Completed piece should measure 4½" from 1st row to center st of last row.

TO ASSEMBLE CENTER PANEL: Following diagram (half of afghan shown), assemble circles and

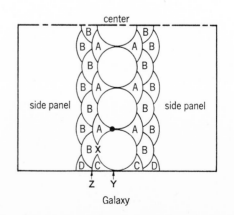

Galaxy

148

circle sections to form complete center panel. Pin, then baste circles together first, joining about 2″ of edges. Pin, then baste circle sections in place, tucking points of A and C sections slightly behind circles.

Using black yarn and working from wrong side, sl st motifs together with crochet hook, being careful to keep pieces flat.

STRIPED SIDE PANEL (make 2): With white, starting at one end, ch 50. **1st row:** Dc in 4th ch from hook and in each ch across (48 dc, counting ch 3 as 1 dc). Break off and turn. (**Note:** To avoid having to weave yarn ends through panel later, crochet over them as you go.) **2nd row:** With black, work dc in each st across; ch 1, turn. **3rd row:** Sc in each dc across (48 sc). Break off and turn.

4th row: Mark beg of this row as shaped edge next to circle sections. With brown, work 2 dc in 1st sc, dc in each sc across (49 dc); ch 1, turn. **5th row:** Sc in each dc across (49 sc); ch 3, turn. **6th row:** Work dc in 1st sc and in each sc across (50 dc); ch 1, turn. **7th row:** Sc in each dc across, working 2 sc in last st (51 sc). Break off and turn.

8th row: With white, work 2 dc in 1st sc, dc in each sc across (52 dc); ch 1, turn. **9th row:** Repeat 7th row (53 sc). Break off and turn.

10th row: With black, repeat 8th row (54 dc); ch 1, turn.

11th row: Repeat 7th row (55 sc). Break off and turn.

12th row: Repeat 8th row (56 dc); ch 1, turn. **13th row:** Repeat 7th row (57 sc). Break off and turn.

14th row: With brown, repeat 8th row (58 dc); ch 1, turn. **15th row:** Repeat 3rd row (58 sc); ch 3, turn. **16th row:** Skip 1st sc directly below ch 3, dc in each sc across (58 dc); ch 1, turn. **17th row:** Repeat 3rd row (58 sc). Break off and turn.

18th row: With white, make lp on hook; y o and insert hook in 1st sc, y o and draw up lp, y o and draw through 2 lps on hook, y o and insert hook in next sc, y o and draw up lp, y o and draw through 2 lps on hook, y o and draw through remaining 3 lps on hook (1 dc dec); dc in each sc across (57 dc); ch 1, turn. **19th row:** Sc in each dc to within last 2 dc, draw up lp in each of last 2 sts, y o and draw through all 3 lps on hook (1 sc dec; 56 sc). Break off and turn.

20th row: With black, repeat 18th row (55 dc); ch 1, turn. **21st row:** Repeat 19th row (54 sc). Break off and turn.

22nd row: Repeat 18th row (53 dc); ch 1, turn. **23rd row:** Repeat 19th row (52 sc). Break off and turn.

24th row: With brown, repeat 18th row (51 dc); ch 1, turn. **25th row:** Repeat 19th row (50 sc); ch 3, turn. **26th row:** Repeat 16th row (50 dc); ch 1, turn. **27th row:** Repeat 19th row (49 sc)m Break off and turn.

28th row: With black, repeat 18th row (48 dc); ch 1, turn. **29th row:** Sc in each dc across (48 sc). Break off and turn.

30th row: With white, work dc in each sc across (48 dc); ch 1, turn. **31st row:** Sc in each dc across. Break off and turn. Repeat 2nd through 31st rows until piece is long enough to fit along side of assembled center panel.

FINISHING: Pin and baste, then sl st side panels in place. Using black, and with right side facing you, work 1 row sc across ends of afghan.

MEDIEVAL ART BEDSPREAD**

Time-consuming but terrific: Every round within the square modules is a different color and many stitches are used. Scalloped border.

SIZE: About 77″ × 90″.

MATERIALS: Coats & Clark's Pearl Cotton No. 5, 88 (50-yard) balls black No. 12 (color B), 42 balls Spanish red No. 126 (color R), 39 balls hunter's green No. 48 (color G), 25 balls steel blue No. 108 (color S), 16 balls orange No. 11 (color O), 13 balls white No. 1 (color W), and 12 balls canary yellow No. 10-A (color Y) (see note below); steel crochet hook No. 1 **or the size that will give you the correct gauge;** tapestry needle.

Note: If you want to adjust the size of the bedspread or if you plan to make something else using this module, for each square you will need the following number of yards per color: 27 black, 14 red, 13 green, 8 blue, 4½ orange, 4 white, 4 yellow. For a less expensive

bedspread you can use a fingering-weight yarn (about 160 yards per 1-ounce skein). For the whole bedspread you will need 29 ounces black, 14 red, 13 green, 8 blue, 5 orange, 4 each white and yellow.

GAUGE: Each module measures 6¼" square.

SQUARE MODULE (make 148): Starting at center with R, ch 4. Join with sl st to form ring. **1st rnd (right side):** Ch 1, work 5 sc in ring; join with sl st to 1st sc.

2nd rnd: Ch 1, work 2 sc in each sc; join.

3rd rnd: Ch 1, * sc in next sc, 2 sc in next sc. Repeat from * around (15 sc); join. Piece should measure ¾" across.

4th rnd: * Ch 3, in next sc work joined tr as follows: ** (Y o hook) twice, insert hook in st and pull up lp, (y o and pull through 2 lps on hook) twice **. Repeat from ** to ** twice more. Y o and draw through all 4 lps on hook (joined tr made); make 3 joined tr in next sc, ch 3, sc in next sc. Repeat from * around, omitting sc on last repeat (5 petals made); join to 1st ch of ch 3. Break off.

5th rnd: With B sc in any sc between petals, * ch 3, 2 sc in next petal, ch 3, sc in next sc between petals. Repeat from * around, omitting last sc on last repeat; join.

6th rnd: Ch 4, work 2 tr in same st as sl st, * ch 2, skip next sc, sc in next sc at top of petal, ch 2, work 3 tr in next sc between petals. Repeat from * 3 times more; ch 2, skip next sc, sc in next sc at top of last petal, ch 2; join.

7th rnd: Ch 1, sc in same st as sl st and in each of next 2 tr, * work 2 sc in ch-2 lp, sc in next sc at top of petal, work 2 sc in next ch-2 lp, work sc in each of next 3 tr. Repeat from * 3 times more, 2 sc in next lp, sc in next sc, 2 sc in last ch-2 lp (40 sc); join. Break off. Piece should measure 2¼".

8th rnd: With S sl st in sc above any petal, * ch 3, in same sp work joined tr, ch 3, sl st in same sp (cl made); ch 3, skip 3 sc, sl st in next sc. Repeat from * around, joining at end (10 cl). Break off.

9th rnd: With B work sc in joined tr of any cl, * ch 3; working over next ch-3 S lp of last rnd, work sc in each of next 3 B sc on 7th rnd, ch 3, sc in joined tr of next cl. Repeat from * around, omitting last sc on last repeat; join. Break off.

10th rnd: With O sc in sc above any cl, * work 2 tr in next sc, ch 1, skip next sc, work 2 tr in next sc, sc in sc above next cl. Repeat from * 8 times more; 2 tr in next sc, ch 1, skip next sc, 2 tr in next sc; join. Break off.

11th rnd: With B sc in sc above any cl, * sc in each of next 2 tr and, working in front of ch-1 on last rnd, work tr in skipped B sc on 9th rnd, sc in each of next 2 tr, sc in next sc. Repeat from * around, omitting last sc on last repeat; join. Break off.

12th rnd: With W work h dc in sc above any cl, * 2 h dc in next sc, h dc in next sc, ch 1, skip tr, h dc in next sc, 2 h dc in next sc, h dc in next sc. Repeat from * around, omitting last h dc on last repeat; join. Break off.

13th rnd: With B work sc in any h dc before a ch-1 sp; * working in front of ch-1 sp, work h dc in skipped B tr on 11th rnd, work sc in each h dc to next ch-1 sp. Repeat from * around, ending with 6 sc (80 sts); join. Break off. Turn work.

14th rnd (wrong side): With G establish 4 corner sections as follows: Sl st in sc to the left of any h dc, * sc in each of next 8 sts, in next st work sc, ch 2 and sc; sc in each of next 8 sts, sl st in next st. Break off. Skip next sc, with G sl st in next st. Repeat from * 3 times more, omitting last sl st on last repeat. Turn work.

15th rnd (right side): With G sc in 1st sc of corner section and in each of next 2 sc, h dc in next sc, dc in each of next 2 sc, 2 dc in each of next 2 sc, 2 tr in next sc; in corner ch-2 sp work 3 tr, ch 1 and 3 tr; 2 tr in next sc, 2 dc in each of next 2 sc, dc in each of next 2 sc, h dc in next sc, sc in each of last 3 sc on corner section. Break off. Work across remaining 3 corner sections in same manner.

16th rnd: With B sc in 1st sc of any corner section, * sc in each st to ch-1 sp and, working in front of ch-1 sp, work tr in ch-2 sp of 14th (G) rnd, sc in each remaining st of corner section (30 sc and 1 tr per corner section); 2 h dc in next skipped sc on 13th (B) rnd, sc in 1st sc of next corner section. Repeat from * around, omitting last sc on last repeat; join. Break off. Mark 9th sc from each corner tr (8 markers).

17th rnd (multicolor rnd): In each marked sc with S work sl st and cl; break off (8 cl). **Circlet (make 4):** With Y ch 3 and join with sl to form ring; ch 3, work 11 dc in ring (mark 5th dc); join. Break off, leaving 1" end. Using end, tie each circlet to B tr at each corner. **R Section:** * Working along 1 side of square, skip corner tr and 1 sc, with R sl st in next sc, ch 4, work tr in each of next 4 sc, ** ch 2, skip next 2 sc, sc in cl, ch 2, skip 2 sc **, tr in each of next 10 sc Repeat from ** to ** once more; tr in each of next sc. Repeat from ** to ** once more; tr in each of next 5 sc. Break off. Repeat from * 3 times more.

18th rnd: Starting in marked st on circlet at any corner, * work 2 sc each in marked st and next st on circlet, sc in each of next 3 sts on circlet, tr in next B sc on 16th rnd, sc in top of R ch-4, sc in each of next 4 tr; ** working in front of ch-2 lp, tr in 1st skipped B sc on 16th rnd, sc in ch-2 lp, sc in sc at top of cl, sc in next ch-2 lp, tr in 2nd of next 2 skipped B sc on 16th rnd **, sc in each tr to next ch-2 lp. Repeat from ** to ** once more; sc in each of next 5 tr, tr in next B sc on 16th rnd, sc in each of 3 sc before marked st on next circlet. Repeat from * around; join. Break off.

TO ASSEMBLE: Hold 2 squares together with

right sides facing. Using B, sl st together across 1 side. Break off. Join squares to form rectangle 12 squares wide × 14 squares long.

BORDER: 1st rnd (right side): With B work 43 dc across each square, working ch 1 across each joining and 4 dc in each of 2 sc at the 4 corners.

2nd rnd (multicolor rnd): S section: With S work as follows in the 8 dc at each of 4 bedspread corners: Sc in each of 1st 3 dc, 2 sc in each of next 2 dc, sc in each of last 3 dc. Work circlets as for 17th rnd of square (mark 5th dc) and tie one at each ch-1 sp at joinings. Mark the 21st dc from each circlet along each square. **G Fans:** With G work as follows along each square: Sl st in marked st, ch 4, in same st work tr, ch 1, 2 tr, ch 1 and tr; in next st work tr, ch 1, 2 tr, ch 1 and 2 tr. Break off. One G fan per square. **Small W Clusters:** Along each square with W work in 6th st to each side of G fan as follows: Sl st in st, ch 3 and, holding back last lp on hook, work a 2-joined-dc in same st, ch 3, sl st in same st. Break off. 2 small W clusters per square. **O Shells:** Along each square in 5th st from each small W cluster work with O as follows: Sl st in st, ch 4, in same st work 3 tr, ch 2 and 4 tr. Break off.

3rd rnd: With B start in marked st on circlet at middle of 1 side. * Work sc in marked st and in each of next 4 sts on circlet, skip 3 B sts, h dc in each of next 4 sts; across O shell work sc in ch 4 and in each of next 3 tr, work 2 sc in ch 2, work sc in each of next 4 tr; skip 2 sc, h dc in next st, ** ch 2, sc in joined dc on small W cluster, ch 2 **, h dc in next 4 sts; across G fan work sc in ch 4 and tr and, working in front of ch 1, work tr in 1st G fan st, sc in each of next 2 tr, tr in 1st G fan st, sc in next tr, ch 3, sc in 2nd ch from hook (picot made), sc in next tr, (tr in 2nd G fan st, sc in each of next 2 tr) twice; skip 1st h dc in each of next 4 sts. Repeat from ** to ** once, skip 1 st, h dc in next st, work across O shell as before, skip 2 sc, h dc in next 4 sts and, starting in 4th dc from marked st on next circlet, work sc in each stitch to marked stitch. Repeat from * around, working as follows at corners: After working across O shell, skip 2 sts, sc in each of next 5 sc; across S corner section work 5 sc, picot and 5 sc; sc in each of next 5 sc to next O shell.

BIG STAR PILLOW

A single giant granny module starts with a circular motif, develops a bold star in popcorns, then finishes in double crochet.

SIZE: 21″ square.

MATERIALS: Spinnerin 4-Ply (Orlon acrylic knitting-worsted-weight) yarn, 1 (4-ounce) skein each sand No. 3237 (color A), beige No. 3205 (color B) and cinnamon No. 3257 (color C); aluminum crochet hook size G (or international size 4.50 mm) **or the size that**

will give you the correct gauge; 22″ × 44″ piece or ⅝ yard 45″-wide red-orange felt for cover; 1¼ yards 36″-wide muslin for pillow; Dacron® polyester for stuffing; 18″ zipper (optional).

GAUGE: 2-dc shell, ch 1 = 1″.

Following Star Motif directions, below, work 1 square in the following color sequence: **1st rnd**—sand; **2nd and 3rd rnds**—beige; **4th through 6th rnds**—cinnamon; **7th rnd and popcorns on all other rnds**—beige; **8th through 17th rnds**—for corner sections work alternate 1 rnd sand, 1 rnd cinnamon.

STAR MOTIF: These directions are for a 3-color motif as shown. You can, if you wish make the motif all in one color; simply omit all references to joining new colors or carrying a color across back.

Starting at center with color A, ch 4. Join with sl st to form ring. **1st rnd:** Ch 4, work 15 tr in ring (16 tr, counting ch 4 as 1 tr); join with sl st in top of ch 4. Break off. **2nd rnd:** Make lp on hook with color B; sc in any tr, * ch 4, skip next tr, sc in next tr. Repeat from * 6 times more; ch 4, join with sl st to 1st sc (8 ch-4 lps). **3rd rnd:** Sl st in 1st lp, ch 4, work 4 tr in same lp for 1st shell, * ch 1, work shell of 5 tr in next lp. Repeat from * around; ch 1, join. Break off. **4th rnd:** Make lp on hook with color C; sc in center tr of any shell, * ch 4, sc in next ch sp, ch 4, sc in last sp; ch 4, sc in center tr of next shell. Repeat from * 6 times more, ch 4, sc in lost sp; join (16 lps). **5th rnd:** Sl st to center of 1st lp and work sc in lp, * ch 4, sc in next lp. Repeat from * 14 times more; ch 4, join (16 lps). **6th rnd:** Sl st in 1st lp, ch 3, in same lp work dc, ch 3 and 2 dc (1st corner made), * (ch 1, 3-dc shell in next lp) 3 times; ch 1, in next lp work 2 dc, ch 3 and 2 dc (corner). Repeat from * twice more; (ch 1, 3-dc shell in next lp) 3 times; ch 1, join. Break off.

7th rnd (popcorn rnd): Make lp on hook with color B; make popcorn as follows: Y o and insert hook in any ch-3 sp, draw up lp and complete dc, make 3 more dc in same sp, remove hook from lp, insert hook in 1st dc, catch loose lp and draw it through st on hook, ch 1 to complete popcorn; ch 3, work another popcorn in same sp for corner; * (ch 1, popcorn in next sp, ch 1, popcorn in center dc of next 3-dc shell) 3 times; ch 1, popcorn in next sp, ch 1, in next corner sp work popcorn, ch 3 and popcorn (another corner). Repeat from * twice more; (ch 1, popcorn in next sp, ch 1, popcorn in center of next shell) 3 times; ch 1, popcorn in next sp; ch 1, join (36 popcorns). Break off.

8th rnd: Divide B into 4 balls. Make lp on hook with A; y o and work dc in any corner sp, in same sp work 1 more dc, ch 3 and 2 dc for 1st corner; break off A. To attach B, draw lp from 1 ball B through lp on hook, *(ch 1, work popcorn in next sp between popcorns) 8 times; drop B, attach A and ch 1; in next corner sp work 2 dc, ch 3 and 2 dc; break off A, attach another ball B. Repeat

from * twice more; (ch 1, popcorn in next sp) 8 times; ch 1, join and fasten but do not break off (32 popcorns). **9th rnd:** Make lp on hook with C; y o and work 2-dc shell in sp after last popcorn in any group, * ch 1, work corner in corner sp as for last rnd, ch 1, shell in next sp; break off C, pick up B at opposite end of next popcorn group and draw it loosely across backs of popcorns, draw B lp through lp on hook; (ch 1, working over long B lp, work popcorn in next sp) 7 times; drop B, attach C and ch 1, shell in next sp. Repeat from * twice more; continuing color sequence, ch 1, shell in next sp, (ch 1, popcorn in next sp) 7 times; ch 1, join and fasten but do not break off (28 popcorns). **10th rnd:** Make lp on hook with A; y o and work 2-dc shell in sp after last popcorn in any group, ch 1, shell in next sp, ch 1, * corner in corner sp, (ch 1, shell in next sp) twice; break off A, draw B from other end of popcorns across popcorns and through lp on hook, (ch 1, working over lp work popcorn in next sp) 6 times; drop B, attach A and ch 1, (shell in next sp, ch 1) twice. Repeat from * twice more; continuing color sequence, work corner in corner sp, (ch 1, shell in next sp) twice; (ch 1, popcorn in next sp) 6 times; ch 1, join and fasten but do not break off (24 popcorns).

Continue working in same manner for 5 more rnds, working 1 less popcorn on each side of square on each rnd. Work popcorns with B and alternate rows of A and C in corner sections. Break off all yarns.

16th rnd: Make lp on hook with A; work corner in any corner sp, * ch 1, shell in next sp. Repeat from * around, working corner in each corner sp; ch 1, join. Break off. **17th rnd:** With C, work as for last rnd. Do not break off.

18th rnd (border): With cinnamon, work dc in each dc and ch sp, working 3 dc in each corner sp; join. Break off.

TO MAKE PILLOW: See the last paragraph of "Rose Trio Pillows."

ROSE TRIO PILLOWS**

The same granny square is used for each, but with different color emphasis. The delightful raised-texture rose pattern is mostly double and single crochet.

SIZE: Each pillow measures 11″ square.

MATERIALS: For pink pillow: D.M.C. Pearl Cotton No. 5, 1 (53-yard) ball each No. 604 (rosy pink, color A) and No. 818 (pale pink, color B), 2 balls each No. 3326 (dusty pink, color C), No. 893 (bright pink, color D), No. 3347 (loden green, color E) and No. 919 (rust-brown, color F). **For peach pillow:** D.M.C. Pearl Cotton No. 5, 1 (53-yard) ball each No. 604 (rosy pink, color A) and No. 818 (pale pink, color B), 2 balls each No. 353 (pale peach, color C), No. 352 (peach, color D), No. 3347 (loden green, color E) and No. 919 (rust-brown, color F). **For yellow pillow:** D.M.C. Pearl Cotton No. 5, 1 (53-yard) ball each No. 973 (bright yellow, color A) and No. 744 (pale yellow, color B), 2 balls each No. 743 (golden yellow, color C), No. 741 (yellow-orange, color D), No. 3347 (loden green, color E) and No. 919 (rust-brown, color F). **For all pillows:** Steel crochet hook No. 0 **or the size that will give you the correct gauge;** 12″ × 25″ piece or ⅜ yard 36″-wide loden green felt for each pillow cover; ⅜ yard 36″-wide muslin for pillow; Dacron® polyester for stuffing; 10″ zipper (optional).

GAUGE: Each motif measures about 3½″ square.

Following directions for Flower Motif, make 9 squares, joining as you work (see photograph for placement).

FLOWER MOTIF: These directions are for a 5- or 6-color motif as shown on our pillows. You can, if you wish, make them in fewer colors or in 1 color, relying on texture alone for interest.

1st Motif: Starting at center with color A, ch 4. Join with sl st to form ring. **1st rnd:** Ch 3, work 11 dc in ring (12 dc; counting ch 3 as 1 dc); sl st in top of ch 3 to join. Break off. **2nd rnd:** Make lp on hook with B, sc in any dc on last rnd, * ch 4, skip 2 dc, sc in next dc. Repeat from * around, ending with sl st in 1st sc to join (4 ch-4 lps). **3rd rnd:** Ch 1, sc in same st as sl st, * work petal of 6 dc in next lp, sc in next sc. Repeat from * around, ending with sl st in 1st sc. Break off (four 6-dc petals made). Piece should cup. **4th rnd:** Make lp on hook with C; inserting hook through back of st, work sc in sc between any 2 petals,* ch 3, sc in back of center dc of next petal, ch 3, sc in back of next sc between next 2 petals. Repeat from * around, ending with sl st in 1st sc (8 ch-3 lps behind petals). **5th rnd:** Ch 1, sc in same st as sl st, * work 6 dc over each of next 2 lps (12-dc petal made); sc in next sc. Repeat from * around, ending

with sl st in 1st sc (four 12-dc petals made). Break off. **6th rnd:** Make lp on hook with D; sc in back of sc between any 2 petals, * (ch 4, skip 3 dc, sc in back of next dc) twice; ch 4, sc in back of next sc. Repeat from * around, ending with sl st in 1st sc (12 lps behind petals). **7th rnd:** Ch 1, sc in same st as sl st, * work 4 dc in next lp; in next lp work corner of 2 dc, sc and 2 dc; work 4 dc in next lp, sc in next sc. Repeat from * around, ending with sl st in 1st sc. Break off. **8th rnd:** Make lp on hook with E; y o, insert hook in 1st dc on last rnd and complete dc; * ch 3, skip 2 dc, sc in next dc, ch 3, skip 2 dc, work 2 dc in next sc, ch 1 (corner sp), 2 dc in next dc, ch 3, skip 2 dc, sc in next dc, ch 3, skip 2 dc, dc in next sc, dc in next dc. Repeat from * around, omitting last dc on last repeat; sl st in 1st dc. Break off. **9th rnd:** Make lp on hook with F; y o, insert hook in any corner sp and complete dc, in same sp work another dc, ch 3 and 2 dc (1st corner made); * ch 5, sc in next sc, ch 5, dc in each of next 2 dc, ch 5, sc in next sc, ch 5, in next corner sp work 2 dc, ch 3 and 2 dc (another corner). Repeat from * around, omitting corner on last repeat; sl st in 1st dc. Break off.

2nd Motif: Work as for 1st motif through 8th rnd. **9th rnd (joining rnd):** With F, work 2 dc in any corner sp, ch 1; hold both motifs tog, wrong sides facing, and sl st in center ch of adjacent corner on 1st motif; ch 1, 2 dc in same corner sp on 2nd motif, ch 2; sl st in center ch of next ch-5 lp on 1st motif; ch 2, sc in next sc on 2nd motif, ch 2; sl st in center ch of next lp on 1st motif; ch 2, dc in each of next 2 dc on 2nd motif, ch 2; sl st in center ch of next lp on 1st motif; ch 2, sc in next sc on 2nd motif, ch 2; sl st in center ch of next lp on 1st motif; ch 2, 2 dc in next corner sp on 2nd motif, ch 1; sl st in center ch of next corner sp on 1st motif; ch 1, 2 dc in same corner sp on 2nd motif (1 side joined). To complete remaining sides, repeat from * on 9th rnd of 1st motif; join. Break off.

Remaining Motifs: Work as for 2nd motif, joining 1 or 2 sides of each new motif to previous motifs as needed, and completing 9th rnd in pattern.

Border: 1st rnd: With F, work sc in each sc and dc around, working 4 sc in each ch-5 lp and 5 sc in each corner lp; join. **2nd rnd:** Ch 1, sc in each sc; join. Break off.

TO MAKE PILLOW AND COVER: Cut 2 pieces of cover fabric and 2 pieces muslin to same shape as crocheted pillow top, adding ½″ seam allowance all around. Stitch muslin pieces together, leaving 1 side open. Stuff; sew open side. With right sides facing, stitch cover fabric pieces together, leaving 1 side open; turn. Insert zipper if desired. Insert pillow and zip or sew closed. Tack crocheted piece to one side of pillow.

IN-THE-CLOVER PILLOW

A stylized four-leaf clover is the motif for these grannies; there are solid-color squares on the back.

SIZE: 14″ square.

MATERIALS: Coats & Clark's Speed-Cro-Sheen, 4 (100-yd.) balls nu-ecru No. 61-D (color A), 1 ball each mid-rose No. 46-A (color B), watermelon No. 122 (color C), Spanish red No. 126 (color D) and hunter's green No. 48 (color E); aluminum crochet hook size F (or international hook size 4.50 mm) **or the size that will give you the correct gauge;** 14″-square pillow form.

SOLID-COLOR SQUARE (make 25): Starting at center with E, ch 6. Join with sl st to form ring. **1st rnd:** Ch 3, work 2 dc in ring, ch 1, (work 3 dc in ring, ch 1) 3 times; join with sl st in top of ch 3. **2nd rnd:** Sl st to next ch-1 sp, ch 3, work 2 dc, ch 1 and 3 dc in same sp (corner made), ch 1, (work 3 dc, ch 1 and 3 dc for corner in next sp, ch 1) 3 times; join. **3rd rnd:** Sl st to next sp, ch 3, work 2 dc, ch 1 and 3 dc in same sp (corner made), ch 1, work 3 dc in next sp, ch 1, (work 3 dc, ch 1 and 3 dc in next corner sp, ch 1, work 3 dc in next sp, ch 1) 3 times; join. Break off.

THREE-COLOR SQUARE (make 4 with B, D, A; 5 with E, C, A; 3 with D, B, A; 4 with E, D, A; 3 with B, C, A; 3 with E, B, A; 2 with C, D, A; 1 with D, C, A): With 1st color, work as for Solid-Color Square through 1st rnd. Break off. **2nd rnd:** With 2nd color, form lp on hook, work 3 dc, ch 1 and 3 dc for corner in any sp, ch 1, (work 3 dc, ch 1 and 3 dc for corner in next sp, ch 1) 3 times; join. Break off. **3rd rnd:** With 3rd color, form lp on hook work 3 dc, ch 1 and 3 dc in any corner sp, ch 1, work 3 dc in next sp, ch 1, (work 3 dc, ch 1 and 3 dc in next corner sp, ch 1, 3 dc in next sp, ch 1) 3 times; join. Break off.

FINISHING: Pillow Front: Following photograph, sew 3-color squares together, being sure alternate squares have E at center. **Pillow Back:** Sew solid-color squares together. Sew 3 sides of front and back together, insert pillow form and sew 4th side closed.

SAMARRA RUG

The undulating design works up quickly; it's an easy repeat pattern composed of single-, half double- and treble-crochet stitches.

SIZE: 23″ × 39″, not including tassels.

MATERIALS: Kentucky Soft Spun rayon-and-cotton Rug Yarn, 10 (70 yd.) skeins copper No. 667 (color C), 4 skeins each red-brown No. 651 (color B) and Indian orange No. 668 (color O); aluminum crochet hook size H (or international hook size 5.00 mm) **or the size that will give you the correct gauge.**

GAUGE: 3 sts = 1″.

RUG: With color B, starting at one end, ch 71 to measure about 23″. **1st row:** H dc in 3rd ch from hook, sc in each of next 2 ch, h dc in each of next 2 ch, (dc in each of next 3 ch, tr in each of next 4 ch, dc in each of next 3 ch, h dc in each of next 2 ch, sc in each of next 2 ch, h dc in each of next 2 ch) 4 times; ch 2, turn. **2nd row:** Skip 1st st (directly below ch 2), h dc in next st, sc in each of next 2 sts, h dc in each of next 2 sts, (dc in each of next 3 sts, tr in each of next 4 sts, dc in each of next 3 sts, h dc on each of next 2 sts, sc in each of next 2 sts, h dc in each of next 2 sts) 4 times. Break off B, attach C; ch 3, turn. **3rd row:** Skip 1st st, tr in each of next 4 sts, dc in each of next 3 sts, h dc in each of next 2 sts, sc in each of next 2 sts, (h dc in each of next 2 sts, dc in each of next 3 sts, tr in each of next 4 sts, dc in each of next 3 sts, h dc in each of next 2 sts, sc in each of next 2 sts) 3 times; h dc in each of next 2 sts, dc in each of next 3 sts, tr in each of next 4 sts, dc in last st; ch 3, turn. **4th row:** Repeat 3rd row, ending with break off C, attach O; ch 2, turn. **5th row:** Repeat 2nd row, ending ch 2, turn. **6th row:** Repeat 2nd row; break off O, attach C; ch 3, turn. Repeating 3rd through 6th rows for pattern, work 2 rows each C, B, (C, O, C and B) 7 times or as necessary for desired length. Break off B.

TASSELS (make 34): Wind C around a 6″ piece of cardboard 17 times. Cut strands at one end and remove from cardboard. Lay strands flat and tie together at center with another piece of yarn. Fold strands in half and tie another strand 1″ from folded end. Tie 17 tassels to each end of rug.

155

PERUGIA RUG

Stripes in a subtle color play in shades of blue are done in single- and half- double crochet stitches.

SIZE: 23″ × 39″.

MATERIALS: Kentucky Soft Spun rayon-and-cotton Rug Yarn, 6 (70-yd.) skeins royal blue No. 639 (color R), 4 skeins parakeet (turquoise) No. 691 (color P) and 3 skeins colonial blue (light blue) No. 636 (color C); aluminum crochet hook size H (or international hook size 5.00 mm) **or the size that will give you the correct gauge.**

GAUGE: 3 sts = 1″.

RUG: With color C, starting at one end, ch 56 to measure about 19″. **1st row (wrong side):** Sc in 2nd ch from hook and in each ch across (55 sc); ch 2, turn. **2nd row:** Working in back lps only skip 1st sc (directly below ch 2), h dc in each sc across; break off C, attach R; ch 1, turn. **3rd row:** Sc in back lp of 1st h dc, * sc in next sc one row below, sc in back lp of next h dc. Repeat from * across ending last repeat with sc in top of turning ch; ch 2, turn. **4th row:** Working in back lps only, skip 1st sc, h dc in each sc across; break off R, attach P; ch 1, turn. **5th row:** Working in back lps only, sc in each h dc across, sc in top of turning ch; ch 2, turn. **6th row:** Working in back lps only, skip 1st sc, h dc in each sc across; break off P, attach R; ch 1, turn. **7th row:** Repeat 3rd row. **8th row:** Repeat 4th row, ending with break off R, attach C; ch 1, turn. **9th row:** Repeat 5th row. **10th row:** Repeat 6th row, ending with break off C, attach R; ch 1; turn. Repeat 3rd through 10th row 10 times or as necessary for desired length. Break off.

BORDER: 1st rnd: With P, with right side facing you, sc 1 rnd, evenly spaced, around outer edges, working 3 sc at each corner; join. **2nd rnd:** Working in back lps only, sc in each sc around, working 3 sc in center sc at each corner; join. Break off P, attach R. With R, repeat 2nd rnd 3 times more. Break off.

PETIT-POINT NOSEGAYS RUG

This handsome traditional design has thirty-five squares, three motifs and uses a form of single crochet that produces a thick, knitted look.

SIZE: About 40″ × 55″, not including fringe.

MATERIALS: American Thread Aunt Lydia's Heavy Rug Yarn, 11 (2½-ounce 70-yard) skeins cream (main color—MC) No. 558; 21 skeins emerald (contrasting color—CC) No. 655; 1 skein each for the accent colors: phantom red No. 140, antique gold No. 565, tangerine No. 315, sunset No. 550, yellow No. 510; aluminum crochet hook size K (or international size 7.00 mm) **or the size that will give you the correct gauge;** tapestry needle.

GAUGE: 3 sc = 1″; 3 rows = 1″. Each module measures 7½″ square.

GENERAL DIRECTIONS: We suggest making a sample square in MC first to get the right gauge and to learn the stitch.

To Work Squares: Always work with right side facing you. Do not join but mark beg of rnds.

To Work V Sts and Corners: A V st is a sc worked to look like a stockinette st. Work V sts along sides of square by inserting hook into center of V formed by st below. Corners are scs worked in usual manner by inserting hook in top lps of st below. See stitch diagram. Always pull up sts to form a long V-shape.

To Change Colors: Work last st of old color until there are 2 lps on hook. Drop old color, draw new color through the 2 lps of old color. After 2nd rnd, always carry 2 strands of yarn across back of piece, working sts over carried strands. Pull these strands every 3 or 4 sts to keep the tension even and the square firm.

FLOWER SQUARE: Using MC and CC for the major portion of each square (see directions which follow list below), make one square each using these accent colors (mark each square with numbered tag):

1. A—tangerine; B—red.
2. A—antique gold; B—sunset.
3. A—phantom red; B—antique gold.
4. A—sunset; B—buttercup.
5. A—buttercup; B—antique gold.
6. A—tangerine; B—buttercup.
7. A—antique gold; B—tangerine.
8. A—phantom red; B—buttercup.
9. A—sunset; B—tangerine.
10. A—buttercup; B—phantom red.
11. A—tangerine; B—sunset.
12. A—antique gold; B—phantom red.
13. A—phantom red; A—sunset.
14. A—sunset; B—antique gold.
15. A—buttercup; B—sunset.
16. A—tangerine; B—antique gold.
17. A—antique gold; B—buttercup.
18. A—phantom red; B—tangerine.

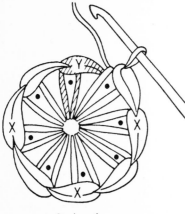

2nd rnd

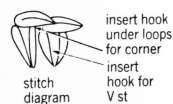

stitch diagram

insert hook under loops for corner

insert hook for V st

Starting at center with A, ch 3. Join with sl st to form ring. **1st rnd:** Work 7 sc in ring; insert hook in center of ring, y o and draw up lp, drop A but do not break off (carry A across back of work through 8th rnd only, working sts over carried strands); with B, make lp and draw through the 2 lps on hook (8 sc).

2nd rnd: With B work V st in next sc (dot in shaded st on diagram for 2nd rnd), V st in next sc (next dot), * work 2 sc in next st for corner (under lps marked X), V st in each of next 2 dots. Repeat from * twice more, work 2-sc corner in the top lps (Y) of 1st st (16 sts).

3rd rnd: With B, V st in each of next 3 sts, changing colors to CC in 3rd st, (carry B through to end of rnd; from now on you will be working over 2 carried colors); work corner with CC; (V st with B in each of next 4 sts, work corner with CC) twice; V st with B in each of next 4 sts; work corner with A; V st with B in last st, changing to CC. Break off B (24 sts).

4th through 10th rnds: Following diagram 1 from 4th rnd, V st in each st across to corner (1st of these sts is marked with white dot), * work 2 sc in corner, V st in each st across to next corner. Repeat from * twice more; work last corner, V st in each st to beg of rnd (80 sts at end of 10th rnd). (**Note:** At end of 8th rnd, break off A and attach another strand of MC to carry across work through to last rnd.) Place safety pin in corner marked X on diagram.

"X" SQUARE (make 7): Starting at center with MC, ch 3. Join with sl st to form ring. **1st rnd:** Work 8 sc in ring. Attach CC and carry through to last rnd. **2nd rnd:** With MC, work as for flower square. **3rd through 6th rnds:** Attach another strand of MC and carry all 3 strands through to last rnd. Following diagram 2, work V st in each st on each side of square and 2 sc in each corner.

"½ X" SQUARE (make 10): Following diagram 3, work as for "X" square. With pin, mark corner X shown on diagram.

FINISHING: Following Diagram 4 for placement, arrange all squares, placing those with X-marked corners as shown. Using tapestry needle and MC, cross-stitch squares together with right sides facing you, working through front lps only. Turn rug over and cross-stitch seams again to reinforce them, working through back lps only.

Border: With CC work 2 rnds of V sts around rug, working 2 sc in each corner. Continuing to work corners, work 2 rnds V st with MC, then 1 rnd with CC. With CC work a rnd of sl sts.

Tassels (make 34): Cut thirteen 12" strands of CC. Tie together at center and fold in half. Knot another strand around all strands 1" from fold. Trim. Attach 1 tassel to each corner, then space remaining tassels about 2½" apart along each end of rug.

Color Key

Diagram 1   Petit Point Nosegays

Diagram 3
Petit Point Nosegays

Diagram 2   Petit Point Nosegays

Square Placement Diagram 4
Petit Point Nosegays

POPCORN BEDSPREAD

You can carry these big squares along with you to work on (they take time but aren't difficult), but keep joining the motifs as they're completed to avoid endless sewing later on.

SIZE: 63″ by 99″.

MATERIALS: Fingering yarn, about 45 2-ounce skeins. Steel crochet hook size 2 **or the size that will give you the correct gauge.**

GAUGE: 6 dc = 1″. Each square measures approximately 12″.

Note: Bedspread is made of 40 squares sewn together, 5 squares by 8 squares and a crocheted border around outside edge.

PATTERN: Popcorn Stitch: 7 dc in same st, remove hook from work, insert in top of 1st of 7 dc, pick up dc st just dropped and pull this through lp on hook.

To Work 1st Corner Only of Each Rnd Except Rnd 1: Work (1 sc, ch 3, 3 dc, ch 3, 4 dc) in 1st ch-3 lp.

To End Each Rnd: After last ch-1, join with sl st to 3rd ch of the 1st ch-3 of that rnd, work 1 sl st in each of next 3 dc.

POPCORN SQUARE: Make 40. Ch 10, join with sl st to form ring.

1st rnd: (Ch 3, 3 dc, ch 3, 4 dc) in ring, ch 1, work * (4 dc, ch 3, 4 dc) in ring, ch 1 repeat from * twice more, end rnd—see Pattern.

2nd rnd: Work 1st corner—see Pattern—ch 1, 1 dc in next ch-1 lp, ch 1, * (4 dc, ch 3, 4 dc) in next ch-3 lp—corner made, ch 1, 1 dc in next ch-1 lp, ch 1, repeat from * twice more, end rnd.

3rd rnd: Work 1st corner, [ch 1, (1 dc in next ch-1 lp, ch 1) twice], * work corner in next ch-3 lp, work bracketed portion along next side of square, repeat from * twice more, end rnd.

4th rnd: Work 1st corner, [ch 1, 1 dc in next ch-1 lp, ch 1, 3 dc in next ch-1 lp, ch 1, 1 dc in next ch-1 lp, ch 1], * work corner in next ch-3 lp, work bracketed portion along next side of square, repeat from * twice more, end rnd.

5th rnd: Work 1st corner, [ch 1, 1 dc in next ch-1 lp, ch 1, 2 dc in next ch-1 lp, 1 dc in next dc, 1 popcorn—see Pattern, 1 dc in next dc, 2 dc in next ch-1 lp, ch 1, 1 dc in next ch-1 lp, ch 1], * work corner in next ch-3 lp, work bracketed portion along next side of square, repeat from * twice more, end rnd.

6th rnd: Work 1st corner, [ch 1, 1 dc in next ch-1 lp, ch 1, 2 dc in next ch-1 lp, 1 dc in each of next 7 dc the completion of the popcorn stitch, 2 dc in next ch-1 lp, ch 1, 1 dc in next ch-1 lp, ch 1], * work corner in next ch-3 lp, work bracketed portion along next side of square, repeat from * twice more, end rnd.

7th rnd: Work 1st corner, [ch 1, 1 dc in next ch-1 lp, ch 1, 2 dc in next ch-1 lp, 1 dc in next dc, (1 popcorn, 1 dc in each of next 3 dc) twice, 1 popcorn, 1 dc in next dc, 2 dc in next ch-1 lp, ch 1, 1 dc in next ch-1 lp, ch 1], * work corner in next ch-3 lp, work bracketed portion along next side of square, repeat from * twice more, end rnd.

8th rnd: Work 1st corner, [ch 1, 1 dc in next ch-1 lp, ch 1, 2 dc in next ch-1 lp, 1 dc in each of next 15 dc, 2 dc in next ch-1 lp, ch 1, 1 dc in next ch-1 lp, ch 1], * work corner in next ch-3 lp, work bracketed portion along next side of square, repeat from * twice more, end row.

9th rnd: Work 1st corner, [ch 1, 1 dc in next ch-1 lp,

ch 1, 2 dc in next ch-1 lp, 1 dc in next dc, (1 popcorn, 1 dc in each of next 3 dc) 4 times, 1 popcorn, 1 dc in next dc, 2 dc in next ch-1 lp, ch 1, 1 dc in next ch-1 lp, ch 1], * work corner in next ch-3 lp, work bracketed portion along next side of square, repeat from * twice more, end row.

10th rnd: Work 1st corner, [ch 1, 1 dc in next ch-1 lp, ch 1, 2 dc in next ch-1 lp, 1 dc in each of next 23 dc, 2 dc in next ch-1 lp, ch 1, 1 dc in next ch-1 lp, ch 1], * work corner in next ch-3 lp, work bracketed portion along next side of square, repeat from * twice more, end row.

11th rnd: Work 1st corner, [ch 1, 1 dc in next ch-1 lp, ch 1, 2 dc in next ch-1 lp, 1 dc in next dc, (1 popcorn, 1 dc in each of next 3 dc) 6 times, 1 popcorn, 1 dc in next dc, 2 dc in next ch-1 lp, ch 1, 1 dc in next ch-1 lp, ch 1], * work corner in next ch-3 lp, work bracketed portion along next side of square, repeat from * twice more, end row.

12th rnd: Work 1st corner, [ch 1, 1 dc in next ch-1 lp, ch 1, 1 dc in next ch-1 lp, ch 1, sk 2 dc, 1 dc in each of next 27 dc, ch 1, 1 dc in next ch-1 lp, ch 1, 1 dc in next ch-1 lp, ch 1], * work corner in next ch-3 lp, work bracketed portion along next side of square, repeat from * twice more, end row.

13th rnd: Work 1st corner, [ch 1, 1 dc in next ch-1 lp, ch 1, 3 dc in next ch-1 lp, ch 1, 1 dc in next ch-1 lp, ch 1, sk 2 dc, (1 dc in each of next 3 dc, 1 popcorn) 5 times, 1 dc in each of next 3 dc, ch 1, 1 dc in next ch-1 lp, ch 1, 3 dc in next ch-1 lp, ch 1, 1 dc in next ch-1 lp, ch 1], * work corner in next ch-3 lp, work bracketed portion along next side of square, repeat from * twice more, end row.

14th rnd: Work 1st corner, [ch 1, 1 dc in next ch-1 lp, ch 1, 2 dc in next ch-1 lp, 1 dc in each of next 3 dc, 2 dc in next ch-1 lp, ch 1, 1 dc in next ch-1 lp, ch 1, sk 2 dc, 1 dc in each of next 19 dc, ch 1, 1 dc in next ch-1 lp, ch 1, 2 dc in next ch-1 lp, 1 dc in each of next 3 dc, 2 dc in next ch-1 lp, ch 1, 1 dc in next ch-1 lp, ch 1], * work corner in next ch-3 lp, work bracketed portion along next side of square, repeat from * twice more, end rnd.

15th rnd: Work 1st corner, [ch 1, 1 dc in next ch-1 lp, ch 1, 2 dc in next ch-1 lp, 1 dc in each of next 7 dc, 2 dc in next ch-1 lp, ch 1, 1 dc in next ch-1 lp, ch 1, sk 2 dc, (1 dc in each of next 3 dc, 1 popcorn) 3 times, 1 dc in each of next 3 dc, ch 1, 1 dc in next ch-1 lp, ch 1, 2 dc in next ch-1 lp, 1 dc in each of next 7 dc, 2 dc in next ch-1 lp, ch 1, 1 dc in next ch-1 lp, ch 1], * work corner in next ch-3 lp, work bracketed portion along next side of square, repeat from * twice more, end rnd.

16th rnd: Work 1st corner, [ch 1, 1 dc in next ch-1 lp, ch 1, 2 dc in next ch-1 lp, 1 dc in each of next 11 dc, 2 dc in next ch-1 lp, ch 1, 1 dc in next ch-1 lp, ch 1 sk 2 dc, 1 dc in each of next 11 dc, ch 1, 1 dc in next ch-1 lp, ch 1, 2 dc in next ch-1 lp, 1 dc in each of next 11 dc, 2 dc in next ch-1 lp, ch 1, 1 dc in next ch-1 lp, ch 1], * work corner in next ch-3 lp, work bracketed portion along next side of square, repeat from * twice more, end rnd.

17th rnd: Work 1st corner, [ch 1, 1 dc in next ch-1 lp, ch 1, 2 dc in next ch-1 lp, 1 dc in each of next 15 dc, 2 dc in next ch-1 lp, ch 1, 1 dc in next ch-1 lp, ch 1, sk 2 dc, 1 dc in each of next 3 dc, 1 popcorn, 1 dc in each of next 3 dc, ch 1, 1 dc in next ch-1 lp, ch 1, 2 dc in next ch-1 lp, 1 dc in each of next 15 dc, 2 dc in next ch-1 lp, ch 1, 1 dc in next ch-1 lp, ch 1], * work corner in next ch-3 lp, work bracketed portion along next side of square, repeat from * twice more, end rnd.

18th rnd: Work 1st corner, [ch 1, 1 dc in next ch-1 lp, ch 1, 2 dc in next ch-1 lp, 1 dc in each of next 19 dc, 2 dc in next ch-1 lp, ch 1, 1 dc in next ch-1 lp, ch 1 sk 2 dc, work 3 dc tog, ch 1, 1 dc in next ch-1 lp, ch 1, 2 dc in next ch-1 lp, 1 dc in each of next 19 dc, 2 dc in next ch-1 lp, ch 1, 1 dc in next ch-1 lp, ch 1], * work corner in next ch-3 lp, work bracketed portion along next side of square, repeat from * twice more, end rnd. Fasten off. When 40 squares have been completed sew them together on the wrong side working through the back lps of the sts.

CROCHETED EDGING: Attach yarn in any corner of bedspread in ch-3 lp, **1st rnd:** (Ch 6—counts as 1 tr, ch 2 on all other corners of bedspread—, 1 tr, ch 2, 1 tr, ch 2, 1 tr) in ch-3 corner lp, ch 1, [sk 3 dc, work (1 tr, ch 2, 1 tr) in next dc, ch 1, sk 2 sts, (1 tr, ch 2, 1 tr) in next ch-1 lp, * ch 1, sk 3 dc, (1 tr, ch 2, 1 tr) in next dc, repeat from * 4 times more, ch 1, sk 3 dc, (1 tr, ch 1, 1 tr) in next ch-1 lp, ch 1, (1 tr, ch 2, 1 tr) in next dc, ch 1, sk 2 sts, (1 tr, ch 2, 1 tr) in next ch-1 lp, * ch 1, sk 3 dc, (1 tr, ch 2, 1 tr) in next dc, repeat from * 4 times more, ch 1, sk 3 dc, (1 tr, ch 2, 1 tr) in next ch-1 lp, ch 1, sk 2 sts, (1 tr, ch 2, 1 tr) in next dc, ch 1, ** (1 tr, ch 2, 1 tr) in ch-3 sp of joined corner of this square, ch 1, repeat from ** in joined corner of next square], repeat bracketed portion along each square on each side edge of bedspread, working the remaining three corners of the bedspread as for the 1st corner at the beginning of Rnd 1, join with sl st to 4th ch of starting ch-6.

Note: To Work Tr Cluster: In working each tr, pull yarn through lps on hook only twice instead of three times, keeping last lp of each tr on hook. After working required number of tr in this way, y o and pull through all lps on hook.

2nd rnd: Work (1 sc, ch 4—counts as 1 tr on other 3 corners—2 tr cluster) in 1st ch-2 lp, (ch 3, 1 sl st in top of tr cluster—picot made), ch 3, (3 tr cluster, 1 picot, ch 3, 3 tr cluster, 1 picot) in next ch-2 lp, ch 3, (3 tr cluster, 1 picot) in next ch-2 lp, * ch 3, 3 tr cluster, 1 picot in next ch-2 lp, repeat from * around entire bedspread, working each corner of bedspread in manner established on 1st corner of this rnd, join with sl st to 4th ch of starting ch-6. Fasten off.

JUTE BASKETS

You can do one of these casserole baskets for the table in an evening, working with heavy macramé cord and a large hook.

MATERIALS: For each basket: Ludlow Macramé Welt Cord (⁵⁄₃₂''-diameter jute, available in craft and hardware stores), 1 (280-foot) spool natural; wooden crochet hook size 16 **or the size that will give you the correct gauge.**

GAUGE: 3 sts = 2''.

CASSEROLE BASKET

SIZE: Fits 2-quart round casserole.

Starting at center of base, ch 2. **1st rnd:** Work 10 sc in 2nd ch from hook; sl st in 1st sc to join. **2nd rnd:** Ch 1, work 2 sc in each sc (18 sc); join. **3rd rnd:** Ch 1, * 2 sc in next sc, sc in each of next 2 sc. Repeat from * around (24 sc); join. **4th rnd:** Ch 1, sc in each sc; join. **5th rnd:** Ch 1, * sc in next sc, 2 sc in next sc. Repeat from * around, ending sc in last sc (36 sc); join. **6th through 10th rnds:** Repeat 4th rnd. **11th rnd:** Ch 14 for handle, skip 7 sc, sl st in each of next 12 sc, ch 14 for other handle, skip 7 sc, sl st in each of next 10 sc. **12th rnd:** Sl st in each sl st and ch st. Break off.

LOAF-PAN BASKET

SIZE: Fits 3'' × 5'' × 9'' loaf pan.

BOTTOM: Starting at 1 end of base, ch 8. **1st row:** Sc in 2nd ch from hook and in each ch across (7 sc); ch 1, turn. **2nd through 15th rows:** Sc in each sc; ch 1, turn. Base rectangle made. Do not break off but continue in rounds.

SIDES: 1st rnd: Ch 2, work 7 h dc across end (15th row) of bottom, 13 h dc across long edge, 7 h dc across other end and 14 h dc across other long edge; sl st in top of ch 2 to join. **2nd and 3rd rnds:** Ch 2, h dc in each h dc (41 h dc); join. **4th rnd:** Ch 1, sc in same place as sl st, sc in next h dc, ch 12 for handle, skip 6 h dc, sc in next 14 h dc, ch 12 for other handle, skip 6 h dc, sc in each remaining h dc; join. **5th rnd:** Sl st in each sc and ch st around; join. Break off.

MITT POTHOLDERS

The fancy but fast and easy single- and double-crochet pattern can be worked in stripes or solid colors.

SIZE: 8½'' from lower edge to top.

MATERIALS: Aunt Lydia's Heavy Rug Yarn. **For solid-color mitt:** 1 (70-yard) skein each peacock No. 740 and spring green No. 605. **For striped mitt:** 1 (70-yard) skein each peacock No. 740, spring green No. 605, brown No. 420, phantom red No. 140 and cerise No. 115. **For both mitts:** Aluminum crochet hook size G (or international size 4.50 mm) **or the size that will give you the correct gauge.**

GAUGE: In pattern st 5 groups = 3''; 3 rows = 1''.

STRIPED MITT

FIRST SIDE OF MITT: Starting at wrist edge with

peacock, ch 17 to measure about 5½". **1st row:** In 3rd ch from hook work 1 sc and 1 dc (1st group made), * skip next ch, in next ch work 1 sc and 1 dc. Repeat from * across (8 groups); ch 1, turn.

2nd row: * Skip dc, in next sc work 1 sc and 1 dc. Repeat from * across; ch 1, turn.

Repeat 2nd row 4 times more. **7th row:** Work across in pattern, ch 3 at end of row. Mark this edge for thumb. **8th row (thumb inc):** In 3rd ch from hook work 1 sc and 1 dc, continue across row in pattern as established; break off peacock, attach green; ch 1, turn.

Working in pattern with green, work even on 9 groups for 3 rows more, ending at marked edge. Do not ch 1 at end of last row. Break off green, turn.

Next row: Make lp on hook with brown. Skip 1st 2 groups, work 1 sc and 1 dc in sc of next group, continue across in pattern to end of row (7 groups); ch 1, turn. Working even in pattern on 7 groups, work 1 row more with brown, 3 rows red and 3 rows cerise.

Next row (dec row): With cerise, work in pattern across to within last group, work 1 sc in sc of last group; ch 1, turn. **Following row (dec row):** Skip 1st sc, work 1 sc and 1 dc in sc of next group, work in pattern across to within last group, work 1 sc in sc of last group; ch 1, turn. Repeat last row twice more, omitting ch 1 at end of last row. Break off.

Thumb: 1st row: Make lp on hook with brown. Starting at outer edge, work in pattern st across free green sts (2 groups); ch 1, turn. Continue in pattern on these 2 groups only for 3 rows more. **5th row (dec row):** Skip 1st dc, draw up lp in each of next 3 sts, y o hook and draw through all lps on hook. Break off. With brown, work 1 row sc evenly on all edges of thumb sts only. Break off.

SECOND SIDE OF MITT: Make another piece in same manner.

FINISHING: Edging: With red, work 1 row sc all around edges, except wrist edge, of both pieces.

Joining: With red, sew both pieces together from the right side.

Wrist Edging: With red, work around wrist edge as follows: Work 2 sc in each sc around. Break off.

Loop: Attach red with sl st to wrist at seam edge and crochet 2" chain. Sl st in each st of ch. Sew end of ch to mitten to form loop.

SOLID-COLOR MITT

FIRST SIDE OF MITT: Using only peacock, work as for Striped Mitt.

SECOND SIDE OF MITT: Using only green, make another piece in same manner.

FINISHING: Using only green, work as for Striped Mitt for edging, wrist edging, joining and loop.

LACY PLACE MAT

The pretty open pattern of long double-crochet stitches has a scalloped border and a grosgrain ribbon insert.

SIZE: 12" × 18".

MATERIALS: Coats & Clark's Speed-Cro-Sheen, 1 (100-) ball white; 2 ⅜"-wide pink grosgrain ribbon; aluminum crochet hook size I (or international hook size 5.50 mm) **or the size that will give you the correct gauge;** spray starch.

GAUGE: 4 sp and 5 long dc = 4".

CENTER SECTION: Starting at one end, ch 37 loosely to measure about 10". **1st row:** Y o, draw up 1" lp in 7th ch from hook, (y o and draw through 2 lps on hook) twice (1 long dc made). Work all long dc with 1" lp. * Ch 2, skip 2 ch, long dc in next ch. Repeat from * across (11 sp made); ch 6, turn.

2nd row: Skip dc below turning ch and 1st ch-2 sp, work long dc in next dc, * ch 2, skip next sp, long dc in next dc. Repeat from * across, ending with ch 2, long dc in 3rd ch of turning ch; ch 6, turn.

Repeat 2nd row for pattern until 18th row is completed. When stretched, piece should measure 15" from beg. At end of last row ch 5 but do not turn or break off.

BORDER: Work dc in regular manner (not long dc). **1st rnd:** Work across one long edge to 1st corner as follows: Dc in 1st sp, ch 1, dc in top of next long dc, * ch 1, dc in next sp, ch 1, dc in top of next long dc. Repeat from * across to within corner sp. In corner sp work (ch 1 and dc) 3 times; ch 1, dc in next long dc. Repeat from * around, working a corner in each of next 2 corner sp, and ending rnd with (ch 1 and dc) twice in last corner; ch 1, join with sl st in 4th ch of ch 5.

2nd rnd: Sl st in 1st sp, ch 4, dc in same sp, work (ch 1 and dc) 3 times more in same sp, * skip next sp, sc in next sp, skip next sp, work (ch 1 and dc) 4 times in next sp (4-dc shell made). Repeat from * around, working a

5-dc shell in each corner sp; join with sl st and break off.

FINISHING: Spray lightly with water or spray starch. Mark off a rectangle 12″ × 18″ on brown paper. Place paper on ironing board or hard surface for pinning. Using rustproof pins, stretch and pin place mat face down to size of rectangle. Spray back of mat until thoroughly saturated with spray starch. Let dry completely. Remove pins.

Starting at 1 corner, weave ribbon in and out of 1st rnd of border. Tie ends in bow.

MIGHTY MOUSE

All single crochet, kitty's toy has big ears, string whiskers, cotton stuffing, no feet. He's cute enough to be a child's toy, too.

SIZE: About 6¼″ long.
MATERIALS: Small amount of gray sport-weight yarn for body and ears; pink yarn for inner ears; scrap of red yarn for eyes; white string for whiskers; steel crochet hook No. 0 **or the size that will give you the correct gauge;** small amount of cotton or gray yarn for stuffing.

GAUGE: 6 sc = 1″.

Starting at tip of nose with gray, ch 2. **1st rnd:** Work 4 sc in 2nd ch from hook. Do not join but mark beg of each rnd. **2nd rnd:** (Work sc in 1st sc, 2 sc in next sc) twice (6 sc). **3rd rnd:** (Sc in each of next 2 sc, 2 sc in next sc) twice (8 sc). **4th through 10th rnds:** Sc in each sc around, increasing 2 sc evenly spaced every rnd (22 sc). **11th rnd:** Sc in each sc around. **12th rnd:** Sc in each sc, increasing 4 sc evenly around (26 sc). Repeat 11th and 12th rnds 3 times more (32 sc). **19th and 20th rnds:** Sc in each sc. Stuff half of mouse completed, then continue to stuff mouse as you work. **21st rnd:** Sc in each sc, decreasing 4 sc evenly spaced around (**to dec 1 sc,** draw up lp in each of 2 sc, y o and draw through all 3 lps on hook). **22nd rnd:** Sc in each sc around. Repeat 21st and 22nd rnds 6 times more (4 sc). Do not break off.

Tail: Sl st in next sc, ch 8, sl st in 2nd ch from hook and in each ch across. Break off.

Inner Ear (make 2): With pink ch 5. Join with sl st to form ring. **1st rnd:** Work 8 sc in ring. **2nd rnd:** Work 2 sc in each sc around. Break off. **Outer Ear (make 2):** With gray work as for inner ear. **3rd rnd:** * Sc in each of 1st 2 sc, 2 sc in next sc. Repeat from * around, ending sc in last sc (21 sc). **4th rnd:** Sl st in each of 1st 3 sc, sc in each sc around to within last 3 sc. Break off. Sew an inner ear to center of each outer ear. Following photograph for placement, sew ears along sl-st edge to body.

Eyes: With red work small straight stitches.

Whiskers: Cut three 3″ lengths of string. Fold in half and pull loop through face on 1 side of nose. Draw ends through loop and pull to tighten. Work whiskers on other side of nose in same manner.

4

Fashions For Men

FATHER-SON CARDIGANS

Instructions for this classic cardigan with raglan sleeves and two worked-in pockets allow you to adopt it for mother and daughter as well.

CHILDREN'S SIZES

SIZES: Child's 4 [6–8–10–12–14] fits chest size 23″ [24″–26″–28″–30″–32″]. Sweater measures 12½″ [13″–14″–15″–16″–17″] across back at underarms and 15″ [16½″–18″–19½″–21″–22½″] from back of neck to lower edge.

MATERIALS: 3 [3–4–4–5–5] (4-ounce) skeins knitting-worsted-weight yarn; aluminum crochet hook size G (or international size 4.50 mm) **or the size that will give you the correct gauge;** tapestry needle; five ¾″-diameter buttons.

GAUGE: 4 sts = 1″; 11 pattern rows = 4″.

Note: To inc or dec in pattern: Work regular dc instead of tr cross at beg or end of row; work increased sts into pattern later. Turning ch 3 always counts as 1st dc.

To inc 1 sc at beg and end of row: Work 2 sc in 1st st (1 sc inc); sc in each st across to within last st; 2 sc in last st (1 sc inc); ch 3, turn.

To inc 1 dc at beg and end of row: Dc in 1st st (1 dc inc); work across in pattern to within last 2 sts (working tr crosses over previous tr crosses); work 2 dc in next st; dc in turning ch; ch 1, turn.

To dec 1 sc at beg and end of row: Draw up lp in each of 1st 2 sts, y o and draw through all 3 lps on hook (1 sc dec); sc in each st across to within last 2 sts, dec 1 sc; ch 3, turn.

To dec 1 dc at beg and end of row: Skip 1st st (the one directly below turning ch); (y o, insert hook in next sc and draw up lp) twice, (y o and draw through 2 lps on hook) 4 times (1 dc dec); work across in pattern to within last 2 sts; dec 1 dc; ch 1, turn.

BODY: Back, left front and right front are worked in one piece without side seams. Starting at lower edge inside border, ch 101 [107–113–119–131–137]. **1st row (right side):** Dc in 4th ch from hook and in next ch, * skip next 2 ch, tr in next ch; working behind tr, dc in 1st of the 2 skipped sts, then in 2nd skipped st (1 tr cross made); dc in each of next 3 ch. Repeat from * across (99 [105–111–117–129–135] sts, counting ch 3 as 1 dc); ch 1, turn. **2nd row:** Sc in each st across; ch 3, turn. **3rd row:** Skip 1st sc (directly below ch 3), dc in each of next 2 sc; * work tr cross over next 2 sc as follows: Y o hook twice, insert hook from right to left around post of 2nd st (center st) of tr cross 2 rows below (see direction of arrow in diagram, below), y o and draw up lp, (y o and draw through 2 lps on hook) 3 times; working behind tr, dc in each of 2 skipped sc on last row (1 tr cross made); skip next sc, dc in each of next 3 sc. Repeat from * across; ch 1, turn.

Repeat last 2 rows for pattern until piece measures 3″ [3½″–4″–4½″–5″–5″] from beg, ending with a wrong-side (sc) row. Do not break off; set piece aside.

Pocket Liners (make 2): Starting at lower edge of liner with another skein of yarn, ch 16 [16–18–18–20–22]. **1st row (right side):** Dc in 4th ch from hook and in each ch across (14 [14–16–16–18–20] dc); ch 1, turn. **2nd row:** Sc in each dc across; ch 3, turn. **3rd row:** Skip 1st sc, dc in next sc and in each sc across; ch 1, turn.

tr cross

Repeat last 2 rows until piece measures 2½" [3"–3½"–4"–4½"–4½"], ending with a wrong-side (sc) row. Break off.

Pocket Opening: Next row (right side): Pick up body piece and work 3rd pattern row across 1st 6 [7–7–8–8–8] sc; pick up and work in pattern across 14 [14–16–16–18–20] sts of last row of right pocket liner, skipping corresponding 14 [14–16–16–18–20] sc on body; work in pattern across next 59 [63–65–69–77–79] sc on body; work across left pocket liner as before, skipping corresponding sts on body; work across remaining 6 [7–7–8–8–8] sts on body (99 [105–111–117–129–135] sts); ch 1, turn.

Work even in body pattern until piece measures 8½" [9½"–10½"–11½"–12½"–13½"] from beg or 1" less than desired length to underarms, ending with a right-side (dc) row.

To Divide for Back and Fronts: Left Front: Next row (wrong side): Sc in next 22 [23–25–26–30–31] sts for left front (do not work over next 5 sts but mark them for left underarm); ch 3, turn. Keeping in established pattern and **working on left front sts only,** dec 1 st at arm edge every row 14 [15–16–17–20–21] times and **at the same time** dec 1 st at neck edge every other row 7 [7–8–8–9–9] times (working neck edge even after decs are completed). At end of arm-edge decs fasten off remaining st. (**Note:** Armhole should measure about 5" [5½"–6"–6½"–7"–7½"] vertically.)

Back: Next row (wrong side): Skip marked sts for underarm on dividing row; sc in next st and in each of following 44 [48–50–54–58–62] sts for back (mark next 5 sts for right underarm); ch 3, turn. Keeping in established pattern and **working on back sts only,** dec 1 st at each arm edge (beg and end of row) every row 14 [15–16–18–20–21] times (17 [19–19–19–19–21] sts). Break off.

Right Front: Next row (wrong side): Skip marked sts for underarm on dividing row; sc in next st and in each st across. Work as for left front, reversing all shaping.

SLEEVES: Starting at lower edge above border, ch 29 [29–29–35–35–35]. Work pattern as for body, increasing 1 st at beg and end of row every 1½" [1½"–1½"–2"–2"–2"] 5 [6–7–5–6–7] times. Work even on 37 [39–41–43–45–47] sts until sleeve measures 9½"

[10½"–11½"–12½"–14"–15½"] or 1" less than desired length to underarm, ending with a right-side (dc) row.

To Shape Raglan Armholes: Next row (wrong side): Sl st across 1st 3 sts, sc in next st and in each st across to within last 3 sts (31 [33–35–37–39–41] sts); ch 3, turn. Keeping in established pattern, dec 1 st at beg and end of every other row 1 [1–1–1–3–3] times, then every row 12 [13–14–15–14–15] times (5 sts). Break off.

FINISHING: Sew sleeves into raglan armholes. Sew sleeve seams. Blindstitch remaining 3 sides of each pocket liner to wrong side of each front.

Lower Border: 1st row (right side): Sc in end st of foundation ch at lower left front corner, sc in each of next 5 sts along lower edge, skip next st, * sc in next 6 sts, skip next st. Repeat from * across, sc in any remaining sts to lower right front corner; ch 1, turn. **2nd row:** Sc in each sc across; ch 1, turn. Repeat last row 3 times more, ending at lower right front corner; ch 1, turn work sideways.

Front Border: 1st row (right side): Sc evenly across right front edge, around neck and across left front edge; ch 1, turn. **2nd row:** Sc in each sc across; ch 1, turn. Mark left front for buttonholes on boy's sweater or right front on girl's sweater, placing 1st marker at 1st row of neck shaping, last marker ¾" up from lower edge and the others evenly spaced between. **3rd row:** Sc in each sc across, skipping 2 sc at each marker and working ch 2 over the 2 skipped sts for each buttonhole; ch 1, turn. Repeat 2nd row twice more. Break off. Sew on buttons.

Cuffs: Work as for lower border. Break off.

Pocket Borders: Work 3 rows sc across top of pocket. Break off. Sew sides of border to sweater.

ADULTS' SIZES

SIZES: Chest/bust measurement, 34" [36"–38"–40"–42"–44"–46"–48"]. Sweater measures 18" [19"–20"–21"–22"–23"–24"–25"] across back at underarms and 23" [24"–25"–26"–27"–28"–28½"–29½"] from back neck to lower edge.

MATERIALS: 6 [6–7–8–8–9–9–9] (4-ounce) skeins knitting-worsted-weight yarn; aluminum crochet hook size G (or international size 4.50 mm) **or the size that will give you the correct gauge;** tapestry needle; six 1"-diameter buttons.

GAUGE: 4 sts = 1"; 11 pattern rows = 4".

Note: For all increasing and decreasing see note after gauge under Children's Sizes.

BODY: Back, left front and right front are worked in one piece without side seams. Starting at lower edge inside border, ch 143 [155–161–167–179–185–191–203]. **1st row (right side):** Dc in 4th ch from hook and in next ch, * skip next 2 ch, tr in next ch; working behind tr, dc in 1st of the 2 skipped sts, then in 2nd skipped st (1 tr cross made); dc in each of next 3 ch. Repeat from * across (141 [153–159–165–177–183–189–201] dc, counting ch 3 as 1 dc); ch 1, turn. **2nd row:** Sc in each st across; ch 3, turn. **3rd row:** Skip 1st sc (directly below ch 3), dc in each of next 2 sc, * work tr cross over next 2 sc as follows: Y o hook twice, insert hook from right to left around post of 2nd st (center st) of tr cross 2 rows below (see direction of arrow in diagram, at left), y o and draw up lp, (y o and draw through 2 lps on hook) 3 times; working behind tr, dc in each of 2 skipped sc on last row (1 tr cross made); skip next sc, dc in each of next 3 sc. Repeat from * across; ch 1, turn.

Repeat last 2 rows for pattern until piece measures 5½", [5½"–6"–6"–6½"–6½"–6½"–7"] from beg, ending with a wrong-side (sc) row. Do not break off ; set piece aside.

Pocket Liners (make 2): Starting at lower edge of liner with another skein of yarn, ch 24 [26–26–26–28–28–28–30]. **1st row (right side):** Dc in 4th ch from hook and in each ch across (22 [24–24–24–26–26–26–28] dc); ch 1, turn. **2nd row:** Sc in each dc across; ch 3, turn. **3rd row:** Skip 1st sc, dc in next sc and in each sc across; ch 1, turn.

Repeat last 2 rows until piece measures 4½" [4½"–5"–5"–5½"–5½"–5½"–6"], ending with a wrong-side (sc) row. Break off.

Pocket Opening: Next row (right side): Pick up body piece and work 3rd pattern row across 1st 8 [8–8–9–9–9–9–9] sc; pick up and work in pattern across 22 [24–24–24–26–26–26–28] sts of last row of right pocket liner, skipping corresponding 22 [24–24–24–26–26–26–28] sc on body; work in pattern across next 81 [89–95–99–107–113–119–127] sc on body; work across left pocket liner as before, skipping corresponding sts on body; work across remaining 8 [8–8–9–9–9–9–9] sts on body (141 [153–159–165–177–183–189–201] sts); ch 1, turn.

Work even in body pattern until piece measures 13½" [14"–14½"–15"–15½"–16"–16"–16½"] from beg or 1" less than desired length to underarms, ending with a right-side (dc) row.

To Divide for Back and Fronts: Left Front: Next row (wrong side): Sc in next 32 [35–36–37–40–41–42–45] sts for left front (do not work over next 5 [6–6–6–7–7–7–8] sts but mark them for left underarm); ch 3, turn. Keeping in established pattern and **working on left front sts only,** dec 1 st at arm edge every row 22 [24–25–26–28–29–30–32] times and **at same time** dec 1 st at neck edge every other row 9 [10–10–10–11–11–11–12] times (work neck edge even after neck decs are completed). At end of arm edge decs fasten off remaining st. **(Note:** Armhole should measure about 8"

[8½"–9"–9½"–10"–10½"–11"–11½"] vertically.)

Back: Next row (wrong side): Skip marked sts for underarm on dividing row; sc in next st and in each of following 66 [70–74–78–82–86–90–94] sts for back (mark next 5 [6–6–6–7–7–7–8] sts for right underarm); ch 3, turn. Keeping in established pattern and **working on back sts only,** dec 1 st at each arm edge (beg and end of row) every row 22 [24–25–26–28–29–30–32] times (23 [23–25–27–27–29–31–31] sts). Break off.

Right Front: Next row (wrong side): Skip marked sts for underarm on dividing row; sc in next st and in each st across. Work as for left front, reversing all shaping.

SLEEVES: Starting at lower edge above border, ch 41 [41–41–41–47–47–47–47]. Work pattern as for body, increasing 1 st at beg and end of row every 2½" [2"–2"–2"–2"–2"–1½"–1"] 5 [6–7–8–7–8–10–12] times. Work even on 49 [51–53–55–59–61–65–69] sts until sleeve measures 16½" [16½"–17"–17"–17½"–17½"–18"–18"] or 1" less than desired length to underarm, ending with dc row.

To Shape Raglan Armholes: Next row (wrong side): Sl st across 1st 3 [3–3–3–4–4–4–4] sts, sc in next sc and in each st across to within last 3 [3–3–3–4–4–4–4] sts (43 [45–47–49–51–53–57–61] sts); ch 3, turn. Keeping in established pattern, dec 1 st at beg and end of every other row 3 [4–4–4–5–5–4–4] times, then every row 16 [16–17–18–18–19–22–24] times (5 sts). Break off.

FINISHING: Sew sleeves into raglan armholes. Sew sleeve seams. Blindstitch remaining 3 sides of each pocket liner to wrong side of each front.

Lower Border: 1st row (right side): Sc in end st of foundation ch at lower left front corner, sc in each of next 5 sts along lower edge, skip next st, * sc in next 6 sts, skip next sc. Repeat from * across, sc in any remaining sts to lower right corner; ch 1, turn. **2nd row:** Sc in each st across; ch 1, turn. Repeat last row 3 times more, ending at lower right front corner; ch 1, turn work sideways.

Front Border: 1st row (right side): Sc across right front edge, around neck and across left front edge; ch 1, turn. **2nd row:** Sc in each st across; ch 1, turn. Mark left front for buttonholes on man's sweater or right front on woman's sweater, placing 1st marker at 1st row of neck shaping, last marker ¾" up from lower edge and the others evenly spaced between. **3rd row:** Sc in each sc across, skipping 2 sc at each marker and working ch 2 over the 2 skipped sts for each buttonhole; ch 1, turn. Repeat 2nd row twice more. Break off. Sew on buttons.

Cuffs: Work as for lower border. Break off.

Pocket Borders: Work 3 rows sc across top of pocket. Break off. Sew sides of borders to sweater.

HIS-HER COUNTRY HATS

Use up leftover yarn for these—several strands are held together and worked on a large hook; basically single crochet.

SIZE: Hat is written in one size; it can be adjusted to fit all sizes.

WOMAN'S HAT

MATERIALS: See note below. **For one hat:** 5 ounces of knitting-worsted-weight yarn—about ½ ounce in each of the following colors: light heather gray (color A), dark red (color B), orange (color C), royal blue (color D), rose (color E), yellow (color F), medium green (color G), rosy pink (color H), baby ombre (color I) and black (color J); 3 ounces sport-weight yarn—about ¾ ounce in each of the following colors: magenta (color KK), dark charcoal gray (color LL), Kelly green (color MM) and white (color NN), aluminum crochet hook size K (or international size 7.00 mm) **or the size that will give you the correct gauge;** 1 yard 1″-wide grosgrain ribbon.

Note: We have specified the colors used in our hat, but you can use leftover yarns in any color combination and vary the colors at random. Be sure to use both knitting-worsted-weight yarn and sport-weight yarn together for the correct gauge. For one hat you need a total of 5 ounces of knitting-worsted-weight yarn in 10 colors and a total of 3 ounces of sport-weight yarn in 4 colors.

GAUGE: With 2 strands knitting worsted and 1 strand sport-weight yarn held together: 8 sc = 3″; 8 sc rnds = 2½″.

Crown: Starting at center top with 1 strand each A, B and KK, ch 5; join with sl st to form ring. **1st rnd (right side):** Ch 3, work 9 dc in ring; join with sl st to top of ch 3. Mark beg of each rnd but do not join rnds from now on. **2nd rnd:** Ch 1, work 2 sc in sp before next dc, * skip next dc, work 2 sc in sp before next dc. Repeat from * around, ending with 2 sc in sp before ch 3 (20 sc). **3rd rnd:** Work sc in each sc around. **4th rnd:** * Sc in next sc, 2 sc in next sc (1 sc inc). Repeat from * around (30 sc). **5th rnd:** * Sc in each of next 2 sc, 2 sc in next sc. Repeat from * around (40 sc). **6th rnd:** * Sc in each of next 4 sc, 2 sc in next sc. Repeat from * around (48 sc). **7th rnd:** * Sc in each of next 7 sc, 2 sc in next sc. Repeat from * around (54 sc). **8th rnd:** Sc in each of next 8 sc, 2 sc in next sc. Repeat from * around (60 sc). Piece should measure about 6″ in diameter.

From now on work even on 60 sc in stripe pattern

as follows: **Stripe 1: 1st rnd:** Sc in each of 1st 3 sc; break off B; attach C. With 1 strand each A, C and KK, sc in each sc to end of rnd (60 sc). **2nd rnd:** Sc in each sc around. **3rd rnd:** Sc in each sc around to within last 3 sc of rnd; break off KK; attach LL and sc in each of next 3 sc.

Continue in stripe pattern of 3 rnds each in the following colors, changing colors at various places on hat, either a few sts before or after marker, as before. **Stripe 2:** Use 1 strand each A, C and LL. **Stripe 3:** Use 1 strand each, A, D and MM. **Stripe 4:** Use 1 strand each D, E and NN. **Stripe 5:** Use 1 strand each D, F and NN, ending with last sc of last rnd at marker. Piece should measure about 8″ from center to edge. Break off colors D and F.

Brim: 1st rnd: With 1 strand each G, H and NN, sc in each sc around, increasing 1 sc in every 5th sc (72 sc). **2nd rnd:** Sc in each sc around. **3rd rnd:** With 1 strand each G, I and NN, sc in each sc around, increasing 1 sc in every 12th sc (78 sc). **4th rnd:** Sc in each sc around, increasing 10 sc as evenly spaced as possible (88 sc). **5th rnd:** With 1 strand each G, J and NN, sc in each sc around, increasing 1 sc in every 8th sc (99 sc). **6th rnd:** Sc in each sc around; join with sl st in each of next 2 sc. Break off.

Sew ribbon to inside of hat, adjusting it to fit head size.

MAN'S HAT

MATERIALS: See note below. **For one hat:** 5 ounces knitting-worsted-weight yarn—about 1 ounce in each of the following colors: black (color A), light heather gray (color B), light rust (color C), brown (color D) and beige (color E); 3 ounces sport-weight

169

yarn—about ¾ ounce in each of the following colors: camel (color FF), dark rust (color GG), light brown (color HH) and natural (color II); aluminum crochet hook size K (or international size 7.00 mm) **or the size that will give you the correct gauge;** 1 yard 1″-wide grosgrain ribbon.

Note: We have specified the colors used in our hat, but you can use leftover yarns in any color combination and vary the colors at random. Be sure to use both knitting-worsted-weight yarn and sport-weight yarn for the correct gauge. For one hat you need a total of 5 ounces knitting-worsted-weight yarn in 5 colors and a total of 3 ounces sport-weight yarn in 4 colors.

GAUGE: With 2 strands knitting worsted and 1 strand sport-weight yarn held together: 8 sc = 3″; 8 sc rnds = 2½″.

Crown: Work as for crown on woman's hat but use the following colors: 1 strand each A, B and FF until 8th rnd is completed (60 sc). From now on work even on 60 sc in stripe pattern as follows: **Stripe 1: 1st rnd:** Sc in each of 1st 3 sc; break off B and FF; attach C and GG. With 1 strand each A, C and GG, sc in each sc to end of rnd (60 sc). **2nd rnd:** Work 1 sc in each sc around. **3rd rnd:** Sc in each sc around to within last 3 sc of rnd; break off A and C; attach B and D; then with B, D and GG, sc in each of next 3 sc.

Continue in stripe pattern of 3 rnds each in the following colors, changing colors at various places on hat, either a few sts before or after marker, as before. **Stripe 2:** Use 1 strand each B, D and GG. **Stripe 3:** Use 1 strand each B, E and HH. **Stripe 4:** Use 1 strand each E, D and HH. **Stripe 5:** Use 1 strand each D, B and II, ending with last sc of last rnd at marker. Piece should measure about 8″ from center. Break off color II.

Brim: Work as for brim on woman's hat but use the following colors: **1st, 2nd, and 3rd rnds:** Use 1 strand each B, D and GG. **4th, 5th and 6th rnds:** Use 1 strand each D, A and GG.

Sew ribbon to inside of hat, adjusting it to fit head size.

NATTY CAP*

Easy as well as quick, it's all single-crochet stitch worked in one piece.

SIZE: Fits 22″ head.

MATERIALS: Lily Sugar-'n-Cream (100% cotton yarn), 3 (125-yd.) balls rust No. 129; aluminum crochet hook size K (or international hook size 7.00 mm) **or the size that will give you the correct gauge.**

GAUGE: 7 sc = 3″.

Note: Use 2 strands yarn held together.

CROWN: Starting at top, ch 2. **1st rnd:** Work 6 sc in 2nd ch from hook; join with sl st in turning ch 1. **2nd rnd:** Work 2 sc in each sc around (12 sc); join. **3rd rnd:** Ch 1, (sc in next sc, 2 sc in next sc) 6 times (18 sc); join. **4th rnd:** Ch 1, (sc in each of next 2 sc, 2 sc in next sc) 6 times (24 sc); join. **5th through 9th rnd:** Continuing in same manner, inc 6 sc on each rnd (54 sc). **10th rnd:** Ch 1, sc in each sc, increasing 3 sc; join. **11th rnd:** Ch 1, sc in each sc around; join. Repeat 11th rnd 13 times. Turn.

CUFF: With wrong side of crown facing you, repeat 11th rnd 6 times for cuff. Break off. Block to desired shape.

170

BULKY SCARF

Work lengthwise and crochet the thick fringe as you go.

SIZE: Scarf measures 9″ × 70″, including fringe.

MATERIALS: Knitting-worsted-weight yarn: 10 ounces camel (color A), 2 ounces each orange (color B) and rust (color C); aluminum crochet hooks sizes I and K (or international sizes 5.50 mm and 7.00 mm) **or the sizes that will give you the correct gauge.**

GAUGE: With I hook, 2 dc = 1″; 2 rows = 1″.

CROCHETED BASE: With size I hook and color A, ch 301 for foundation chain. Break off and set aside. **1st row (right side):** With I hook and A, ch 15 for fringe, pick up foundation chain and work dc in 16th st from end (15 free ch sts at beg of foundation ch form another fringe), * ch 1, skip next st on foundation chain, dc in next st. Repeat from * across to within last 15 sts, ch 15 for fringe. Break off (2 chain fringes at each end). **2nd row (right side):** Ch 15 for fringe, dc in 1st dc, * ch 1, dc in next dc. Repeat from * across, ch 15 for fringe. Break off. Repeat 2nd row 15 times more.

STRIPE PATTERN: Always work with right side facing you and begin at same end of scarf for each stripe.

To Work Stripe: With K hook and yarn double follow Color Sequence (below) and ch 12 for fringe. Insert hook in sp between 1st 2 dc; working loosely, y o and bring lp through scarf and through lp on hook (1 sl st made), * insert hook in next sp between dcs, y o and bring lp through scarf and through lp on hook (another sl st made). Repeat from * across, working sl st around last dc; ch 12 for fringe. Break off.

Color Sequence: Work 1 sl-st stripe over each dc row in the following colors: 1 row each A, B and A, 2 rows C, 1 B, 2 A, 1 C, 2 A, 1 B, 2 C, 1 row each A, B and A.

TWEEDY SLIPPERS

Slippers that are accented with solid color and worked in single-crochet stitch need only a bit of shaping.

SIZE: Man's medium (9–10).

MATERIALS: Knitting-worsted-weight yarn, 4 ozs. each blue (color A) and beige (color B); aluminum crochet hook size J (or international hook size 6.00 mm) **or the size that will give you the correct gauge;** tapestry needle.

GAUGE: With 2 strands held together: 3 st = 1″; 6 rows = 1″.

SOLE: With 2 strands A and 1 B held together, starting at toe, ch 6. **1st row:** 2 sc in 2nd ch from hook, sc in each of next 3 ch, 2 sc in last ch (7 sc); ch 1, turn. **2nd row:** Sc in each of 1st 3 sc, 2 sc in next sc (inc made), sc in each of next 3 sc; ch 1, turn. **3rd row:** Inc in 1st sc, sc in each of next 6 sc, inc in last sc (10 sc); ch 1, turn. **4th row:** Sc in each sc across; ch 1, turn. Repeat 4th row

22 times more. **27th row:** Draw up lp in each of next 2 sc, y o and draw through all 3 lp on hook (1 sc dec); sc in each of next 2 sc, dec 1 sc, sc in next 2 sc, dec 1 sc (7 sc); ch 1, turn. **28th row:** Repeat 4th row. **29th row:** Dec 1 sc, sc in each of next 3 sc, dec 1 sc. Break off.

BACK AND SIDES OF UPPER: With 1 strand each A and B held together, starting at middle of 1 side, ch 16. Work in vertical rows as follows: **1st row:** Marking beg of row for lower edge, sc in 2nd ch from hook and in each ch across (15 sc); ch 1, turn. **2nd row:** Sc in each sc across; ch 1, turn. Repeating 2nd row, work even for 26 rows more.

VAMP: 29th row: Sc in each of 1st 8 sc; ch 1, turn. Work 2 rows even. Dec 1 sc at upper edge on next row (7 sc). Work 7 rows even. Dec 1 sc at upper edge on next row (6 sc). Work 1 row even. Dec 1 sc at upper edge on next row (5 sc). Work 14 rows even. Inc 1 sc at upper edge on next row (6 sc). Work 1 row even. Inc 1 sc at upper edge on next row (7 sc). Work 7 rows even. Inc 1 sc at upper edge on next row (8 sc). Work 3 rows even. Break off, leaving 12" end. Matching lower edges, sew last row to 1st row to form ring.

FINISHING: Fold vamp in half. Mark fold at 5-sc end for center of toe and at 15-sc end for center of heel. Pin, then sew vamp to sole.

Upper Edging: 1st row: With 2 strands A and right side facing you, starting at center back, work 1 rnd sc evenly spaced around entire upper edge of slipper, working 3 sc at each outer corner, decreasing 1 sc at each inner corner and decreasing 1 sc 5 times around toe; join. **2nd rnd:** Sc around, working 3 sc at each outer corner; join. Break off. With A, sew top edges of vamp together. Right slipper is made like left.

HIS-HER ARAN PULLOVERS

Magnificent crew-neck pullovers for both of you, crocheted to resemble the cables and popcorns typical of Aran fisherman sweaters.

SIZES: (34–36) [(38–40)–(42–44)–(46–48)]. Sweater measures 18" [20"–22"–24"] across back at underarms, 17" [18"–19"–20"] from underarm to lower edge.

MATERIALS: Coats & Clark's Red Heart Cashelle (Civona Orlon acrylic knitting-worsted-weight yarn) 10 [12–14–16] (3½-oz) skeins fisherman (cream) No. 110 (for woman's sweater) and camel No. 326 (for man's sweater); aluminum crochet hooks sizes H and I (or international hooks sizes 5.00 mm and 5.50 mm) **or the size that will give you the correct gauge.**

GAUGE: On I hook, 4 sts =1" in pattern st.

STITCH DIRECTIONS: Front Post Dc (f dc): Y o; insert hook from front to back and to front again around vertical "post" (upright part) of next dc; y o and draw yarn through, y o and complete dc in usual manner. Horizontal ridge will form across opposite side (wrong side) of work.

Back Post Dc (b dc): Y o; reaching over top of piece and working on opposite side (right side) of work, insert hook from right to left around vertical "post" of next dc, y o and draw yarn through, y o and complete dc in usual manner. Horizontal ridge will form across side facing you (wrong side).

Popcorn: Insert hook in next st, y o and draw lp through, y o and draw through 1 lp on hook, (insert hook in same st, y o and draw lp through, y o and draw through 1 lp on hook) 4 times, y o and draw through all 6 lps on hook, ch 1 tightly.

172

PATTERN STITCH: 1st row (right side): Sc in each of 1st 2 sts, f dc around each of next 4 sts, * sc in each of next 5 sts, f dc around each of next 4 sts. Repeat from * to last 2 sts, sc in each of last 2 sts; ch 1, turn. **2nd row:** Sc in each of 1st 2 sts, b dc around each of next 4 sts, * sc in each of next 2 sts, popcorn in next st, sc in each of next 2 sts, b dc around each of next 4 sts. Repeat from * to last 2 sts, sc in each of last 2 sts; ch 1, turn. **3rd row:** Sc in each of 1st 2 sts; work cable over next 4 sts as follows: Skip next 2 sts, f dc around each of next 2 sts, f dc around each of 2 skipped sts (cable made); * sc in each of next 2 sts, sc in top of popcorn, sc in each of next 2 sts, make cable over next 4 sts. Repeat from * to last 2 sts, sc in each of last 2 sts; ch 1, turn. **4th row:** Repeat 2nd row, being careful that 1st 2 past dc cross over 2nd 2 past dc of each cable. Repeat 1st through 4th rows for pattern st.

BACK: Lower Border: Starting at lower edge with size H hook, ch 73 [82–91–100] to measure about 18″ [20″–22″–24″]. **1st row:** Dc in 4th ch from hook and in each ch across (71 [80–89–98] dc, counting ch 3 as 1 dc); ch 1, turn. **2nd row (right side):** Work f dc in each dc across f dc in top of ch 3 ch 1, turn. **3rd row:** Work b dc in each dc across, b dc in top of ch 3; ch 1, turn. Repeat 2nd and 3rd rows 3 times more.

Change to size I hook and work even in Pattern Stitch until piece measures 17″ [18″–19″–20″]. Place marker at beg and end of last row for underarm. Continue in pattern for 7″ [7½″–8″–8½″]. Break off. Mark center 31 [32–31–32] sts for back neck.

FRONT: Work same as back until armholes measure 5″ [5½″–6″–6½″], ending on wrong side.

To Shape Neck: Left Side: 1st row: Work in pattern across 1st 22 [26–31–35] sts; turn. **2nd row:** Sl st in 1st st (1 st dec), work in pattern across. **3rd row:** Work in pattern to within 1 st of sl st (1 st dec); ch 1, turn. Work even in pattern on 20 [24–29–33] sts until armhole measures same as back. Break off. Skip center 27 [28–27–28] sts on last full row worked.

Right Side: 1st row: Work in pattern across remaining 22 [26–31–35] sts. **2nd row:** Work in pattern to last st (1 st dec); turn. **3rd row:** Sl st in 1st st (1 st dec), work across row. Work even on 20 [24–29–33] sts until armhole measures same as back. Break off.

SLEEVES: Starting at lower edge with size H hook, ch 38 to measure 9½″. **Cuff:** Work as for lower border of back on 36 sts. Change to size I hook. **To establish pattern st: 1st row:** 2 sc in 1st st, f dc around each of next 4 sts, * sc in top of last st worked, 2 sc in next st, f dc around each of next 4 sts. Repeat from * across, ending 2 sc in last st (50 sts); ch 1, turn. **2nd row:** Sc in each of 1st 2 sts, b dc around each of next 4 sts, * 2 sc in next st, popcorn in next st, 2 sc in next st, b dc around each of next 4 sts. Repeat from * to last 2 sts, sc in each of last 2 sts (62 sts); ch 1, turn. **3rd row:** Starting with 3rd pattern row, work in pattern on these 62 sts, increasing 0 [1–1–1] sts at beg and end of next 0 [1–2–3] rows. Then, working increased sts in sc, work even on 62 [64–66–68] sts until sleeve measures 18″ [18″–19″–19″]. Break off.

FINISHING: Sew shoulder seams. Sew sleeves between markers. Sew side and sleeve seams.

Neckband: 1st rnd: With right side facing you, starting at right shoulder seam with size H hook, work 74 dc evenly around neck edge; sl st in 1st dc. **2nd rnd:** Ch 3, f dc around each st around; sl st in ch 3. **3rd rnd:** Repeat 2nd rnd. Break off.

INDEX